BLOCKBUSTER!

The Sweet Story

Martin Popoff

BLOCKBUSTER!

The Sweet Story

Martin Popoff

WP
WYMER
PUBLISHING
Bedford, England

First published in Canada by Power Chord Press in 2021
under the title *Rebel Rouser: A Sweet User Manual.*
This revised edition published in 2025 by Wymer Publishing, Bedford, England
www.wymerpublishing.co.uk Tel: 01234 326691
Wymer Publishing is a trading name of Wymer (UK) Ltd.

Print edition (fully illustrated): **ISBN: 978-1-915246-69-1**

Edited by Jerry Bloom.

A catalogue record for this book is available from the British Library.

eBook formatting by Lin White at Coinlea Services.
Typeset/Design by Andy Bishop / Tusseheia Creative.
Cover design: Tusseheia Creative.
Front cover photo: Pictorial Press Ltd / Alamy Stock Photo.

Contents

Introduction

The glam-shiny volume you now hold in your hands (or peer at upon your screen, faithful eBook reader), came about in the manner of which many of my books get generated. Although all too often these days, it seems mortality has entered into the mix. First off, before we get dark, a few years ago now, I had written these long individual essays on my favourite albums by this vastly underrated and frankly besieged band of glamsters turned metal. Some of that material has appeared in my old out-of-print *Ye Olde Metal* series, and some only at zunior.com, where the lion's share of my eBook material is, including many of these short documents that have never appeared in print.

Now, when those things hang around, I usually think, maybe I could jump back into that band's life and get to finishing the tale, turn what I've already started into a full book. Which is what I did, with the first version of this tome emerging as *Rebel Rouser: A Sweet User Manual* back in 2021.

Now to the darkness. Sweet bassist and so much more, Steve Priest (and by more, I mean excellent lead vocalist and songwriter), died in 2020, leaving Andy Scott as the last man standing, as it were, from the classic four-piece Sweet line-up. But of course, on the happy side, it's inspiring that Andy went and delivered an entire new Sweet album in 2024, entitled *Full Circle*, an album which demonstrates that Andy's energy and skill-level remains boundless, despite rocking and rolling at 75 years of age.

But back into the darkness for a moment, Steve's death had put in motion the writing of a retrospective article for *Goldmine* magazine, for which I looked up Andy again, who graciously consented to an interview.

To be sure, I had chatted with Andy before and found him to be nothing but genial, plus refreshingly intelligent and introspective on the subject of what he had accomplished in life, namely the commandeering of a career that was way bigger than what the band's US album sales would have you believe. The thing is, I've talked to Steve as well, and what is quite remarkable to me, I'd actually seen his modern-day Californian version of Sweet, not once but twice in person, and had met up with him and the band in person on both occasions. One of these was at an idyllic classic rock festival in the wilds of Nakusp, British Columbia, and the other time was right here in Toronto. It was a pleasure and honour meeting a very friendly Steve and the rest of his band, somewhat casually interviewing them, and then also talking to Steve on the phone for more formal interviews over the years.

But again, on the mortality trip, writing this book reminded me of putting together *Beer Drinkers and Hell Raisers: The Rise of Motörhead* (hmm, just noticed the hell raiser thing), which covered only the early years of that band, up to 1982's *Iron Fist* album. What I still can't get my head around is that between the time of finishing that book and it actually coming out through the typically laborious publication process, all of those guys—Lemmy, Phil and Fast Eddie—were still alive and well when I finished writing but were all gone like the Ramones by the time the book appeared in the shops.

So yes, here we are once again pondering mortality, with this book really being motivated by the exact same sense of purpose that had me ask *Goldmine* editor Pat Prince if I could write up something for the mag reminding people how rich an experience listening to Sweet was and still is. Fortunately for the book, the band's career is a singularly weird one (pardon the pun), with the band moving from pop puppets through strident ambitious metal into one of the unheralded purveyors of pomp rock, at the end, utterly and completely ignored. Topsy-turvy and circuitous it was, so be sure, a case study in the music business, with pretty much everything good and bad happening to these guys along the way.

And what of the music?

Well, the one thing I wanted to get across with this book... well, two things, actually... Anybody who might potentially read more than a couple of my books knows how great the band were from *Sweet Fanny Adams* through to *Off the Record*. But I wanted to reiterate how, really, most of the early stuff, when they were a quote unquote singles band, with songs written by Mike Chapman and Nicky Chinn, a lot of that stuff is a hoot and a lesson in songsmithing to boot. It's only the really, really early material—say, 1970, '71, into '72—that is what you might call embarrassing, too silly for consumption. And then the second thing I wanted to get across, for the ages, i.e., put in the evergreen form that a book is (and why I like to write books, frankly), is that the later material by the band, when Brian was quietly shown the door, deserves the attention of serious musicologists as well.

So, there you go, right? Just like a bunch of books I write, there's a swathe of writing that serves as a platform where if I can put shoulder to the grinding stone, I can get over the top and produce a book. And then there is the motivation to celebrate these people's lives so there is something out there that their kids and grandkids can maybe discover one day.

And then finally there's the DJ in me, the proselytizer of good music in me, that guy that wants to apply serious analysis to the pre-*Sweet Fanny Adams* material and the post-*Off the Record* material, so that all of us current Sweet fans and potential Sweet fans can realise that there is more to the catalogue beyond the stuff that surely the most casual music fan can agree upon as genius, most notably *Give Us a Wink*!

Just one more quick thing—quick because I probably allude to this a bit later on in situ, in the proper chapter—but I gotta stress how magical Sweet was to me and my buddies precisely when the North American version of *Desolation Boulevard* came out and it was all about "Fox on the Run" and most especially "Ballroom Blitz," which lit a fire under our 12-year-old asses like you wouldn't believe. Everything about that song just spoke to us about how and why we loved hard rock and heavy metal—and Peter Criss. Indeed, the mania about Sweet—at least for a brief instant—was as heady and dizzying as it ever was around Kiss. I'm trying to wrack my brains, but I believe it corresponded with the *Rollerball* movie and the rollerskate/roller-rink craze as well. Yes, I can picture it… roller-ing around the rink, and then Sweet would come on and we'd go insane.

And if you can believe that—believe it or not—on a tighter level, i.e. maybe with more serious music fans only, when "Action" came out and was quite a hit as well, we all went nuts for this band all over again. I say "Action" and not *Give Us a Wink* because I remember the reception for the album was more sober and serious. But absolutely, I remember, whatever, grade 5 or 6, thinking that these guys were geniuses when we heard "Action."

Which was absolutely reinforced by Canuck B-side "Medusa" (or, weirdly, "Medussa"), a song almost as mythical and talismanic as the story itself. In any event, this was the golden period for us as kids, never to be experienced again, not even with *Off the Record*, which I only grew to love quite a bit later in life. Same goes for "Love Is Like Oxygen" and "Discophony," which I absolutely adore now, but I don't recall being a big deal to us as teenagers.

In any event, yeah, there's the multiple reasons I had to do this book, not the least of which is connecting on a level with Andy and Steve which I felt at least—from my end—seemed a little higher than acquaintance, although not at a level that I would be so presumptuous as to call friendship. I mean, that's certainly going too far, as in either case, this was not the usual type of notch above acquaintance with a rock star when you've interviewed them eight or ten times. It was more like the few times you've talked to them, it's like you knew them longer and better than you had. Maybe it's only because of how deeply special the band were to us as pre-teens in 1975. Who knows? Not me, but there you go.

Martin Popoff
martinp@inforamp.net, martinpopoff.com

CHAPTER 1:

The Early Years
"Somebody is writing all these things to order."

It's a tale of talent blooming and then subsumed unlike any other. Or maybe it's a story that happens often, except once the industry has its way with you, you are thrown away and the public never hears of you. Sweet's convoluted story of considerable early success but ultimately a crash falls somewhere in-between, with a little bit of both, a certain whiff of sweet success, if localised, followed by heady creative heights accompanied by "some" success followed by a fast fade to obscurity.

In essence this is the story of Sweet—Brian Connolly, Andy Scott, Steve Priest and Mick Tucker—coalescing after a jumble of bands into a foursome of fierce talent that quickly got tangled in a world of outside writers and producers and singles and charts. Once extricating themselves, well, as fans we got to see extra dimensions to those talents as the guys created the superlative records they will always be remembered for. What followed, sadly, was a steep decline in commercial impact, then bickering between parties and, alas, in the end, three of the four members of this exquisite band leaving us too soon.

And how did this all start? Well, the same way all our favourite bands from the '70s did, climbing the ranks through the late '60s while watching your hair get longer and your clothes more colourful. We may as well begin at the lip of the stage, with Brian Francis Connolly, born October 5th, 1945, in Govanhill, Glasgow, Scotland, to an unidentified father and a teenage waitress who gave Brian up for adoption. He was raised by Jim and Helen McManus and was singing early.

Moving to Harefield, Greater London to attend school at the age of 12, he did a spell with the Merchant Navy before getting into a number of bands. His break came when he joined West London R&B/beat group Wainwright's Gentlemen, where he made the acquaintance of drummer Mick Tucker. Connolly was co-lead vocalist with one Ann Cully, who should be credited as the person who replaced none other than Ian Gillan of Deep Purple fame in the band, despite Brian often getting the credit—Ian had left in April of '65, at which time Ann joined, to be accompanied by Brian in September of '65.

Michael Thomas Tucker, born July 17th, 1947, in Kingsbury in North London, was a self-taught drummer, picking up the sticks at 14 and grooving to the jazz greats, which would put him in good stead later in life to be sure. He'd been playing London since '65 at the age of 18, but later in Wainwright's Gentlemen, in January of 1968 now with Brian, the two would leave the band, having not been happy with the dismissal of guitarist Frank Torpey from the fold. Other versions of the story have Brian's days numbered anyway, with Mick already on the outs, criticised for playing too flamboyantly.

Born February 23rd, 1948 in Hayes, Middlesex, England, Stephen Norman Priest had whacked together his own bass guitar and started gigging with local bands fired up by the exploding music scene in Britain in the mid-'60s. Steve, acquiring a reputation with his act The Army, was soon invited to join Brian and Mick and Frank Torpey in what was then going by the name of The Sweetshop, formed January 26th, 1968 at a meeting at The Swan Inn (now Café Rouge at The Swan), in Ruislip, northwest London. Steve in fact came on the following week, and then in July of '69 Torpey was gone, replaced on guitar by Mick Stewart.

"We were pretty heavy when you look at it," reflects Steve. "We were all brought up by the same bands. I loved Cream, the Yardbirds, the Stones. In fact, I saw them when I was 15 and I was knocked out with it. I mean, they're still going (laughs). But we all had the same sort of upbringing, and we all had the same sort of heroes. Mick Tucker loved Ginger Baker. He loved his attitude, and we all loved Cream. And Andy wasn't our first guitarist—Frank Torpey was. We were around doing the circuit for three years before Andy was the guitarist. We were doing pretty heavy stuff, but at the time in England, reggae was the choice of the month, so we didn't go over too well doing 'I Feel Free.'"

Further on the band's secret weapon at the back of the stage, Priest told me that, "Mick was amazing, an underestimated drummer, completely underestimated. People are going now, 'Oh, he's the best drummer' and all this, and it's like, why didn't you say this at the time? But he was the power point of the whole band. If you ain't got a good bass player and drummer, you might as well give up. And his influences... I'm talking about guys from the '30s and '40s. Oh God... Gene Krupa, Buddy Rich. Buddy Rich, mainly; he loved Buddy Rich. And he wanted to be as good as Ian Paice. I said, 'You are. You've got a different style.' Because I can listen to him and I could listen to Mick, and I could tell which was which, and I said, 'You are as good as him.'"

The mention of Ian Paice is crucial here. The Sweet played gigs early on with the psychedelic version of Deep Purple. And Steve's band, The Army, had even played with The Maze once, featuring Rod Evans and Ian. Steve says that Mick right from the beginning had his sights on Ian Paice, studying his style, vowing to compete.

"And Brian… Brian was incredibly unique," continues Priest. "He had a very distinctive voice, a good command of the stage. He was very self-confident. Or at least he looked it. No, he was a great front man. He was like the orchestra leader. Brian was a wonderful person, very streetwise. Not the brightest tool in the shop. He was very clever in his own way, and had a heart, a huge heart. But Mick, incredibly underrated. I think he's one of the best drummers who came out of England. Amazing technician, and he pounded the hell out of them. He had so much stamina."

May 22nd, 1968, the band officially change their name to The Sweet. An acquaintance of the band, Mark Wirts, had already put out—as arranger, conductor and producer—a single under the band banner The Sweetshop. "Barefoot and Tiptoe," backed with "Lead the Way," was issued on Parlophone in 1968, and unfortunately for the other Sweetshop, Wirts had registered the name.

But on July 19th of that year, Steve and Brian, now operating as The Sweet, had their own record out, a single on Fontana, pairing "Slow Motion" with "It's Lonely Out There." At this point the band is a mildly psychedelic outfit, image-wise dressed in upscale but understated psychedelic frill, with matching haircuts not long and not short. For the pleasant and professional A-side, a sort of mid-tempo Stones ballad, given its piano and acoustic guitar, Brian adopts a surprisingly insistent vibrato.

The B-side is altogether different, essentially up-tempo psychedelic rock with an R&B vibe, pushed by a beat with snare on the one and three, cut through with fuzzy guitar licks. Nonetheless there's nothing wild about it—The Sweet sound positively sober on their first record, maybe even a bit establishment.

Producing the single was one Phil Wainman, who begins a long association with the band, or rather parachutes in here but then is gone from their lives for a while. Wainman had worked with The High Grades, The Paramounts and The Quotations previously, but was most known at this point for co-writing The Yardbirds' "Little Games" with pianist Harold Spiro. At this juncture, having been a drummer, he was working as a songwriter and music publisher. The single is supported by a trip the following month to a radio show hosted by David Symonds, where the band conduct their first live BBC radio broadcast.

September 5th, 1969, the guys shift from Fontana over to Parlophone for a second single, pairing A-side "Lollipop" with "Time," the latter serving as the band's first songwriting credit. The guys were pleased to be able to record at Abbey Road but were none too happy with the song choice. Amusingly, despite a fairly limp and behaved psychedelic musical track, sort of Small Faces, "Lollipop Man" sports the type of humorous novelty lyric that would soon make the band famous. As well, there are the early vestiges of the band's patented professional and blended high harmonies. "Time" sports an excellent Brian vocal over a mildly rumbling rock track, this one marking a slight uptick in the band's psych intensity, especially come solo time. As well, we get to hear Mick Tucker starting to stretch out a bit with a few licks, a few fills, and toward the end, a spot of busy bass drum work.

In January 1970 there's another Parlophone single pairing "All You'll Ever Get From Me," a true pop number, with "The Juicer," which is pretty much the band's first heavy rocker, even if they didn't write it. But yes, this sounds like heavy Steppenwolf, a bit bluesy, a bit R&B, a bit hard Guess Who, with Connolly sounding like Burton Cummings. Again, we get to hear Mick stretch out but also Brian, who peels off a few nice screams and is part of some strong signature Sweet harmonies, albeit in their infancy. Both of these songs got worked up for radio broadcast. This single gets issued by Odeon in Germany (the band's first picture sleeve) and in Spain and on Paramount in the US.

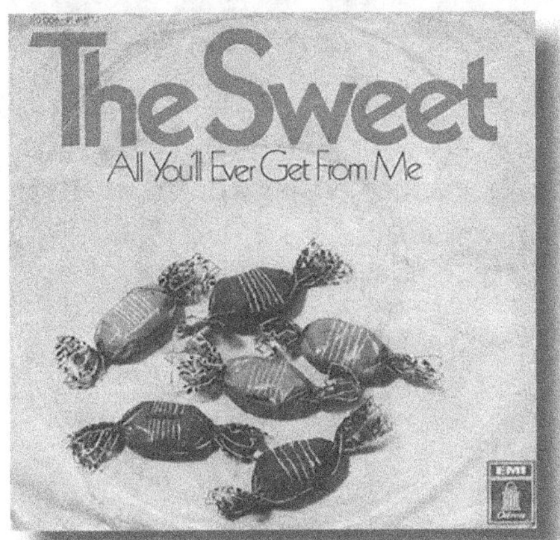

Another 1970 single, issued in June, pairs "Get on the Line" with "Mr. McGallagher." Steve affirms that Brian is the only member of the band performing on "Get on the Line," and that female backup singers were brought in for the harmonies, even though the guys were more than capable to perform that task.

The A-side is breezy, sunny days hippie pop, but again, one can hear the spare arrangement and hookiness of the band's hits to come in the not too distant future—in fact, this is a cover of fictional band The Archies, from 1969's *Jingle Jangle* album. The B-side is slow-moving but quite resplendent psych, showcasing Brian's thespian vocal skills over a lyric and in fact music track that sounds like pastoral Kinks.

At this point in the story, Sweet is about to get a new guitarist and complete their "classic" line-up. Andrew David Scott, born June 30th, 1949, in Wrexham, Wales, is in London town in August of 1970, and his plan is to audition for two bands on the same day, The Alan Bown Set and Sweet. Andy has been through a bunch of bands, actually beginning on the bass, but now was a guitarist of some experience. Having played with the likes of The Rasjaks, Guitars Incorporated, the 3Ds, The Fore-Winds, Missing

Links and The Strangers, it was a gig with the Silverstone Set supporting Jimi Hendrix in January of 1967 that sent Andy back to the guitar. Next was The Elastic Band (featuring Andy's brother Mike on bass), The Scaffold and Mayfields Mule, with whom Andy recorded three singles. The Elastic Band actually put out a full album, in 1969, called *Expansions on Life*.

Andy's audition for The Sweet was conducted with the band as well as managers Nicky Chinn and Mike Chapman, who are soon to figure prominently in the Sweet story. Things didn't look so good when Andy blew a fuse on Sweet's amp, but he eventually got through the process and was hired.

"I didn't actually get to do the audition for The Alan Bown, or The Alan Bown Set as they were then," clarifies Andy. "They just became The Alan Bown in the end. But I think that's when Jess Roden had left. We used to do gigs with The Alan Bown Set, when I was in a band called The Silverstones and then The Elastic Band. So, they kind of knew me, or they knew who I was. And when I got there, their road manager took me on one side and he said, 'Well, we're just not going to be ready today.' And I said, 'Oh, it's a shame.' 'Cause I said that I'd made a special journey, which back then, you know, took a little bit of doing, getting on and off buses with a bloody guitar and all that. And he said, 'Look, we know who you are; we'll give you a bell, all right?' I said, okay."

"I went back to, to Shepherd's Bush where I was living. 'Cause that's where the audition for Sweet was. And I walked in there and well, as we now know, the rest is history. The situation with Alan was that, I think, you see, this is the other side of that coin. Maybe that guy was just trying to be as nice as he could, because I think they'd already made their mind up when they realised that Robert Palmer from Vinegar Joe was actually available to join that band. I think he'd been standing in for somebody. He'd been in this other band with Elton John, the Bluesology thing, that actually had Rod Stewart from time to time and people like that. And I think Robert Palmer was right on the fringe of doing something. So, when they heard that he was available, I think that they had the blinkers on. I'm not even sure whether they did go through the motions of holding auditions. I think that the job was his."

On the subject of blowing a fuse with Sweet, Andy says, "Well, for me it was sarcasm, and it was funny. I plugged my guitar in and whoever has been using the amp previously, they'd just turned all the volumes right the way up. So, God knows how that sounded when they were auditioning. 'Cause I mean, in a room of that size, it was too loud. And so, my 335, just feedbacked like you wouldn't believe. And I basically said to Mick—because Steve was laying on the top of his 4x12 at that point, and then he realised, oh somebody in the room woke him up—and I said, 'Should I carry on?' Then that met with 'Absolutely.' So, it wasn't a bad moment. It wasn't that 'Oh, well, you know, I guess I've blown it' moment."

As for what was played that day, Andy explains that "They were asking people to record an old rock song and I think it was 'Summertime Blues.' And, well, I wanted to introduce… I played one of my own compositions, a song called 'Now Is the Time to Rise,' which never appeared on any Sweet album. But we'd done a couple of things. I think we'd done 'Great Balls of Fire' or 'Good Golly Miss Molly' or something like that. And we'd done 'Summertime Blues' and there was another song as well. Spooky Tooth had a song called 'Better by You.' And they knew it, so we did that and then I did a song that I sang myself. 'It's in G, follow me;' you know, that kind of thing."

Steve says that it was Mick who put his foot down and said that Andy was the guy for the job, while Mike Chapman didn't think so, remarking that this guy seemed like he was only in it for the payday. It had been a long night by this point and Brian had already gone down to the pub. Steve says after narrowing it down to three candidates, a second audition was held a few days later and Andy got the job.

Andy Scott played his first gig with the band on September 26th, 1970, at the Windsor Ballroom in Redcar.

Notes Steve, "Both Mick and Andy were, let's say, very serious, too serious at times, and everything had to be perfect, perfect. I like perfection, but I also like a little mistake here and there, like the Stones. A little kink in there somewhere… 'Ah, you can let that go.' Oh, they couldn't handle that. Playing-wise though, I think you're hearing the tip of the iceberg. We were very controlled. We didn't go nuts. Our full potential was never met, because we were so controlled. Not by ourselves, but management and the record company."

Now dropped by Parlophone and close to splitting up, things pick up for The Sweet when the band ink a deal with RCA, early 1971. They also make their UK TV debut on a show called *Lift Off*, and as mentioned are working with Chapman and Chinn, plus a returning Phil Wainman.

"Chapman came from Australia," explains Steve. "He was in a band called Tangerine Dream, I think (ed. actually Tangerine Peel). Chapman came over from Australia and came to London to make his way. He met Chinn at a club in London, and Chapman was waitering. Chinn was looking for something to get into. He needed to prove himself or something. Chapman thought of himself as a songwriter, and Chinn thought that he was too, so they got together. And that's Chinn and Chapman. Chapman did most of the writing, I have to admit. He was very good. He could write very catchy little things. He proved that when he went off on his own."

"Sweet were rather an enigma," muses Andy. "We came through the tail end of the '60s. Just before I joined, there were a couple of singles released that were extremely commercial. They didn't get anywhere, but one of them was a radio success, and they were at a turning point in their lives. I think the guitar player had already left, and it was this chance meeting with Brian, meeting a record producer who had worked with them, who said he had a couple of songwriters who have some songs and would Brian mind singing on them. And from then it spiralled a little bit out of control, and they realised that there was the basis of a band here, even though there was no guitar player."

"Hence, enter Andy Scott," chuckles Andy, "and I come from a progressive rock band. It was not really my absolute thing, but having jammed with Mick and Steve, the bass player and drummer, I realised that we all liked The Who, we all liked Cream, we all liked Deep Purple, we all liked Led Zeppelin, so there was absolute common ground. Just because the singles you were hearing were one type of music, as soon as we had our opportunity, you turn the record over and listen to the B-side, and you had some completely different sounding band on the other side."

"I knew Slade when I was in the band previous to Sweet," explains Andy, asked to chart any similarities there with the act that would become Sweet's main rival and comparative very shortly. "I was in a band called The Elastic Band. And they were called The In-Betweens, and they then had a change of name, to Ambrose Slade, and that's when they were being managed by Chas Chandler who was looking after Jimi Hendrix. And the problem at that time, when I say problem, there was a lot of skinhead kind of stuff going on, and I remember talking to Dave about this. He had a problem where he lost his hair, and he had to have a shaved head for a while. So, they all did it, for like an image thing, in 1970. And they were like really looking hard on the front cover of the pop magazines and things, and I thought to myself, that's a little bit radical."

"And it was around the time when Jimi Hendrix died, so Chas then concentrated himself completely and utterly on Slade. The next thing we knew, their hair had grown again and they were on the charts with 'Coz I Luv You.' And yes, I think their attitude was very similar to mine. We've been at this since our teenage years, 16, 17, there's a chance of some success here, we're going to grab it with both hands; we're not going to let go, if we can."

"Early days of Sweet, we were probably on a circuit that many bands were on," continues Scott, asked if looking the way they did had them fighting their way out of clubs. "Everything from playing colleges through to the equivalent of working men's clubs, which on the weekend turned into music halls for the teenagers of the town. And so, it was never quite as bad as you probably would think. You came out with a statement there—I don't remember it being quite as bad as that. But I do remember the audience as being like sponges, and willing to absorb and get involved with everything and anything that was coming to their town. And when they were confronted with a band like Sweet or Slade, who were slightly different, that's probably why, having done the groundwork, and then having released the records, there was a fan base already there for it."

Next for the band was a single with all the pieces in place. For "Funny, Funny," issued in March of '71, first off, we've got the classic Sweet line-up in place, namely Brian, Andy, Steve and Mick. As well, we've got an A-side written by Mike Chapman and Nicky Chinn (Chapman has said the inspiration for the song was "Sugar, Sugar" by The Archies), a B-side written by Sweet and all of it produced by Phil Wainman.

As Steve mentioned, Mike Chapman had come to London from Australia, working his way through the Downliners Sect and Tangerine Peel, who had records out. Soon he found Nicky Chinn and together they started writing, at first for Mickie Most's RAK label. "Funny, Funny" is pure, innocent pop, an up-tempo song with hooks for miles, built on a frame of drums, bass and acoustic guitars, with a few light electric licks thrown in for colouring. Already on display is a strong Brian plus assured vocal harmonies. The B-side, "You're Not Wrong for Loving Me" is essentially a folk song, with a slight psychedelic bent, like acoustic Led Zeppelin. The single was issued by an aggressive RCA all over the world and did well, putting Sweet on the map (everywhere). On home turf, by May of 1971, it had risen to No.13 in the charts.

Even up into late 1973, "You're Not Wrong for Loving Me" was serving a purpose, as part of the band's meticulously planned revamped "act," in which, mid-show, the guys would plunk themselves down on stools and do an acoustic set, which previously had included things like a soft version of "Eight Miles High" by The Byrds.

The team was back the following month with "Co-Co," again written by Chapman and Chinn, with a B-side, "Done Me Wrong All Right," by The Sweet. The Caribbean flavour of "Co-Co" was inspired by a vacation trip Mike had made to the Bahamas. Again, it was all session musicians with Brian providing a lead vocal and the guys, this time, being allowed to add backing vocals. "Co-Co" went all the way to No.2 in the British charts, prevented from reaching the top position by fellow RCA artists, Middle of the Road's "Chirpy Chirpy Cheep Cheep." "Co-Co" certifies in the home country as a gold single, bettering the silver status of "Funny, Funny."

Reviewing the track for the *New Musical Express*, Derek Johnson wrote, "This is an obvious hit if I ever heard one! It's much better than 'Funny, Funny,' which was strictly teenybopper, and it took me back to the heyday of bubblegum, The Archies and all! This is still an instant pop disc, aimed at the young and the young-at-heart. But there's more substance and sheer guts to it. The depth is provided by a captivating Latin flavour and a mellow steel drum sound. The tune is as catchy as 'Funny Funny' and its tailor-made for discotheques and jukeboxes. An old Sweet track was reissued by EMI last week, but now that this official follow-up is on sale, the former clearly stands no chance at all. There's nothing progressive, experimental, or even very clever about this record— just good, happy pop. Thank goodness!"

"If I knew that I might have written a few," chuckles Andy, when I asked him what the magic ingredients were to these songs by Mike and Nicky. "I always find it difficult to comprehend why somebody, should we say, as talented as Mike could come up with 'ho-chi-ka-ka-ho.' I understand that they were… well, somebody is writing all these things to order. They'd had a meeting with Phil Wainman and I remember Phil telling me, years later, he said, 'I loved that record, "Montego Bay."' He said, 'Your band was the ideal outlet for me to try and record my "Montego Bay,"' and he said, 'We almost achieved it with "Co-Co" and "Poppa Joe."' That Caribbean steel band sound. I mean, there were black players on those records. There was a bass player and the steel band and we just had some fantastic arrangements and players in the studios back then. I'm not saying that we couldn't have done it ourselves, but Phil was definitely a taskmaster who in a three-hour session wanted backtracks for the A and the B side done."

"Look, pop singles back then were very, very finite; it was almost formulaic," continues Scott. "I listen back to some of those singles from the late '60s into the early '70s, some of them, I'm not even sure whether there's drums on there. It's not like what happened a couple of years later where all of a sudden, the drums are right in the front, especially with some of the disco songs that came out. But some of the songs from the late

'60s, the vocal is the all-important thing. And I think handclaps carried the rhythm more than drums. Phil Wainman was a very, very good and very clever record producer."

Indeed, if you look at videos of the band miming "Co-Co" for TV (Sweet did *a lot* of miming over the years!), Mick essentially plays the role of traditional percussionist, rather than keeper of a fat rock 'n' roll beat. The nonsense words of which Andy speaks form the chorus of this song, repeated at length until they are stuck to your head like a big juicy wad of bubblegum. However, flip to the B-side and for the first time we hear Sweet as the accomplished hard rock band they would become. Sounding like a cross between Deep Purple (Brian: "We been all night rocking at the house of blue light") and Black Sabbath (circa that band's cover of Crow's "Evil Woman"), this is the work of a band leaping forward ten steps, magnetic vocalist, thumping bassist, fuzzy licks from the guitarist and a Mick that is manic.

Indeed, there's virtually nothing that ties the style and arrangement of this song to Sweet's early singles. In this respect, the "Co-Co" single serves as a two-track representation of the Sweet conundrum as it exists through to the end of *Desolation Boulevard*, this duality between pop and nascent metal, even if Chapman and Chinn will move in the direction of the latter over time.

Tellingly, for the heavy B-side, Mike and Nicky showed little interest and left Phil Wainman to deal with the guys. Steve says that the song was written at a club gig in Nottingham and that they had banged the lyrics together at an Italian restaurant while waiting for Brian to do his vocals on "Co-Co."

"We were heavily influenced by Deep Purple, Zeppelin and Black Sabbath," says Andy. "And remember, heavy metal, or the rock bands from the '60s, were so influenced by what came previously, with things in the '50s. We all were, even though I didn't realise it. One of the reasons I wanted to play the guitar was bands like Cliff Richard and The Shadows, and of course Elvis Presley. And I think it was Ritchie Blackmore who said one of the reasons why he really wanted to address something… there's a certain guitar solo in, I think it's in 'Jailhouse Rock,' where the guy just hits all the open strings and he goes into the solo. And he says those kinds of things don't just happen. They're the monumental things that change the way we perceive stuff."

"So, in other words, you don't any longer have to be as precise as you want to be, as long as the feel and as long as the energy was good. So I think, when we all come through from that—and we all used to play the Chuck Berry songs—you realise that some of that Howlin' Wolf and

'Smokestack Lightning,' the early stuff, oh God, the guy, there were so many, especially in America, who came through that were like guitar heroes that were making the grade."

"But in the '60s, it became very serious. All of a sudden, the English bands, mainly, had a rather serious way of approaching the blues that had come before. Jimmy Page, I mean, without him, the riffs would never have been as organised as they are now. The riffs would've still been… every time a riff came along, the old bluesmen wouldn't play exactly the same every time. So somebody had to organise it, and as I said, when I sat down with, oh, I was thinking of Bo Diddley for example… you know, we've all got all of this in our backgrounds, and so when it came to the '70s, I think the ongoing things that were being drawn from the '60s, the last thing we wanted to do was be another denim-clad, long-haired, with your head down clone, and I think the dressing-up part of it was a way of putting the fun back into it. In other words, it's like saying, we'll take a Led Zeppelin song and make it more commercial and dress it up a little bit and make it a little bit of fun."

And fun was most definitely something crowds yearned for, in the England of the day. "Yes," agrees Andy. "In England, when we were having some of our biggest hits, we were having this thing called the three-day week where people were being... you know, there was such inflation and hardly any jobs that people were being pressured into working three days a week and sharing jobs, and there were power cuts of all sorts going on here. So, I think the next element that people look for, to maybe help a life that isn't possibly as good as it should be, back then, was obviously the music. Because at that time, I can't think of anything that was actually bigger in Britain."

There are also some pretty advanced examples of Andy's patented harmony leads coming to the fore here. Asked about twinning parts with himself, Andy says, "Well, when there's only one guitarist and you want to do something… you've heard the Allman Brothers or you've heard Wishbone Ash. When Thin Lizzy first came out, they were just a three-piece. They didn't have Scott Gorham; he came a little bit later on. And of course, it then became what everybody wanted, that you started to find the bands were no longer four-pieces. They were five-pieces; they wanted two guitar players so they could play twin leads together."

As for his inspirations to go this way and indeed make these memorable singing and sing-able leads one of Sweet's trademarks, Andy says, "For me there was a band called Spirit, Randy California, and I used to love what he did. He used to do some incredible dubbing, like twin guitar stuff, nothing outrageously fast or anything like that. But I didn't realise that on one of the B-sides I think it was… before I joined Sweet, I had a brief period in a country rock band called Mayfield's Mule, who had one hit record. And while I was in that band, we reworked some of the things that they'd done on their album, and me and the singer, who was also the other guitar player, he loved it 'cause we were doing like a bit of the Allman Brothers twin lead things."

"Around the same time, 1969, 1970, I remember thinking that when we did 'Done Me Wrong All Right,' the main guitar part is a twin lead. But the recording was only four-track, I think, so I'm having to sing and play my guitar at the same time, because my generation just didn't have that; you don't have the tracks. So, what you hear are performances on stuff like that. So, you've got the diddle-diddle-diddle, the twin harmony, and then coming up, you've got a guitar solo to do. So, there's no time to think about it. You have to have all of that kind of thing worked out. Now once the 16- and 24-track machines are in the studio, it's a bit better because I can do a guitar part and then say, I wonder if I could put a harmony to that."

"Whereas before I had no idea whether I could put a harmony with it, because I hadn't had a chance to work it out, because the ones that I had time to work out were done at home on my Revoxes where I'd realised, yes, I can put a harmony with that. And it was always a lot simpler. Whereas some of the stuff that you hear on the Sweet recordings are quite complex, because I played a guitar solo and then thought, hang on, I can add a harmony to the end of that guitar solo, and it was never intentional to put a harmony there. It just takes a bit of finding which note fits where, and then you're away. All of a sudden you sound like you're a genius. But it's not quite like that; for me, a lot of that is on the hoof—it's almost like winging it."

Further on Thin Lizzy connections, Andy says, "I was very lucky to have met Gary Moore, when he first came over from Ireland with Skid Row. Sweet, you would never believe this, we'd just entered the charts with our first record and were put on the bill with Skid Row in a biggish club, but nevertheless a club, in the north of England. But we were playing on slightly different stages. It was one of these clubs that had split levels and things. I walked into the dressing room, because it was always a shared dressing room back then, and we had heard the Skid Row album, *Skid*, because Mick Tucker and I had been trying to learn the riff to 'Mad Dog Woman,' which was extremely fast. In the afternoon, not realising that Skid Row had arrived, when we walked in the dressing room, Gary Moore is now playing a little of our hit that was in the charts, on his guitar, but with a slightly bluesy feel. And I went, 'Touché.' Ever since then, every time… I used to go to Lizzy gigs all the time, and they were absolute gentlemen. I loved Phil."

Back to the A-side, here's a few memories from legendary engineer Phill Brown (Jimi Hendrix, Rolling Stones, Led Zeppelin, Bob Marley, Jeff Beck, and younger brother of Rush producer Terry Brown) on the sessions.

"I was a house engineer at Island, through '76. And I did a lot of stuff with these two guys called ChinniChap, who were writers. We worked with Suzi Quatro and Mud and various things of that era. I did two Sweet tracks. In hindsight it's a bit sad in a way because their B-sides, which they did themselves, were always fantastic, but the A-side they weren't allowed to play on. The business was very constructed. We would do a single in a day basically. So 10:00AM to 1:00PM would be the backing track, which was session players, and then the band would come in 2:00PM to 5:00PM to do the vocals and then we'd mix, you know, 6:00PM, 7:00PM to 10:00PM in the evening and it was finished."

As for Mike and Nicky… "I mean, very camp," says Phill, "in the way they behaved. But they were hot at the time. They were working for Mickie Most and as I say, they did Mud, Suzi, Sweet, all kinds of stuff. Very efficient, very businesslike, a little bit serious, taking the whole process very seriously, which, you know, at Island we would basically try and have a good time and enjoy ourselves. I know that Michael Chapman, when they split up, he went off to America and did these amazing records with Blondie. So, I was impressed with what he did later because the Blondie records I thought were fantastic. But I never really took them that seriously. This whole kind of seriousness and campiness wasn't really my world. Maybe it's just that era with the glam rock thing that they thought they needed to be that way, 'cause they were quite straight looking guys as well. So maybe they just thought that it would help them in their careers. I don't know."

"But yeah, the guys themselves were a little pissed-off because they weren't allowed to play on the records. They got given the backing track at one o'clock in the afternoon and then given the lyrics. It was like, 'Okay, you sing this, you sing here, this is the chorus.' And so, I don't think they'd even heard much of the songs before they were in the studio doing them. And they wanted to play their own stuff, you know?"

Phill says Phil Wainman played the drums and Pip Williams (also a Phil!) played guitars, adding "Straight session, union session, three hours to get the track down and the overdubs and everything sorted. And then vocals in the afternoon, mix it all in the evening and that was it. For the B-sides I wasn't there. Island in those days was actually quite an expensive studio. They were probably put into the cheapest studio and left to their own resources. Some of the B-sides that they made were fantastic; they were doing what they really wanted to do. But yeah, the A-sides, cutting the track with bass, drums, guitar, double tracking vocals and things like that, but very few real tricks. We didn't do backwards reverbs or anything like that. Obviously in that era there were very few effects and things anyway, so they were done fairly honestly—it is what you hear. It's kind of what everyone was doing."

Asked about this notion going around at the time that Brian lacked confidence as a vocalist, Phill figures, "I think perhaps quite shy. I'm not really sure whether it was shyness or as I say this kind of slightly pissed-off attitude that they had to do those kinds of songs. We had three hours in order to get the vocals done. So, it's not an incredibly short amount of time, when you think that you're doing lead vocal, double tracking, backing vocals. I'd say he was shy more than anything else; it wasn't that he was reluctant, or he didn't deliver. Yeah, I think there was a shyness there. After I'd worked with him the first time, we put up screens so he couldn't be seen by anyone and that did seem to improve the situation. 'Cause you know, people in the control room often don't realise, but if you walk out into the live room and you look back and you look through into the control room and it's bright lights, you've got five or six people looking at you. It's not always the best environment for vocals. So, we would just screen it off, so he wasn't visible to the control room, and then peering around if he needed to talk to anyone."

The other guys could sing too, says Phill. "Yes, the guys were doing the backing vocals. ChinniChap were always there the whole day, and Phil Wainman. And they would come in and we would do the lead vocal track, bounce down, and then everyone would get involved in doing backing vocals. I think they were the ones that did the handclaps."

And soberly so… "Yes, well it turns out later, I didn't realise at the time that they were actually quite heavy drinkers. But no, I don't think they were that pissed on the sessions. Probably a few just to lubricate it. Brian got into drinking heavier as time went on. The Island thing was very much smoking; it was a kind of dope studio because of the connection with a lot of reggae stuff with Bob Marley and that era. So, there was a lot of hash around which obviously with ChinniChap and Phil Wainman, that was not really acceptable."

Then Phill found himself wrapped up in the success of the band. "That's what really surprised me. I knew nothing about them when I did the 'Co-Co' track. I'd worked with Harry Nilsson on 'Without You' that year. And then I get this award, you know, from *New Musical Express* and I just obviously thought it would be for 'Without You' by Harry Nilsson, 'cause it was such an amazing track. But it was 'Co-Co' by Sweet. And so, I never took awards very seriously ever since then. But they were a really good kind of rock glam rock band, and as I say the B-sides are fantastic.

They're so much punchier and rock. But the A-sides, novelty pop, which is what ChinniChap made their name on back then. I did Suzi Quatro 'Can the Can.' That's a more credible track but it's still very much of a pop song. But with Sweet, you listen to the B-side and you hear a live rock band. I've noticed over the last couple of years, there's been more and more stuff posted up about Sweet and they seem to be getting the credibility now, which maybe they didn't have at the time."

Next for the band, in October of '71, was another Chinn/Chapman song called "Alexander Graham Bell," which reaches No.33 on the UK charts. A shift is made to a bit more heaviness and increasing ambition to the arrangement, this being a sort of proggy pomp rock with the pageantry of The Kinks. Steve calls the song "terrible" and indicates that it was more or less a direct lift from a song called "Henry Ford." The melody is at times dour and foreboding, and the subject matter flies in the face of pop convention. Priest was unsure that it was right for the band but the guys went along because Nicky and Mike were so gung-ho over it.

Wrote Derek Johnson in his *NME* assessment of the track, "Another song by Nicky Chinn and Mike Chapman, writers of The Sweet's first two hits. They've come up with a novel idea here and have re-written history in the process—the idea being that Bell invented the telephone specifically in order to make contact with his girlfriend! Pounds along with a solid beat, is lustily sung by The Sweet and has a rip-roaring orchestral scoring. It lacks the teenybopper hook chorus of 'Funny Funny' or 'Co-Co' (which is probably a good thing, lest the group becomes stereotyped), but still boasts a catchy refrain with which it's easy to sing along. To sum up, a very commercial disc—not quite so twee as the last two, but still loaded with instant appeal and clearly destined to complete The Sweet's chart hat-trick."

"Alexander Graham Bell" stalled at No.33 in the UK charts. Again, the B-side, "Spotlight," was written by the boys in the band, and here we have Sweet deftly mixing CSNY acoustics with electric punch, not stopping there, but adding on top their professional and glossy vocal harmonies and another dose of twinned lead work from Andy. Add the song's doomy melodies and what you have is something very much akin to Uriah Heep, a far cry from "Funny, Funny," with the seeds of discontent now sown.

CHAPTER 2:

Funny How Sweet Co-Co Can Be
"Look, it's not their album"

Next on tap for Sweet would be the issuance of the band's first full-length album, although typical of Sweet's surreal career, *Funny How Sweet Co-Co Can Be*, out on RCA November 27th of 1971, would soon be overshadowed by additional stand-alone singles, each more exciting than the last.

Like the singles, the guys in the band wedge some writing onto the record. "That was definitely Brian and I talking," relates Andy, "and basically saying, look, it's not their album. It's not a showcase for Chinn and Chapman. So, you know, we would like to propose some material, which is what we did. I think they picked, should we say, the least contentious material. There's one song which is actually quite a good song, that they didn't pick, but I can see why they didn't pick it. 'Cause it's more like a psychedelic pop song, a song called 'Be with You Soon,' which appeared on later versions. It just didn't make the cut for the album at the time. But there was something like six hit records on that album because some of them had been recorded by other people."

Opening the album is the previously released "Co-Co," which is followed up by Chinn-Chapman number "Chop Chop," vocal melody reminiscent of "The Teddy Bear's Picnic," the Sweet variation featuring an arrangement by Fiachra Trench. Still, despite the song's inanity, Mick gets to play his drums, both Andy and Brian are dealt a watery chorus effect and there's some nice (uncredited) Hammond organ work as window dressing.

Next is a cover of Holland/Dozier/Holland classic "Reflections," made famous by The Supremes, here arranged with strings by Pip Williams.

"I see the two cover versions that they chose," recalls Andy. "Luckily, I'd been in a band that had performed 'Reflections' before I joined three years back. So, I knew the parameters of how the vocals should be sung. So, I just sat there with Brian for the afternoon and told him how to just sing it, basically." Steve relates, however, that Brian had a tough time with the vocal, which had become a trend to the point where he was losing confidence in his abilities. Steve recalls the guys being sent out of the studio down to the pub and returning two hours later to find Brian still being routined over the first line of the song.

Next is the first band-written song on the record. Notes Andy, "The 'Honeysuckle Love' thing was mine and Steve's attempt at writing like Marc Bolan. Because that seemed to be de rigueur; that's what was needed. So, we wrote this song that Marc could have written. And it just so happened that right at that moment, Marc Bolan had been kind of messing around with a lot of acoustic stuff, with his first thing, with Tyrannosaurus Rex, and I remember, I actually thought that when I first heard Bolan, that it was David Bowie. And then I realised we were signed to a label that actually had David Bowie on it and *Hunky Dory* was his first album that I turned onto. Plus, by that time, Marc Bolan was just starting to release things like 'Get It On,' in '71, and we found ourselves, not being left behind, but thinking this is what we are."

Indeed "Honeysuckle Love" sounds like T. Rex, but it also sounds a bit dour and droopy, like Creedence Clearwater Revival—not heavy Sweet and not poppy Sweet either. Much poppier is "Santa Monica Sunshine," although here Mike and Nicky have the band sounding like happy Grateful Dead from the rootsy *Workingman's Dead*/*American Beauty* period.

The gasping and grasping at straws continues with a cover of "Daydream," written by The Lovin' Spoonful's John Sebastian and a hit for The Lovin' Spoonful in 1966. Says Andy, "if you wanted to pick some songs that would have been Brian with his name written through them, then give him a Neil Diamond song or an old rock 'n' roll song, like 'Great Balls of Fire' or something like 'Daydream,' because in five minutes he would have knocked those off, you know."

Over to side two of the original vinyl, we have previously issued single "Funny, Funny" (technically now without the comma, but we will retain the song's original, ahem, integrity). "Tom Tom Turnaround," another Chinn-Chapman number, is next. Same time it appears here, Australian pop band New World were having a Top Ten hit with the track. In Sweet's world, the vaguely native American sounding song is part of a through-line started with "Chop Chop" and continuing through "Wig-Wam Bam" and onto the band's fashion disaster use of Indian war paint and head-dresses.

Mid-side two, the guys write up another one for the record, inexplicably going for a combination of bluegrass, country and establishment '60s pop for "Jeanie." Second to last on the original UK issue is Chinn-Chapman number "Sunny Sleeps Late," which sounds like Roy Orbison, complete with soft slide guitar and a horse gallop of a beat. The album closes strong with the aforementioned "Spotlight," the only song on the record that points to the future of Sweet.

Pretty interesting though that the German edition of the album, sporting a different cover and a slightly altered title (*Funny Funny, How Sweet Co-Co Can Be*), underscores this idea of the end of the record pointing to what's next. As Andy says, "'Done Me Wrong All Right' was the B-side of 'Co-Co' but it didn't make it onto the British album. It was considered far too heavy." But there you have it, with the 12-track German issue ending with two songs that would not have been out of place on *Sweet Fanny Adams*.

CHAPTER 3:

Biggest Hits and The Sweet
"The singles did not reflect what we were"

Into 1972, Sweet continue with their winning ways, issuing "Poppa Joe" as a single, backed with "Jeanie," again, seemingly into every corner of the world. All told it's been a pretty impressive onslaught of physical product by this point, with the full-length album also seeing issue in way more exotic territories than most bands would ever enjoy, again, due to the long arm of RCA at that point in time, before what would be a steady decline in stature for the label over the ensuing years.

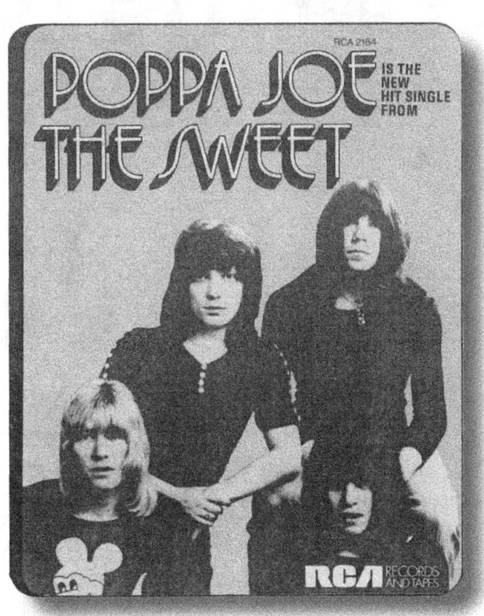

What is equally impressive is that the very Caribbean-flavoured "Poppa Joe" would be the subject of a full-on MTV-styled production video ten years before there'd even be an MTV. Steve recalls the shoot day at Weston-super-Mare as bitterly cold and all told, fairly idiotic, especially the shots of the band running up and down the beach.

And this wasn't the band's first video clip—atop myriad properly produced TV and sundry live-ish clips, both "Co-Co" and "Jeanie" would receive surprisingly adept video treatment. In fact, this represents another area in which Queen might be said to have taken some of Sweet's thunder. Somehow Queen has gotten a bunch of credit for being pioneers of the music video, where surely Sweet were there with the goods five years earlier, even if The Beatles should receive, arguably, the most credit for blazing this trail.

But yes, "Poppa Joe" finds Chapman and Chinn up to their usual tricks, beginning with a chorus full of childish nonsense novelty euphemisms. There's even a crowd participation section of chorus in case you didn't get it the first time. Plus, there are lots of "goes" at this almost rap mouthful of words, backed with steel drums and percussion and handclaps instead of, as Andy has noted, much of Tucker actually tucking into what Tucker does.

As well, 1972 and 1973 find the band with hooks deep into a glam world that is patently ridiculous, generating many pictures of Brian, Andy, Steve and Scott that have got to be some of the most cringe-worthy of any band ever. Still, you gotta laugh—as they have—and still do—over the years. A constant source of controversy came from the guys getting asked if they were gay and then these horniest of heterosexuals playing it up.

The stage show was both lascivious and profane and even landed the guys a stay in a Belgian gaol. The clothes continued to send the wrong message too, but the guys and their managers Mike and Nicky knew this kept them in the entertainment papers despite the constant fast-talking needed to get them out of tight spots at more provincial gigs.

At the music end of The Sweet, things are improving, with each single stronger than the last, and the band's tentative steps into the world of full albums solidifying with a hits compilation in the UK and even a full-length album in the US, albeit that being a hits pack as well, even if it's framed a bit more like an official US debut.

And so, backing it up and breaking it down, February 1972, "Poppa Joe" is released, with the throwback song charting well, at No.11 in the UK while notching a handful of number ones and number twos elsewhere around the planet. Sweet become favoured regulars on BBC TV's *Top of the Pops* show, a happenstance that the band used to intensify the almost Irish show band-ness of their outrageous glitzy costumes.

Still, the guys were straining for credibility, as Brian told Julie Webb in March: "We used to get a bit choked-off, especially with the press abroad, who came up and asked, 'Do you really like the music you play?' We really do seem to be the group everyone has a go at. People are usually so critical of pop or bubblegum bands. We are not bitter about it, because we haven't had the opportunity to do a tour of Britain. So, a lot of the people who knock us probably haven't even seen us live. Obviously, criticism, when you get slated, hurts—you can't ignore or dismiss it all together. I wish, in a way, people would pay more attention to us live. Audiences still expect us to play things like 'Funny, Funny' when we include other things, including a rock medley. We don't do all our work on the continent. It's just that we've had hits there, so we worked there."

May '72, as alluded to, Steve and Brian are taken to court in Belgium by a town objecting to an earlier Sweet concert which had involved the use of an allegedly pornographic film clip among other violations, landing them a stay in gaol (Steve appreciated getting a visit from Nicky after a good four days, with Priest wondering if they'd been forgotten).

Later this month Sweet is kicked out of the Tivoli in Copenhagen after a gig in Krudthuset for more errant behaviour. This is followed by yet another "ChinniChap" song, "Little Willy," issued as a single. This one hits No.4 in the UK. The slight double entendre on the song is often exploited by the band and its audiences, especially during live shows. Later, for what is considered to be an overtly sexual stage act, the band are banned by the Mecca dancehall circuit.

Here's where the tide shifts in the disposition and dispensation of Sweet singles. "Little Willy" sounds like heavy Bachman-Turner Overdrive. Mike's and Nicky's golden touch when it comes to hooks is still on impressive display, but the song is turned up, stacking dependable "Louie Louie" power chords on top of drums whacked hard and foot-stomping like Slade. There's a beautiful pre-chorus that sets up and even shinier chorus on which Brian complains about how Little Willy just does what he wants. And again, in case you didn't get the message, there's a modulated version of the chorus, emphasised by additional percussion tracks. And still… Steve has indicated that even here, on a nascent hard rock song, the band was not allowed to play on the track. This attitude from above would change, says Priest, most likely when Mike and Nicky saw the guys perform it live on *Top of the Pops*.

What's more, on the B-side is the band's own "Man from Mecca," which serves as the band's heaviest song yet, massive of riff like Mountain and the hardest of Led Zeppelin. As a bonus, the song is also scandalous, with a clearly heard "if you wanna fuck" being part of the song's oft-repeated chorus. As mentioned, the band had just been put on a tour of "Mecca"-styled ballrooms around Britain, hence the title.

Come September of '72, "Wig-Wam Bam" doesn't let down the side, sounding like punk rock five years early, even if the band's blinding silver lamé pantsuits, floor-length Indian headdresses and war paint makeup would be the opposite of punk wear (excepting Adam Ant). Once again, we're in that "Louie Louie" sweet spot when it comes to the chord sequence as Mick pounds the war drums—this performance is entirely Sweet for the first time. Also, in deference to the usual formula, the chorus descends into a zone where juvenile word play acts almost as instrument, a combination of voice and additional percussion, given Brian's "slam poetry."

"Wig-Wam Bam" would vault to No.4 on the UK charts, backed with "New York Connection," a similarly punky band-penned rocker, although this one leans a bit toward the meat-and-potatoes American rock of Kiss (as well as the aforementioned BTO).

All the intensifying madness of the band is gathered for sober consideration on an album called *Biggest Hits* issued by RCA in December of '72 across a million territories, the US not being one of them. Basically, the record is what it says on the front of its crappy album cover, a little over half the album being the band's A-sides of all styles, plus pointedly some of the heavier Bs.

Into 1973, it's back to work making small and inexpensive records for what seems like multiple countries on all continents except Antarctica. In January, "Blockbuster!" gives Sweet its first UK No.1, with the explosive anthem remaining at the top of the charts for five weeks. The song has a similar riff to another popular song of the time, David Bowie's "The Jean Genie" which is stopped at No.2 by "Blockbuster!"

Disc—January 13, 1973   5
THE SWEET
BLOCKBUSTER!
DYNAMIC NEW SINGLE RCA 2305
RCA Records and Tapes

This one starts with siren and then Brian signing like a siren, but soon he's climbing his monkey ladder, going thespian in preparation for the performance we'll soon hear on "Ballroom Blitz." The music behind him stays pretty tame, leaving vocals to provide most of the drama, not just Connolly on lead, but the climactic harmony swells of the chorus as well.

To add further context to the "Jean Genie" vs. "Blockbuster!" controversy that erupted (the songs came out within a week of each other, and on the same label), there's the influence on both tracks from Bo Diddley's "I'm a Man," which in turn draws from Muddy Waters' version of "Hoochie Coochie Man," written by Willie Dixon for Muddy. You could add in here also Mickie Most's version of "Money Honey" from 1964, with Mickie being a close associate of Mike Chapman. A fragile consensus however has emerged between the Sweet and Bowie camps that the shared influence was likely the Yardbirds version of "I'm a Man."

"Blockbuster!" was backed by another raver of a proto-metal number in "Need a Lot of Lovin'," which joins "Done Me Wrong All Right" and "You're Not Wrong for Loving Me" as songs with boring and yet weirdly awkward and hard to remember titles that nonetheless hit the listener right between the eyes.

Now we're at the height of the UK glam boom, driven by TV and the grainy pinups in the papers, populated by the likes of Sweet, Bowie, T. Rex, Slade, Mott the Hoople, David Essex, Roxy Music and Mud.

"You know, the glam thing didn't last very long," notes Steve. "A lot of people thought it was the whole of the '70s—it wasn't. It was like 18 months. And then, by the time we got to releasing 'Action,' I'm not… I'll wear stage makeup, but I'm not going to go up there and look like a fairy to sing 'Action.' So that's when we went to the stage-y stuff but not over the top. Yeah, the very worst… I had a pair of silver lamé hot pants once, and I added a silver shirt, and it was a little risqué. Of course I had silver boots. Also, I remember I was doing one TV show, and I had these women's boots on. I have no idea how I got into them. But they were extremely high, and we had been imbibing of champagne before the show, and I nearly fell over; I nearly broke my ankle (laughs). But as always, I got used to them."

"We got dubbed as being a glam rock band, from playing *Top of the Pops*," continues Priest, "where everyone was trying to be more outrageous than everyone else, and it was like, what is that TV show over in the US, can't remember it, where the audience started dressing up? Well, it doesn't matter anyway, but Marc Bolan, I think, started it, and David Bowie was there. We decided to camp it up, and then all of a sudden it was glam rock, and I'm thinking, what the hell are they talking about? It always amazes me that Slade were called glam rock. They were anything but glamorous. They were a middle-class type rock 'n' roll band. It just amazes me that now they go, oh, they were glam rock. It was just because they were there at the time, I think. But they were blue collar workers. And Sweet, we were never really accepted in England. Eventually we were, but reluctantly. And I think people got the wrong idea about us, because of *Top of the Pops*. Yeah, it was a good servant to a bad master."

"Kensington Market, mainly," continues Steve, asked where they'd all go to get glammed up. "That was where everyone went. And then all of a sudden, the single platform turned into a quadruple platform, until you needed a crutch to walk with them. They were dangerous (laughs)." Before Queen became a thing, Freddie Mercury and Roger Taylor ran a stall in the market, which was basically a three-story indoors gathering place for Bohemian culture, located at 49/53 Kensington High Street.

As for the gold and silver jumpsuits and the like, Priest says, "In fact, the wrestlers used to copy us. I'm serious. When we start doing the makeup thing, there was one big wrestler in England, well-known wrestler, Jackie Pallo, and all of a sudden, he would come out (laughs), and he did us! He put makeup on, put silver glitter on and jumped into the ring and everybody was floored. No, we came first. They copied us (laughs)."

"Well, there are a couple of very weird connections here," adds Andy. "There were a couple of wrestlers, in the late '60s and early '70s, who used to wear silver capes and you know, white trunks rather than just ordinary wrestling-type stuff with glitter on them. There was a blond guy called Adrian Street. Mick Tucker and I, we used to laugh our heads off and think he was fantastic (laughs). And there was another guy named Jackie Pallo, in the wrestling world, but that's got nothing to do with music."

Asked about the rumour that there was a manager of multiple glam bands who was really into outer space and aliens and spacesuits and hence all the flash silver, Andy says, "That had nothing to do with us. We were a law unto ourselves. That kind of thing that came after us, within our peer group... we were never part of any Nicky Chinn and Mike Chapman... one of our members of the band nicknamed it the Nicky Chinn and Mike Chapman School of Dancing. I mean, Suzi Quatro came after us, as did a couple of other bands, which I'm not sure they ever meant anything in America, a band called Smokie and a band called Mud. They were building a little roster of bands to write for, but quite frankly, we were set apart, because we were still with the record producer Phil Wainman."

"I remember, Mick Tucker and I... I lived on a road in Shepherd's Bush, where there was a Greek bootmaker who was starting to make these platform shoes, and he had this pair in the window. I went in and I managed to squeeze into them, and I arrived, backstage at the *Top of the Pops*, I remember as quite early days, one of the really bubblegummy-type singles, and all of a sudden, I'm a hell of a lot taller than the rest of them. I said, 'This is the future,' and then we saw Elton John on the show wearing them. Then the Kensington Market started to sell them, but I kept going back to this little Greek guy, because they were half the price, and I was sending Mick and a few other members of bands over. But the clothes thing, it was just to see how outrageous you could actually get. Because one of the members of Slade, Dave Hill, was quite prominent doing this, as was Marc Bolan. And so instead of having just one guy in a band, you had four of us."

"That's why people remember the band," continues Andy, "because it was the whole band, not just Marc Bolan, the lead singer, or Dave Hill, the lead guitar player. You're talking about every one of us was a bit out there doing it; we saw it as a bit of pantomime. I don't know if that means anything in America. Where it's not real; it's more ugly sister than Cinderella. And what people don't remember is, or tend to forget, it's really only '72 to '73, where we were dressing like Christmas trees. Once we hit '74, where we were starting to write our own material and things had moved on, things like 'Fox on the Run,' we were starting to wear what you would probably call what the real rock bands were wearing. It was a mixture of metallic, leather and jeans, jean material, maybe a silk shirt. The whole look had actually changed by then, so really, and truthfully, the look that you think of for bands like Mötley Crüe is definitely from the 'Ballroom Blitz' era in Europe."

And so, off everyone went making this "idyllic" music... "Well, England wasn't at war with anyone, if I remember," laughs Steve. "In the '60s, America had Vietnam so everyone was off about that, in America, at least. But in the '70s, we had nothing to fight about, really. Except the government. They were so bland; it was boring to write songs about them. It was strange, because we were like an era. They called it the glam rock era, which lasted about 18 months. The world thinks it was the whole of the '70s, which it wasn't. But then all of a sudden punk came along, you know, Johnny Rotten and that lot. And so we were old-fashioned."

"But that was one of the things: cart before the horse," figures Steve, on how heavy the band were becoming, despite the glam image. "We were already playing songs like 'Done Me Wrong All Right,' which was the B-side of 'Co-Co,' and we would come out on stage and start the set with that, and everybody would just go, 'What?! Hey?! What's going on here?' So sometimes we were caught between the devil and the deep blue sea, between the glam and what we wanted to play. So, it was a strange situation to be in."

Record Mirror out of the UK perpetuated the link, regularly featuring

Sweet in their hyper glam newspaper... "Yes, you're right—there were a few teeny bop-type magazines, and that was one of them, I vaguely remember. The other ones were in Germany, one called *Bravo*. I was amazed they used to have us and David Cassidy and the Bay City Rollers. That genre, which, you know, you can't not have publicity. But we'd already been doing TV in Holland, Belgium, Germany, and we weren't looked upon as being a glam band. We were looked upon as being a pop band, which is different, believe it or not (laughs). So, they took to us as being more serious than the English did, because we were so outrageous on *Top of the Pops*. I don't know, I don't think they took us seriously. They are now, of course—again (laughs)."

Ask Andy how glam rock happened, and he blames rock scribes, but then he casts it as a natural progression from early strains of rock 'n' roll. "Somebody coined it. It's probably one of the blokes like yourself, somebody with some sort of journalism in their background. It usually starts like that, doesn't it? I guess, the only way I've ever been able to talk about this with other people, has been with other bands like Slade. You see, well, you keep having to calling it glam, because back then, we were just looking to see how we could sell records on *Top of the Pops*, which was the biggest music show in Europe at that time. I remember seeing Marc Bolan on there, early days, and putting this glitter on his face, and the androgyny of it all—is he?, isn't he?, you know, that kind of feel, and it didn't fit comfortably. Especially with us. But a lot of people used to think that we were homosexual anyway, and so it was, 'Okay, you think it's that way, do you? Right.' We all of a sudden became the ugly sisters in the pantomime. The 'How far do you want it to go? We'll show you how far it can go.' It was just a bit of a laugh for us, where I actually think that possibly Bowie took it to an extreme, took it to heart, bless him, but it only lasted for a couple of years."

"See, we were definitely thinking we wanted to go down that heavy rock way, but the way we looked... I don't know, with the long hair, and the fact that we were groomed and not just slobbing about in jeans and tie-dyed T-shirts... that's what other bands like Free were doing—they were still carrying the leftover of the '60s hippie thing, whereas Sweet definitely wanted to glitz it up and glam it up a little bit."

In other words, on top of the "ugly sister in the pantomime" concept (concurrently practiced by the somewhat prettier New York Dolls and later by the squarely ugly Twisted Sister), part of the reason Sweet went glam was to distinguish it from other heavier rock bands image-wise, bands who were going for the scruffy hippie look. But let's not forget, none of the glam bands sounded particularly alike. To be sure, there were narrative and sonic ties between raucous Mud (infamously "Tiger Feet"), Sweet and Slade, but other bands went way off on other tangents. As well, Sweet's closest musical links with glam were with their singles, whereas their own heavier writing was off in a near heavy metal realm, or rather, Sweet were distinguished as the one band doing some quantity of heavy metal while operating in the glam world.

The *Melody Maker*'s esteemed Chris Welch got the balance right already back in January of '73, in describing what Sweet looked like, writing, "What goes on inside the mind of a man who wears eye shadow, silver boots and sports voluptuous red tresses? Does he indulge in the kind of excess that put years on Dorian Gray? Many strongmen, upon viewing the elaborately clad youths who make up Sweet might be forgiven for believing that this highly successful pop group represent a progressive collapse in the morals of modern society, and the final proof that Britain has reverted to the perversions of ancient Rome."

"Most glamorous of all the glam rock bands, Sweet have a kind of outrageous vulgarity that can arouse the ire of the rock press as much as they upset Len Biggles, manly, beer-swigging ruffian with biceps of steel. They expose daring amounts of skin, spend as much on cosmetics as they do on guitar strings, and camp about like a row of bell tents. As they flounce on stage, there is a great tickling of bottoms and laying of hands on hips. And yet the effect created is not so much debauched night at the cabaret in prewar Berlin, but rather a giggle at the new town hop."

Added, in the same article, a droll Andy Scott (who was in fact usually out-drolled by Steve Priest!), "Don't knock what we do. We've made a few mistakes in the past and we learned a few lessons. We started out as a cross between Marmalade and Spooky Tooth. We also did a lot of Motown. We went on to a bubblegum image and it didn't go down too well. After 'Funny, Funny' we thought we were finished. Oh well, that's the end of Sweet. But then we had a big hit with 'Co-Co.' And at the beginning of '72, we knew we had to change with the scene. We elaborated on the makeup and clothes and it has all gotten a bit out of hand. But the kids like it and expect it. We know where we are at."

This would seem to indicate that image-wise, Sweet were attempting a shift away from the less colourful pop and bubblegum look to the in-vogue glam look, to be up to date with current styles, yes, but also to please the fans. What was happening to the music was a concurrent but separate thing. There they were busily moving from pop and bubblegum music to heavy rock, but again, the clothes were neither here nor there. In other words, it hadn't crossed their minds, yet that heavy metal might require a post-glam wardrobe.

As alluded to earlier, Sweet began making inroads in the all-important American market, not that they'd get over for support through touring yet for a while. The band had signed with Bell Records early on, home most notably to The Partridge Family, the (mostly) fictitious TV band who nonetheless scored five gold records in the US, precisely four more than Sweet. "Co-Co" had been issued in the States but only got to No.99 in the charts, but all of a sudden, May of 1973, here comes "Little Willy" storming its way to a No.3 placement as well as RIAA-certified gold record status as a single. It is of no concern to Bell, because holding them off from getting any further is Tony Orlando and Dawn's "Tie a Yellow Ribbon Around the Old Oak Tree," which is also a Bell record.

Continued single success in the UK, now with the irresistible and considerably rockin' "Hell Raiser," issued April of '73 (backed with "Burning"), prompts the release of the band's first LP in the States. "Hell Raiser" hit No.2 in the UK, certifying as a silver single (of note, Steve recalls it being "Hell Raiser" that had been halted by Tony Orlando).

"Tie a Yellow Ribbon Round the Old Oak Tree," arguably one of the longest song titles to make No.1, was actually credited to "Dawn featuring Tony Orlando" (with Tony being a look-alike for his namesake Tony Iommi!). It held the No.1 spot for four weeks and was eventually dislodged by the Wizzard song "See My Baby Jive." Sweet still occupied No.2 when Roy Wood's group took the top spot.

In any event, it's a song that raises the stakes on "Blockbuster!" en route to "Ballroom Blitz" with Connolly vamping enigmatically, playing the restless reprobate about to lose it. Notable on "Hell Raiser," the band had sorted out how to play it when they had been sent to perform a single show in Hong Kong (also on the bill, Tom Paxton), set up because their booking agent wanted to arrange a sort of paid holiday. After the show, the guys were sent to a school to put together the song from Mike's and Nicky's demo.

Remarked Steve, speaking with *Circus*, "'Little Willy' for me was a joke. Lots of times we'd do a basic track for a song that was very heavy and gutsy, but by the time it was mixed and produced, it came out sounding saccharine and prettied up. 'Hell Raiser' was the first thing that sort of sounded like us, but it was much heavier before it was mixed. When we first started, we were a heavy rock 'n' roll band, but we were going on stage, rocking 'n' rolling, and people expected to see The Archies!"

"In the early period, we needed each other," added Mick Tucker, on the penners of "Hell Raiser," namely Mike and Nicky. "But when we started to get more into writing our own material, the relationship with them became detrimental to us. We were brainwashed into believing we were totally dependent on Mike and Nicky. They never took any interest in our own writing. They were only interested in their A-sides, their own songs. The A-sides, against the B-sides, which we wrote ourselves, sounded like two different bands."

Indeed "Burning," one of their own, is the band's heaviest song yet, an almost demonic and doomy metal monster that predicts the invention of power metal. The guys play the heck out of it, taking the opportunity to stretch out, especially Mick. The narrative is most definitely maintained: Sweet is taking the B-side back road toward independence.

Julie Webb, from the *NME*, noted that "Hell Raiser" went down a storm at a Bristol gig she was reviewing, writing, "Sweet, you may remember, got a right slagging off by the critics after their Rainbow gig. Truth is, there seems to be musical conflict in the band. Or that's how it comes off on stage. They play the old hits like 'Co-Co' and 'Poppa Joe' and 'Wig-Wam Bam,' but the feeling hits you between the eyes that they don't really want to play them and in fact would prefer to be shot of them. Now when it's an Andy Scott extravaganza on guitar, or a Mick Tucker drum spot—that's

April 28, 1973
NEW MUSICAL EXPRESS
Page 41
HELL RAISER
RCA 2357
A new single from THE SWEET on RCA
RCA Records and Tapes

when they seem happiest. Like the moment the spotlight was on Scott, he goes into action like a cosmic whirl. And Mick (who incidentally is a good drummer, though he looks like he's trying too hard) can sure hit them skins."

"Recently, we heard that the band had 'altered'—even 'developed.' Certainly, a lot of visual groundwork has been put in. The recent addition of proper lighting—the blue police light during the playing of 'Blockbuster!' for instance—has done much to improve the stage act. The rock 'n' roll medley, including 'Summertime Blues' and 'Lucille,' seemed to have been whipped up to twice the normal speed, and at times the vocal sound harsh, but it was this medley that encouraged that hysteria we're always hearing about at Sweet gigs. Singer Brian Connolly, looking a positive picture of sartorial elegance, did much to work the audience into some kind of participation even if he does have a somewhat over-aggressive manner on stage. The encore, 'Hell Raiser,' was the highlight, with smoke on stage, and the band, interested in their music again, sounding tighter than before. And after that? Well, the surprise of the evening: bright lights all over the stage and the audience, as to the strains of that memorable tune 'The Stripper,' Sweet did a quick 'can-can' and threw out posters. Different."

As a note on the rock 'n' roll medley, this is something that the other vocally blessed heavy metal band, namely Uriah Heep, did on their hit two-LP *Live* album, issued a month previous—Heep even called this insufferable bit "Rock 'n' Roll Medley."

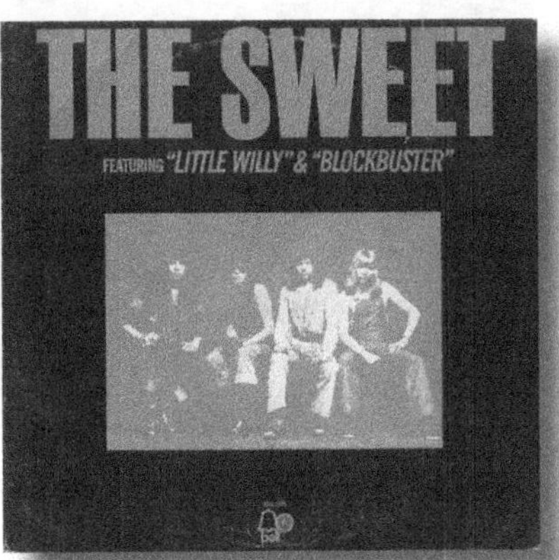

Back to the band's creeping career in the United States, July 1973 sees the release of *The Sweet*, an apt and satisfyingly grounded title for a debut record, even if one is quickly disoriented by the additional text on the cover that blares "FEATURING "LITTLE WILLY" & "BLOCKBUSTER"." The colour palette used for the cover, silver and brown, was picked for its similarity to the colours of the Hershey's Milk Chocolate packaging, i.e. an iconic American sweet.

"Little Willy" a rocking new taste from the Sweet.
RCA RECORDS AND TAPES
RCA 2225

The Sweet in Concert
Top Rank   Swansea   23 June
Top Rank   Bristol   24 June
Top Rank   Cardiff   25 June
Francoise   21 Kings Road   26 June
Top Rank   Liverpool   28 June
Top Rank   Hanley   29 June
Top Rank   Plymouth   30 June
Chelsea Village   Bournemouth   1 July
Rex Ballroom   Bognor Regis   3 July

We don't want to over-emphasise the importance of *The Sweet* because it didn't sell squat. But what is gorgeous about the situation is that Bell had put together a record that stressed the band's heavy rock side and therefore, necessarily, their own songwriting. There were ten songs on the record, with fully six of them written by the band.

Commendably, for the first full-length stateside, there's no "Funny, Funny," "Chop Chop," "Poppa Joe" or any of the non-single nonsense from *Co-Co*. Instead, Chapman and Chin are represented by the sonic punch of "Little Willy," "Wig-Wam Bam," "Hell Raiser" and "Blockbuster" (formerly "Blockbuster!"), the latter of which experienced a little bit of chart action, reaching No.73 on the Billboard charts.

As for the band's own tunes, what we got was "New York Connection" and "Done Me Wrong Alright" (a.k.a. "Done Me Wrong All Right") on side one, and then "Need a Lot of Lovin'," "Man from Mecca," "Spotlight" and "You're Not Wrong for Loving Me" on side two, the latter the only ballad on the album.

"We were already there," says Steve, asked about the band's heaviness at this point. "We were inspired by Cream, with a lot of blues inspiration. Phil Wainman's forte was the fact that he was a session drummer, and that's all he did. He played in studios, so he knew what he was doing. Chinn and Chapman had no idea. Chapman wrote songs; Chinn needed a career and went along for the ride. But Wainman was the only one with any actual studio acumen and knew what he was doing. The only problem with him, he was a bit old-fashioned. He wanted me to use a Fender bass, which was fine, because that was a good old one you used in studios, but I hated it (laughs). He would make me put foam rubber under the end of the guitar I was using to dampen the sound. I would rip it out (laughs)."

"Sweet were brought into an area by a record producer," continues Andy, tying it all together, "and introduced to a couple of songwriters who quite frankly thought, these will be successful, but they were completely and utterly wrong for what our band's ideals with me were, by the time I joined. But the singles did not reflect what we were. And it wasn't until '72, we were already in the slipstream, that we actually took a bit more control. In fact, if you turn the records over, and quite a few DJs did, and critics of the band, were always saying, in the magazines like the *Melody Maker* and the *NME*, if you turn the records over, you'll probably get a bit more indication as to what possibly the band could do. Because, you see, for the masses, the seven-inch single that was selling a million every time we released one, that's not what journalists and critics wanted."

Rolling Stone reviewed *The Sweet*, almost filling the page with their analysis, framing it in a keyline and providing a picture.

"The Sweet is already on its way to US triumph," wrote James Isaacs, "on the strength of last spring's smash 'Little Willy,' an infectious, pounding piece of highly formulaic pop that substantiated the group's place in the grand tradition of such English bubblegum bosses as the Small Faces, the Herd and Dave, Dee, etc., through its insistent, heel-kicking rhythm and melody, vocals bolstered by chorus and heavy guitar underpinnings. Ohio Express confections meet the early-charging Led Zep, and therein lies the joy of listening to almost every cut on The Sweet's American debut LP, which is composed of the recent English hit singles and B-sides."

"Whoever they are," continues Isaacs, "The Sweet are predictably comely; their collective look of pristine pop stars from working-class origins is, of course, perfect. Musically, the singer has assimilated the past of Marriott and Plant (listen to 'New York Connection,' which sounds like a Small Faces raver, or 'Need a Lot of Lovin',' a dead ringer for Zep's 'Communication Breakdown'). The band has most assuredly done its homework while listening to the Beck Yardbirds (guitar break on 'Man from Mecca,' a feedbacker that reincarnates vintage 'Happenings 10 Years Time Ago' Beck), the Zep, the Who, the Small Faces and (thankfully), to a lesser degree, Jethro Tull and Black Sabbath."

"Of the ten cuts, eight are bonafide time bombs, set to explode within three minutes and performed with diabolical calculated flash. The only two duds are the mannered 'Spotlight' and a stiff, out-of-place bow to CSN&Y called 'You're Not Wrong for Loving Me.' 80% of the material herein would make you want to crank up the car radio and do wheelies for hours on end."

Jon Tiven, reviewing the album for Florida's short-lived music paper *Zoo World*, proclaimed, "(FANFARE) HERE they are (blast of fuzzbox trumpets) the NEW (cannon-fire) ENGLISH (fireworks explode to form a Union Jack) HEAVIES! The Sweet have a weighty problem, namely, what is The Sweet Sound? Is it the heavygum sound of their singles (written by Nicky Chinn and Mike Chapman), or the superheavy Purplish sound of their B-sides (penned by the band)? Stepping into the shoes of The Who we find the Sweet, a band that's had to put up with all kinds of image problems in their home country, England. They started off as a total bubblegum band, but after a few singles they broke away from the acoustic guitar almost entirely and turned up the volume on the electrics for 'Little Willy,' their first hit in America. England still loved them, but they were stuck with the Pop label. In America they were just getting called The Ohio Express with fuzzboxes."

"Unfortunately, by the time 'Little Willy' dominated the United States record charts, they had already put out three singles in England which were considerably better, not to mention heavier. But in America they were getting put into the Pop Slot by snot-nosed clots who dismissed 'Blockbuster!' as a steal from David Bowie, not even realising that 'The Jean Genie' was a lacklustre version of The Yardbirds' 'I'm a Man' (taken from the Bo Diddley book of licks) while 'Blockbuster!' was rock power incarnate. They've been compared to Grand Funk Railroad but that's just a load of hogwash. First off, The Sweet can play their instruments quite well, they can sing well, their own material (although derivative) is fine, their arrangements are incredibly good, and they aren't self-indulgent."

"*The Sweet* can clearly be separated into three categories," mused Alan Betrock, in *Phonograph Record*. "The first, and best, group of songs fall into the 'power-pop' genre, and were all hit A-sides: 'Wig-Wam Bam,' 'Little Willy,' 'Hell Raiser' and 'Blockbuster!' The second category fall into the Black Sabbath heavy-thud mould, and were all Sweet B-sides: 'New York Connection,' 'Done Me Wrong All Right,' 'Need a Lot of Lovin'' and 'Man from Mecca.' The third, and least important category are the remaining two tracks, 'Spotlight' and 'You're Not Wrong for Loving Me,' which, for simplicity's sake, shall be deemed melodic-ballad-fillers. The 'heavy B-side category' is the one that puzzles me most. Obviously back in the days of Sweet's early hits like 'Funny Funny,' 'Co-Co' and 'Poppa Joe,' the group was mercilessly harassed for being no-talent bubblegum hitsters, so in an attempt to show the undergrounders where they were really at, they made their B-sides forays into realms better governed by Black Sabbath and Uriah Heep. Unfortunately, these B-sides never reached the ears for which they were intended, so the Sweet's change of image had to come via their A-sides. And as these A-sides got progressively heavier, and the Sweet began to gain more respect in their homeland (though they are still joked about), I would have expected the B-sides to get more original."

Continues Betrock, "The final UK hit, 'Hell Raiser,' alternates with 'Wig-Wam Bam' as the best cut on the album. It is their heaviest success, and their tightest effort. In some ways, I feel that the success of 'Hell Raiser' paved the way in Britain for the success of 10CC's 'Rubber Bullets.' The Sweet are the only group who have combined all that's 'best in the British 'progressive-commercial' sound (Herd, early Move, Zombies, etc.) with the superlatives of the British 'power-pop' genre (Who, Small Faces, etc.), and if that wasn't enough, they manage to add a creative impetus of their own. So, what this boils down to is that the Sweet are masters of the 45."

Curiously, in an earlier feature article for *Zoo World* written in the summer of '73, no mention is made of *The Sweet*. However, there is a surprising report direct from Brian on how the band's next record was to be a concept album! But before we hear that interesting nugget, Brian demonstrates a clear understanding of the band's mixed messages and how they might jeopardise success in the US.

"I think a hit single is the hardest thing to write," begins Connolly. "You've really got to know how to find that extra magic. So actually, there's a very good reason why we only write the B-sides. The writers of the A-sides have never written a miss. We can't compete with them. I mean really, who'd want to? If you get eight big ones on the charts, they haven't done wrong. Besides, as things are at the moment, we co-wrote the last two, 'Blockbuster!' and 'Hell Raiser,' with Mike Chapman. So now it's not quite the writers writing for us. We write with them, and anything or any ideas we sort of have for ourselves are used."

Concerned that prospective fans are buying the band's old records on import, Brian says, "I don't think that's a good idea, because we don't really want to go back on any of the old singles. I mean, 'Little Willy' is old enough. I really don't know why it took so long to come over there. I believe they did release 'Co-Co' over there but I'm glad they haven't released any of the earlier stuff. I Even for myself, I know it was a hit and everything, but I would have preferred to have released something a little more up to date. 'Little Willy' isn't really too bad, but it still isn't the Sweet as they are today. Have you heard, 'Blockbuster!?' It's going to be the next big one, the next single you're getting. That is the Sweet as they are now. It's quite a bit different. We're cutting out all the in-between ones. Then you're getting 'Hell Raiser,' which is currently out in England. The way we've planned it is by November or maybe when we come on tour in September, we'll catch up."

"You see, in the beginning, the single was more important than the group," continues Connolly, "and now it's swung the other way and they don't really knock us now. Because the face of the group is far stronger. It represents the singles, whereas the singles used to represent the group. I think the act's got better as well. Our music is harder. Basically, it's just modern rock 'n' roll, really. This is why I'm glad we're breaking now in the States instead of a year ago, because we would've broken with even more poppy jingle jangle stuff. I'm pleased that none of the earlier singles are going to be released in the States. It just doesn't figure. It's just not the group. It's taken us three good years to get ourselves out of that bubblegum bracket and I hate to get pushed right back into the bracket in the States."

And the next record, as it was planned back in the summer of '73?

"It's the story of rock 'n' roll, not just a pop album with singles. Sort of rock 'n' roll from 1956 to 1976. We're going to finish it with a futuristic track. The songs are original. Basically, it's our interpretation of what was around over those years. What was leading the era, '56, '59, '63, '65, you know, Beatles and so on. The name of the album is *From the Grave of*

Ocker the Rocker. And the idea is that Ocker becomes famous in 1956 and hits the big rock scene, the pop bit, and here's ten years of his life. We go from sort of early Elvis to Little Richard, right up to '64, when Ocker gets killed. Then there's a Beatles thing, then an interpretation of Phil Spector, which was an era all on its own. Then we come right up to date and finish the album with a futuristic track of what we think '76 will be about."

Fortunately, we never got *From the Grave of Ocker the Rocker*. As Steve told Genny Hall in April '74, "We got halfway through writing the album with the help of Mike Chapman and Nicky Chinn, but when we listened to it in the cold light of day, we didn't find the songs very inspiring. So now we've shelved the whole idea."

Unfortunately, the public didn't show up at the record store to purchase copies of *The Sweet* either, perhaps in part turned off by the compilation-look album cover. But indeed, this was a record that the critics—as well as music fans who liked their rock hard—could get behind. Fact is, for 1973, *The Sweet* was a fairly loud 'n' proud record, the work of a British band but somewhat American-sounding, albeit graced with a bit of the UK's big three at the time, namely Uriah Heep, Deep Purple and Led Zeppelin.

Stateside, all we had were the likes of Cactus and Mountain, with new offerings from Blue Öyster Cult in 1972 and in 1973, Aerosmith and Montrose. Amongst that lot, *The Sweet* sounds just fine, thanks. The strength of the record should have been followed up with a tour of the States but that was not to happen.

In a story that is eerily similar to that of guitarist Brian Robertson and Thin Lizzy on the eve of an important world tour, just as the band was supposed to capitalise, Brian got himself into a pub brawl in Staines with someone who considered his good looks perfect for a Nazi recruiting poster. Like Robertson who had his hand sliced up, Connolly also took damage to his "money-maker" when outside and mixing it up, he was stomped on the throat. The result was that he couldn't speak for six months.

In total, this injury was to scotch a US tour, a British tour, a marquee show at Charlton Football Stadium supporting The Who, and some of his potential contribution to the upcoming second album.

As Brian told *Melody Maker*'s Jeff Ward in mid-'74, "Give me any song and I'll sing it, but something like 'Teenage Rampage' is a bit difficult because it really is screaming. I never realised until I lost my voice how high we sing, because it's so easy to sing anything else. I think it'll be a few months yet before my voice comes back 100%. If you'd seen the treatments I had to have, needles and all…"

"The biggest choker was Charlton," continues Connolly. "We were booked, and everything was confirmed. We knew we were doing it weeks and weeks ago, but nobody wanted to say anything until The Who had made their arrangements. We were chuffed about it for a couple of months. Basically, Townshend asked us to do the gig. We dig The Who and know them fairly well, and I think they were aware of the fact that we'd always dug them over the years. I think maybe it was Townshend's way of saying that Sweet is underrated musically. The band has always been underrated but I suppose we're going to be tied with it for God knows how long. I mean, The Who were a singles band once—we've got so much in common with them, I think. Charlton would've been about the best gig we could've done. I don't yet know if we're on the world tour or not when the whole package goes out again. But the last I heard was that we would be on it. It's still not the same as playing in England, though. I would've got more out of playing at Charlton than I would have California, because everything you want to do, you want to do first in England."

Arguably most ruinous to The Sweet's career was the effect on the band's stature in the States. The success of "Little Willy" in America would stand as a curious rock 'n' roll story, brief, with a whiff of novelty and one-hit wonder to it, until, that is, Sweet mania would erupt on the backs of "Fox on the Run" and a military snare-strafed rave-up heard 'round the world called "Ballroom Blitz."

Still, one could sense in Brian's words the cantankerous attitude toward careerism that seemed to be a commonality within the ranks of the band. As he told Cameron Crowe in 1974 (seemingly without a sense of irony!), "Those Rollers. Just look at them with their funny clothes and nervous determination to become the biggest band in the world. The Sweet just don't care. Everyone tells us we have to scheme on an American audience, if we really want to hit it big. Ha! When we get there, we'll play what we want to play. And if we don't go over well, we'll do concerts here. This is a rock 'n' roll band, not an army."

"I'm not surprised these other groups failed," continues Brian, ready to take another swipe. "They're average bands. Not outstanding at all. Look at Slade. They're just an English football band that had a few hits, aren't they? On the other hand, we're not just some artificial singles band. We thought the only reason 'Little Willy' was a hit in the States was because people thought it was a black record. Besides, at the time we were wearing makeup and dressing up like four Christmas trees. It was a giggle for us. People like Bowie were taking it really seriously, and we were just a bunch of tarts having a good time. If we'd gone to the States two years ago, when the glitter rat race was on, we would've been misunderstood. It would've killed us. We did the right thing by staying away. No question."

The band would only record the one album for Bell. Manager Ed Leffler got them out of the deal with the help of a record executive named Richard Perry. Perry had recently transferred from EMI in England over to Capitol on the Sunset Strip in LA, and so he was well aware at how big Sweet were in Europe. For once, the band would find a spot of luck across the pond in their quest for world domination.

CHAPTER 4:

Sweet Fanny Adams
"Like somebody taking the reins of a racehorse"

While Sweet was busy not executing a much-needed assault on America, it did the next best thing, and that's unleash upon the world its statement for the ages.

Emerging from Audio International Studios in London, the band carried with them the tapes for "Ballroom Blitz," a story inspired by a gig the guys played in Scotland, January 27th, 1973, where they were "bottled" off the stage. The song opens with Mick on military snare and bass drum whacks, while Brian coyly utters the immortal words, "Are You Ready Steve?" This intro was inspired by producer Phil Wainman demonstrating for the guys, Sandy Nelson's "Let There Be Drums." Explained Mick to *Circus*, "We always wanted to make a drum record, and when we were routining the song, it all revolved around my drum pattern, like a Sandy Nelson record."

Then we're into a song that sounds like an update on the poppy punk of "Hell Raiser." Except here we've got Chapman and Chinn writing an expert ramp-up through a couple of pre-chorus shapes toward a cloud-break of a chorus that could not be resisted. The vocals are fun as well, with Brian ratcheting up in intensity from a staid and sombre verse persona to what is a metaphor for the mania and chaos of the fight discussed in the song. In this aim, he is helped by Steve who hysterically reports on the mayhem. Later on, Andy gets into the brawl, but on guitar rather than vocal, busting out a choppy chord-based guitar solo.

The "Ballroom Blitz" single was issued in September '73, backed with the band-penned "Rock & Roll Disgrace," a noisy, tribal hard rocker that is a little less technical and more glam than the band's usual B-sides.

Disc—September 15, 1973   11
THE SWEET
THE
BALLROOM
BLITZ
NEW SINGLE   RCA 2403
RCA Records and Tapes

Mick just pounds away, although Andy does do a twinned guitar solo. The single hit No.2 in Britain, kept out of the top spot by Simon Park Orchestra's "Eye Level," a song from a popular TV show at the time called Van Der Valk. It quickly went silver and then gold in the UK and was issued, again, true to the usual plan, all over the world—it must be noted, the single, at the equivalent of a dollar or even less, was a way for a larger amount of fans to participate in patronising their favourite bands, and as efficiently as possible, i.e. getting the hit single, which in many cases would be played until the often quite thin vinyl wore out. As well though, fans were being conditioned with Sweet to realise that even if they were going to buy the album, there'd likely be a B-side that wouldn't be on it.

Strength to strength, February '74, "Teenage Rampage" becomes the band's third single in a row to reach number No.2 in the UK. The guys are stalled from reaching No.1 this time by another ChinniChap composition, Mud's irritating yet irrepressible "Tiger Feet." Apparently Sweet might have sold more records, but the sales that were sampled this time were all in the Midlands, where Mud happened to be from.

This gold-selling single features on its B-side, "Own Up, Take a Look at Yourself," written by the band. "Teenage Rampage" sticks obediently to formula, sounding like the mean, median and average of all the previous singles stretching back to "Little Willy." It's heavy, there are handclaps, it's anthemic and there are these memorable "hysterical" vocal passages along with accomplished vocal harmonies. The B-side finds Sweet writing once again, like the previous B-side, somewhat glam and heavy just like Mike and Nicky. In other words, across the band's most current four tracks, everybody is thinking the same. Still, there's a somewhat awkward and

SWEET
TEENAGE RAMPAGE
Get yourself a Constitution
JOIN THE REVOLUTION
SWEET
LPBO 5004
RCA Records and Tapes

choppy chorus with more notes than you'd characteristically get out of Chapman and Chinn. There's also an aggression that isn't part of the band's happier glam numbers. In essence, chalk this one up as another Sweet song that predicts the rise of punk.

And then, before the fans could take a breath from laughing at Sweet's latest gold and silver jump suits, April '74, here they come with a second full-length album, *Sweet Fanny Adams*, a record now considered a classic. It's a small point, but this was also the band's first album as Sweet, as opposed to The Sweet. But more importantly *Sweet Fanny Adams* marked the nexus point where a serious play for rock credibility would take place, the band writing many of their own songs and playing them with then-modern heavy metal aplomb, musicianship to the fore.

Also at this juncture, Sweet brought on board as manager the aforementioned Ed Leffler, later famous for commandeering Van Halen; Leffler is now deceased, having succumbed to thyroid cancer in 1993 at the age of 57.

"I became involved with the group in December of '73," explained Ed to *Record World*'s Eliot Sekuler, "after they had, during the summer of that year, *their* enormous 'Little Willy' record. The three singles that followed 'Little Willy' didn't happen for them. I was friendly with Larry Uttal, who was president of Sweet's label at that time, Bell Records. I knew that Larry might be leaving Bell, and at that time, the group had only six months remaining on their contract. I went to Larry and asked that no other Sweet records be released until his future and that of Bell had been decided. I promised that I wouldn't talk to another label until Larry's plans had been made, and that he would be given the first opportunity to sign them."

"Larry indicated that he still believed very much in Sweet, but he held off on making a final decision on his own plans until there were only a few weeks left on the group's contract. By the time Larry left Bell, all of the group's product reverted back to their own ownership. I was very happy because after Slade and T-Rex had come to the US and had not made it, it seemed better to do nothing for a while than to try something and fail with it. Time would allow the necessary groundwork to be laid down."

"I had already seen Sweet on the stage and knew that they were an exciting performing group. I knew that if I could bring them here in the right manner, they had a good chance at stardom in this country; they had never performed here before. I thought the setting for a Sweet contract tour would be crucial. American audiences are comparatively rude towards performers, unlike audiences in the UK or Europe who will generally be in their seats at 7:30 for a 7:30 show and will be very courteous towards an opening act. Here, if there are three acts on the bill, people will hang out or do whatever until the main act comes on. My feeling was that the only way that I could properly showcase Sweet here would be to let them do their own show, because they're good and they do an hour-and-a-half to two hours on stage."

"In order to do that, we had to get their recordings better exposed. 'Little Willy' had been such a big record that most people thought that was the name of the band. Unfortunately, the record had been classified as a bubble-gum song and Sweet are anything but a bubblegum group. I felt that we had to let 'Little Willy' die, as it were, to re-establish the group's image from scratch. So, we waited; we allowed a certain amount of time to pass with the memories of other English groups that had come here and hadn't made it. We negotiated and finally, last February, we consummated a deal with Capitol Records; almost seven months after, as you can see, it's done very well over here. Capitol Records has really gotten behind the band and has done a great job for them; they've been the cement behind our plans."

Speaking with *Cash Box* about signing on with Capitol, an unattributed member of the band said that "The old company was not behind us, not into us. We didn't know but a few people there, and the one person who was behind us left. Also, at the time we didn't have a US manager. We just bided our time until we found the right record company, the right management, and that time is now."

Added Leffler, "Capitol is interested in building a group. When negotiations were going on with Capitol, there was a rift between the group and their producer/writers Nicky Chinn and Mike Chapman. The material that interested Capitol was mostly written and produced by Chinn and Chapman, but when the break came between the group and the producers, Capitol expressed its faith in the group. They did that by signing a contract."

"We had had enough, and they had had enough," was the sentiment, now back to the band talking. "The split was really made a certainty when we had a miss, a single called 'Turn It Down,' which was turned down by the BBC, by everyone." As for touring the US versus Europe… "Europe's had all the excitement; they want progression. But we are an excitement band, so it's just a matter of picking the right numbers. We're always changing the show. We are progressing. What we're doing now on stage is no big clever thing, but compared to say 'Ballroom Blitz,' yes, it's different. In the UK it's all AM. But the only thing you do when cutting a single there is listen to it through a small speaker to see how it will sound on radio or TV. But we write commercially anyway. Pete Townshend used to say, back in the early days of the Who, that if you go over three minutes on a single, things get a bit touchy, but if you use more than three chords, you get called up before the committee. But we have a really good line-up of singles for '76 already in the can. We wouldn't have chosen 'Ballroom Blitz' as our first single for Capitol. They wanted 'Fox on the Run' first but realised that if 'Ballroom Blitz' made it, 'Fox' was the perfect follow-up, and that if it didn't, then they had another good shot with 'Fox.'"

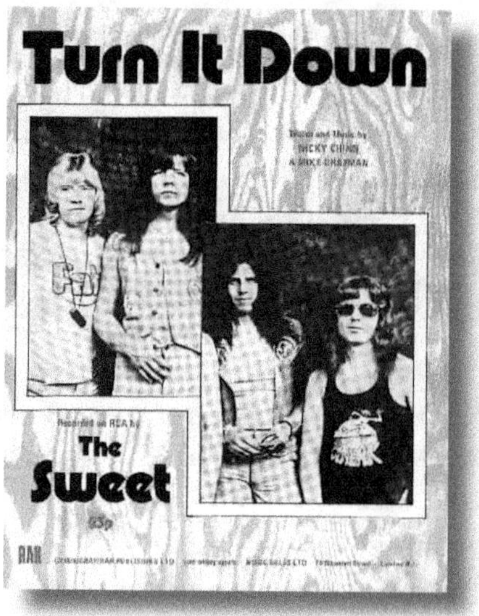

Catching up on the glam scene, now nearing its demise, at the light end of things, there was Bowie, T. Rex, Roxy Music, Bay City Rollers even, and in the middle, Mott and Mud (says Steve of Mud, "They were in the Chinn and Chapman camp, stable. They were writing songs for them same time as they were writing songs for us"). But bringing the clanging power chords, well, that was left to the likes of Sweet and to some extent Slade.

But now there was also Queen, who was making a splash with their 1973 debut and now a second album called *II*, issued a month previous to *Sweet Fanny Adams*.

"I guess you could say that" agrees Andy, who offers a different timeframe, but a valid one, albeit based on the evidence of Sweet's singles more so. "I think that Queen came a fair bit later than Slade and Sweet. I think they were probably three years on, but quite a few people have made the comparison. But the way I see it, we probably kicked off the hard-sounding rock band with the high vocal harmonies, but probably before the public was due to receive it. So, when Queen came along, three or four years later, it was probably the right time. And remember, we had just been through a kind of sexual revolution, so having a Freddie up front of a heavy rock band wouldn't have had the same problems that it would've had in 1970. Because in '75, it was probably considered, 'Yeah, this is quite chic.'"

For his part, Steve doesn't shy away from the idea that Sweet did all of Queen's tricks first. "Oh yeah, well, the idea of the whole band, when we got together, pre-Andy, the idea was to have… there were only three of us at the time who could sing at the time: me, Mick and Brian, because our guitarist couldn't sing. And we wanted three-part harmonies over heavy backing. That was the whole idea, a really rocking heavy backtrack, but with three-part harmonies over it, you know, in front of it. Nobody had done that before."

Fair enough, but why did Queen take it to a very large bank, while Sweet came second fiddle? "Oh, it's all down to timing. And it's also down to whether the press liked you or not, how you handle the press. As I say, it really is down to timing, the fact that we opened the door. As Bo Diddley said, 'I opened the door to rock 'n' roll and got left holding the handle.' And that's what we did in England, because they came along and did exactly the same as what we were doing. But I don't know, they just got accepted. It was one of those things. Hard to explain."

"We felt that we knew better than the Chinn and Chapman situation, and Phil Wainman," continues Andy, onto the subject of taking over the songwriting reins for this landmark record. "They probably would've wanted us to carry on with a few more openly naïve pop singles. But right at that time, it was Phil Wainman who turned around and said, 'Look, there's an album to be made here.' Chinn and Chapman were spending more time in America and following their noses, and we were basically left in England knowing that there's an album spot, and we just got on with it. I wrote a hell of a lot of songs, of which I think half a dozen of them are on *Sweet Fanny Adams*. And I really enjoyed Phil Wainman's enthusiasm, because he threw himself into it. But there is probably another agenda going on there as well.

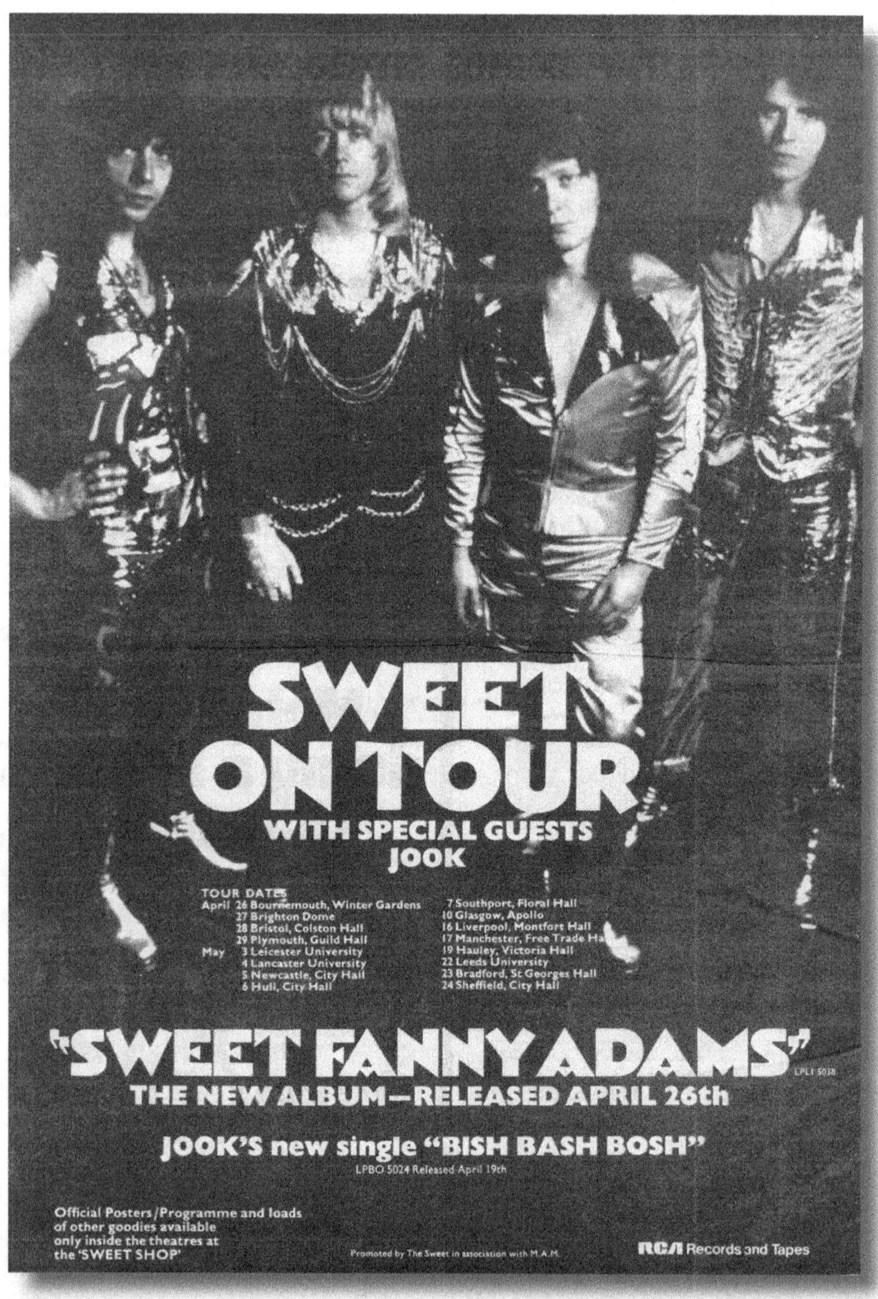
SWEET
ON TOUR
WITH SPECIAL GUESTS
JOOK

TOUR DATES
April 26 Bournemouth, Winter Gardens
27 Brighton Dome
28 Bristol, Colston Hall
29 Plymouth, Guild Hall
May 3 Leicester University
4 Lancaster University
5 Newcastle, City Hall
6 Hull, City Hall
7 Southport, Floral Hall
10 Glasgow, Apollo
16 Liverpool, Montfort Hall
17 Manchester, Free Trade Hall
19 Hauley, Victoria Hall
22 Leeds University
23 Bradford, St Georges Hall
24 Sheffield, City Hall

"SWEET FANNY ADAMS"
LPLI 5038
THE NEW ALBUM—RELEASED APRIL 26th

JOOK'S new single "BISH BASH BOSH"
LPBO 5024 Released April 19th

Official Posters/Programme and loads
of other goodies available
only inside the theatres at
the 'SWEET SHOP'

Promoted by The Sweet in association with M.A.M.

RCA Records and Tapes

He was probably quite happy just to get on with it without having Nicky and Mike breathing down his neck. That was the one and only album of Sweet that didn't actually have one of the singles on it."

"But, as the Americans pointed out, that was probably the one album that was, in a rock music sense, the most commercially viable, even though it didn't have singles on it. So, when we went to America, they loved the title *Desolation Boulevard*, but they didn't really like some of the material on *Desolation Boulevard*. So, they basically cherry-picked *Sweet Fanny Adams*, moved it onto *Desolation Boulevard*, and added the two singles 'Fox on the Run' and 'Ballroom Blitz.' And that was the album in America. Their *Desolation Boulevard* was nothing like the *Desolation Boulevard* for the Europeans."

More on that later, but yes, to clarify, the version of *Desolation Boulevard* for North America, that in fact went RIAA-certified gold, was mostly the classics from *Sweet Fanny Adams* (which wasn't released in the US), plus some well-picked singles. The UK and the US *Desolation Boulevard* shared the same album cover, but the UK version was a straight carry-forward on in the career past *Sweet Fanny Adams*, all new songs, no overlap.

Back to *Sweet Fanny Adams* and first its cover imagery, it was essentially a demonstration of all the glam talk we've generated so far. "The *Sweet Fanny Adams* cover art was the starting point," notes Andy, "because the compilation sleeve that went before that (meaning the UK issue of *Funny How Sweet Co-Co Can Be*) was basically one of the songwriter's ideas of, you know, having a boiled sweet that somebody was unwrapping, and there we were inside it, you know—ha ha. But we wanted to show that we had two sides, so what the guy did, after we had taken a heavy rock pose of us in all the glitter suits, for *Sweet Fanny Adams*, he put in a mirror, and threw some kind of oil and distortion stuff on it, so that you had us standing, and our reflection was this rather disfigured version of the band. And the back sleeve was where all the metal pipes were, with us in our own little cubicle, if you like, all four members of the band. And I thought that was quite an interesting sleeve for a first attempt."

"Sweet were the first glam band ever, and that I ever worked with," recalls photographer Barry Levine, famed for his work with Kiss and Mötley Crüe. "I did the album cover for *Sweet Fanny Adams*. And that was the funniest band around, because, at least Nikki Sixx and these guys were the epitome of, 'You look at me the wrong way and I'll rip your head off.' They were who they were. They didn't try to be anybody else but Mötley Crüe. The name does personify who they are. Whereas The Sweet were just four guys who really didn't write their material; they had those big songwriters writing their material. And then later on down the line they started writing their own material, but basically, they went for the complete Gary Glitter glam look, that whole real... I mean, a lot of people don't really understand that, but Sweet were probably the first real glam band. But the funny thing about it is, they're all street guys in a sense, like if they weren't doing that, they would be bricklayers. Glam was more of a façade than anything else. It was more putting on a costume. I photographed the Dolls when they were starting out, and with the Dolls, at least you had an attitude that reflected their image and their music and it was integrated. The Sweet didn't have any of that."

"Like I was saying, they were bricklayers," continues Levine. "Especially the lead singer, who died of alcoholism. And I remember shooting AC/DC, who had that same kind of attitude. Sweet, I remember once in Germany, when they were doing their album, and at one point John Paul Jones was helping on a track with them, and he came into the studio, in Germany, '75, '76, and the lead singer was drunk out of his mind, and he could never get himself straight. Andy Scott, the lead guitarist, was really the leader of that band. He was always a pretty straight-up, nice guy, but don't fuck with me. Steve Priest, really, really a sweet guy, really nice guy, no attitude. He almost had the same attitude as Deke, John Deacon of Queen. Where, with Queen, these were three guys that constantly hated each other. I mean, it was funny to watch. They would get into arguments before every show. And Deacon was the only one who separated himself from the bullshit. He was like the accountant of the band. He was just a nice, sweet guy. And Steve Priest was the same kind of mentality. Quiet, no ego, nothing like that."

As for Mick Tucker, Levine comments that, "It's funny, that drummer reminds me of Tommy Lee. The same technique. Even same physical technique, the way he would swing his sticks above his head and come down with it. If you go back and look at him, and look at Tommy, same technique. But yeah, they were pretty rough around the edges. These boys were from Scotland; they were Newcastle boys, Glasgow boys (ed. Brian, at least, was born in Glasgow), they were pretty rough around the edges. So, people that knew their music, knew the band and knew that. And they just represented a whole other look—flamboyant clothes, big hair—they had a lot to do with influencing people. Plus, at the time, playing in a band, being English, coming over here—that was something special. And the LA bands paid homage to them. But it's funny because when they came back over here, they were managed by this guy who was managing Van Halen for a while, and they came over in the '70s and tried to come off as a pure rock band. Nobody gave them any attention or any respect, which was sad because they were really good musicians. When they took off the costumes it was like Clark Kent as opposed to Superman."

As for the title of the *Sweet Fanny Adams* album, it's a bit of a circuitous tale, but there had been a brutal murder of an eight-year-old girl back in 1867 named Fanny Adams, and somehow this lurid bit of headline news moved into British Navy vernacular for downtime at work or idleness, essentially "nothing." From this comes "sweet F.A." or "sweet fuck all." Of course, underscoring this narrative, the song that opens side two of the original vinyl version of the album is called "Sweet F.A." Steve indicates that it was manager Ed Leffler that thought this would be a good name for the album.

Explained Mick at the time, speaking with *Melody Maker*, "The title of the album was originally *Sweet FA*, which summed it all up, and then Nicky went 'round to the BBC and one of the guys there on the panel said he wouldn't say he wasn't going to play the album, but he wouldn't encourage it to be played with a title like that. We compromised and called the album *Sweet Fanny Adams*. I suppose you have to do that sort of thing, really, like 10CC had to. Yet when they get things like Lou Reed's 'Walk on the Wild Side,' they don't even worry! Some of the lyrics—even Bowie—if they read them…"

Sweet Fanny Adams opens with a rock 'n' roll atomic blast.

"Set Me Free" emphatically ushers in the new Sweet with a percussive maelstrom in ten seconds from the band's musical secret weapon Mick Tucker. After a few surging and punctuated power chords, the song converts into a proto-speed metal that would have been a highlight on any Deep Purple album, had Ritchie, Ian and Roger written it.

"I remember locking myself away in my garage, much to the chagrin of my family, because I didn't really have a studio in the house at that time," recalls Andy. "So, I remember hanging carpets up all around the edge of the garage, and creating little booths within, so I could still use my amplifiers without disturbing the neighbours too much. And I had a couple of Revox tape decks in there, and I just got on with it. And the things that kind of came out, I think Mick put his finger on it, we wanted to write about experiences, and 'Sweet F.A.' is about things that have happened on the road. And 'Set Me Free' was me, shall we say, not quite parodying, but saying, well, there you go Deep Purple and Ian Gillan. We can do a song like that equally as well."

"We had never lost that in our own heads," continues Scott. "We always wanted to make albums like *Sweet Fanny Adams*. So, they rose inside, and the first real opportunity that you get to do that is like somebody taking the reins of a racehorse. You kick about a little bit and see what you've got, don't you? I don't think there was any major strategy going on or sitting down to make an absolute plan—'This is the kind of album'—which I probably think, in today's market, there will be people who have done polling and marketing and saying, 'That kind of an album won't work in this climate.' But back then you were just making music because you wanted to make music. And if it struck a chord, I think you were very lucky. *Sweet Fanny Adams*, especially at that time, struck a chord."

"But yeah, for me, always, 'Set Me Free' and 'Sweet F.A.' are the favourites, which are always stalwarts of what we've done over the years. But when you delve into the album, you realise that there are songs like 'No You Don't' and 'Restless' and 'AC-DC,' and the list just keeps growing. It's all good stuff."

"'Set Me Free,' Andy wrote that, basically," chuckles Steve. "I don't know what it's saying (laughs). It was Deep Purple-inspired, definitely. But that's fine—we were good friends with Deep Purple."

"We were very lucky," continues Andy on the subject of Mick and how important he was now going to be within the context of Sweet 2.0. "I think a lot of rock bands, if you don't have the drummer, it can be difficult. And I think we were very, very lucky to have Mick. He adored people like Ian Paice, and in the end, I remember saying to him, I think you're every bit as good as that, mate. And when you listen to some of those pop records, the interaction between the guitar and the drums is a lot of the secret of it."

Indeed, with rocket fuel such as "Set Me Free"—and it sounded like a rocket even more so late in the track, given a bit of phase-shift effect—the band could feel almost smug in the face of comparisons with other heavy rock acts of the day, especially in the glam ghetto.

"Oh, let's put it this way," says Andy, admitting as much. "We had the kind of attitude to think that we were superior. We certainly didn't take any prisoners. Whether we actually were or not, I would have to throw myself back to being 22 again, and probably as obnoxious and as know-it-all as a 22-year-old, up-and-coming guitar player probably would be. I'm not saying that that's got much to do with it, but I think sophistication and rock music don't make good bedfellows all the time."

Back to the record, *Sweet Fanny Adams* then coughs up the lesser-known but equally detail-oriented "Heartbreak Today," which places inside a deftly pop environment chugging, shuffling power chords, tons of vocal harmonies and some more of Andy's tasteful and memorable guitar harmonies. The performances are tight and confident, and it's well and impressive to see that the deep album tracks hold up the side amongst the massive songs for which the band was to become increasingly known. Apparently, this one was influenced by Steely Dan.

Next, it's "No You Don't," a malevolent metal classic with all the pathos and drama of later Sweet classics like "Action" and "Medusa." "'No You Don't,' Chapman wrote that," points out Steve. "I think he was having a go at his girlfriend, basically. Brian was supposed to have sung it, but he was attacked in the street. He got his throat kicked in. So, I ended up singing it."

There's the reference to Brian's near tragic stomping, with Priest letting on that Connolly's hoped-for recovery was still happening during the making of the album. What is fortunate is that Steve was in possession of a lead singer's voice as laden with personality as Brian's was. And here he was playing the psycho, perfect for this dark and twisted metal monster. Essentially what happened was that Brian's diagnosis of a badly bruised larynx meant that he couldn't sing the likes of "Restless" and "No You Don't" and indeed, that's why Steve was ushered in to do some lead vocals. A sub-plot, however, had Mike Chapman growing increasingly exasperated with having to coach Brian. Mick Tucker goes so far as to say that Mike was trying to mould Brian in his own image, constantly haranguing Brian to sing it exactly the way Mike would do it. All the while, Brian was worried—quite sensibly, unfortunately—that his injuries had limited his range.

"No You Don't" was covered five years later on Pat Benatar's platinum-certified *In the Heat of the Night* album. Indeed, that record was co-produced by Mike Chapman, who also brought to the project the title track, which he wrote for post-glam popsters Smokie. Also written by Mike and previously recorded for Smokie was "If You Think You Know How to Love Me."

While we're on the subject of covers, "Set Me Free" saw two fairly high-profile renditions up into the hair metal era, first by Saxon on 1984's

Crusader album and then by Vince Neil on his first solo album, *Exposed*, from 1993. Thrashers Heathen also saw some success with the song, recording it for their Ronnie Montrose-produced 1987 debut, *Breaking the Silence*.

"I think the only band that they ever wrote anything of any kind of weight with were us," says Andy, upon being proposed the idea that Chinn and Chapman were perfectly capable of writing cutting-edge metal as well as pop, as evidenced by their penmanship of "No You Don't." "I can't think of another. I mean, Suzi's songs were a mixed bag. I suppose 'Can the Can' had a bit of edge to it, maybe 'Devil Gate Drive.'"

"They only provided most of the singles and I did most of the albums myself," answered Suzi, when I asked her about Chapman and Chinn in 2019. "That was our arrangement. I was always the writer, and I liked that arrangement because it took the pressure off me to fit it into a three-minute… I quite enjoyed just writing. We had a good arrangement and we stuck to it. I've not been close with Nicky for a long time now. Of course they haven't been together for a very long time. But I still work very closely with Mike Chapman; he's a good friend. The last album I did with him was 2011, *In the Spotlight*. He just got my new album to listen to. He was begging me for it because I sent him a few demos on the way and he said, 'Oh my God, this is great.' We're really close. Mike and I always worked wonderfully in the studio together. We have a mutual respect. Mike is a talented guy. He always was, always will be and I love him to pieces, and I was privileged to have worked with him and still be working with him."

Suzi's worked with Andy Scott as well, issuing in 2017 a self-titled album called *Quatro, Scott & Powell*, the Powell being Slade drummer Don Powell. "Yes, sure. We put out a great album; always so proud of that. Nice collaboration of three musicians, really worked well. I knew Andy better than the rest and I'm close with Andy; we're good friends. I'm close with Don—we're good friends. The three of us, I think we got along particularly because we came from the same era, which I call—maybe stupidly, but I do—I call it the last good era of musicians who came up by way of learning their craft by gigging."

As for her association with the glam scene, Quatro says, "My sound was based in rock 'n' roll and my look was very plain. I think the reason I got mixed in with that term is because my hits started in that era. So, they lumped me in there. But if you listen to what is real glam music and you listen to me, it's not the same."

Continues Andy on the subject of Mike Chapman, "So it was only really with us that I would say that it verged on the real heavy metal. You see, songs... Mike Chapman hadn't seen the band play in three years. Somebody said, 'I think you should get in a car and go to a gig.' Well, when he came back from the gig, he virtually wrote 'Blockbuster!,' 'Hell Raiser' and 'Ballroom Blitz,' having seen the kind of show it was."

And speaking of "Hell Raiser," *Sweet Fanny Adams'* next track, "Rebel Rouser" is a virtual pastiche of that one to "Ballroom Blitz," with a lick from Eddie Cochran's "Something Else" thrown in. It's most definitely one of those songs that couldn't be included on the US *Desolation Boulevard* because of the similarities. Still, it's prime Sweet, and chock full of gooey hard rock bits, nearly to "Action"-busy levels. Again, quite curiously, this one finds the guys in the band writing like Mike and Nicky.

Side one of the original vinyl ends with an embarrassing throwaway, a waste of space, a cover of "Peppermint Twist," even if the arrangement, particularly, around the vocals, is fairly ambitious. One can't help but think this '50s throwback number, as well as "Rebel Rouser," with its similar old-time rock 'n' roll feel, represent remaining vestiges of the historical concept album of which Brian has spoken. Much to the band's amusement, the song was issued by RCA as a single in Australia, where it zoomed to No.1 in the charts. Noted Brian, in *Record Mirror*, "We wanted to use a number from our stage act. So, whenever we did a live gig, we asked the kids which one they liked the best and as it happened, 'Peppermint Twist' turned out to be the favourite."

In any event, with "Peppermint Twist" best forgotten, it's onto side two with "Sweet F.A.," another blistering exercise in craft and precision and yet speed and aggression—Mick remarked that "We played every instrument we could lay our hands on."

"We wanted to call the US *Desolation Boulevard* album *Sweet F.A.*," recalls Andy. "But everybody in America was kind of, 'That's a bit too rude,' and 'You'll never get played' and all this other stuff. To tell you the truth, we wanted to call it *Sweet Fuck All*, but at the time they never would've accepted that. And apparently no one in America knew what *Sweet Fanny Adams* meant."

Similarly profane to that, there's also the lyric of the song, specifically "If she don't spread I'm gonna bust her head." It's not just a one-off. Oddly, Sweet touch down periodically on a sort of aggressive misogyny. Everything is normal song after song, civilised even, and then all of a sudden there's a "Man from Mecca" or a "Someone Else Will." Mick Tucker even went so far as to say, "This one was written for its lyrical content and explains everything about us."

And such rude talk is incongruous with the music, especially here. "Sweet F.A." is the track on the record where you really hear the acumen with which *Sweet Fanny Adams* is produced. There are metal moments within this complex song where no one at the time could touch what Sweet were doing, save for, perhaps, doppelgangers Queen.

"Whenever you to speak to fans, they'll go back to *Sweet Fanny Adams*," muses Andy, asked about the record's palpable sonic magic. "You see, the British version, the European version, did not have any hits on it. It was nine tracks which were very nicely conjoined, and Phil Wainman did a fantastic production job, and they were recorded very quickly. Phil Wainman was not the kind of guy to... if it was a three-hour session, right, this is what we need to get done in these three hours. That kind of the thing. So, when you hear the finished product, and when you think how it came together, with no Chinn and Chapman around, for the simple reason that they were in America—they were either on holiday or doing a little bit of work. However, they did not want to come back to England in the wintertime, so we just got on with it. All the time, people return to this album."

Second track on side two of the album is "Restless," which, like "Rebel Rouser," marries glam to early rock 'n' roll, even if a few metal-ish riffs invade. There's also a bit of a proto-hair metal thump to it. Call this one a bridge track that might have made more sense on the self-titled US album from 1973. Again though, we get stylistic touchstones from an earlier era, a bit of '50s plus the '60s, maybe even The Beatles, suggesting that certain things about the song are there because it was going to be integral to *From the Grave of Ocker the Rocker*.

With respect to the lyrics, Steve says that the key to crafting the song was diving into his Elvis Presley collection and playing everything he had, with the light bulb moment coming when he got to "Heartbreak Hotel." And speaking of hotels, this is one of the first things he wrote in the first house he (and his wife Pat) had ever purchased, for £12,200. This followed

upon Andy and his wife Jackie already getting a place, in Hayes.

Next up on *Sweet Fanny Adams* is "Into the Night," another scorching rocker that would serve as a headbanging highlight to the American *Desolation Boulevard*. Its many metal moods tell a story, and all of the band's many talents are included amongst the fray including both vocal harmonies and considerably sublime guitar harmonies. There's also, late in the sequence, all manner of prog rock fits and starts plus a novel echo effect for the climactic ending.

"'Into the Night' came from a long time previous," says Andy. "It was just one of those songs I had kicking around in my head, and I just put it down and offered it up, and Mike Chapman immediately jumped on it and said that's got to go on the album, because it was so different." As he told *Record Mirror's* Genny Hall, presumably playing it for her on a handy stereo system, "It's like going through a tunnel in a dream. There's a sinister voice, which comes through in a minute, but you won't be able to hear it properly on this set. I suppose you could call it a headphone track."

"The Shadows had done it, so why not?" queries Steve, with respect to Andy's multi-tracked lead guitar work. "He did it on 'Into the Night,' very early on, the harmony guitars. I don't know why exactly—he just wanted to do it (laughs)."

"I grew up listening to people like Randy California and Frank Zappa," offers Andy, on the idea of twin leads, building further on his previous remarks. "You only have to listen to what extra dubbing can do, because it was kind of unheard of. If there was a guitarist in the band, how dare he think about playing a second part? But then you listen to some of the early Shadows records, and there are ghosts of harmonies on the guitars there. Then you think, it's absolutely… when you listen to George Harrison with his bottleneck, it's double-tracked. And when you listen to Jeff Beck, a lot of his solos, he would double-track them, but loosely, so they had a kind of… it was one of those things where you couldn't put a finger on what you were listening to, but you knew it was different. And quite honestly, that's where I certainly got it from. And you know, having spoken to Brian May, it became a very useful tool in the armoury of the guitar. The only difference is, we now need to work out how we're going to do it on stage (laughs)."

"I've always written a song or two," continues Andy, asked about where this fecund creativity came from. "They haven't always been what you would call a Maserati, but you learn, and you find your way. I sometimes think… and you can never unlearn anything. It's like an egg—once it's boiled, you can't put it back in the shell. Songwriting is like that. If only I could transpose myself back to when I was 21, when my head was full of all these great ideas; but I then remember, I knew very little back then. Half the problem is, I can never go back and write a song like 'Into the Night' or 'Rock 'n' Roll Disgrace' again, because my head's not there. I could probably write another 'Love Is Like Oxygen' at some point, but there's no way I can go back."

"But to answer your question, where the music came from, as with all the other bands in the '60s, we were real big fans of people like the early Yardbirds and the early Who, of course. And there were bands that got formed out of other bands like Cream and Deep Purple. We knew a lot of the members of Deep Purple, and because of Jimmy Page's connection with the Yardbirds, I'd also met, along the way, John Bonham when he was in a Birmingham band called The Way of Life. So, all these influences are still pent-up there, but you're not sure, or you don't think, in your mind, that they are commercial enough."

"So, what you're trying to do is you're trying to write… and I guess it probably wasn't until something like 'Whole Lotta Love,' where there was a hook there in the guitar riff, and in the way that the whole thing was performed—it was almost like it was the blending of the new heavy rock with commercialism. Although Led Zeppelin probably wouldn't have seen it in that way, because I know from talking to various people from the past, they've almost put that as a defining moment when... because Deep Purple set about trying to write commercial heavy rock songs, of which 'Black Night' was exactly one of those kinds of compositions."

"No, influences by then had settled," says Scott, asked whether anything more contemporary, say, from the early to mid-'70s was inspiring Sweet at this juncture. "It was whatever we were at that time. Jeff Beck is God to me, and there were little things that people like Hendrix do. But Jeff Beck, if only I could get a tenth of some of his sounds. And like I say, the riffs of Jimmy Page, unstoppable stuff. So, I don't think we were being completely and utterly influenced by any one thing, but I guess the outcome of the album is quite a mixture of a lot of different things."

"And a song like 'No You Don't,' the middle section was completely and utterly ruled by my love of *Tommy* for example. Remember, we had just come out of the '60s where the influences that we were drawing from were bands like Free. So, I think some of the glam ideas, the guitar riffs and the way that they were played, are pure, probably late '50s, even. You can almost see some of it going back to Elvis, but with the '60s musicality. We're only doing what Led Zeppelin did, because that's what all the early '50s bands and prior to that did: blues riffs. And Jimmy Page organised them so you could actually hear a proper guitar riff. Because when you listen to some of the old Robert Johnson recordings, you're aware there's a little riff there, but when you hear Led Zeppelin play a song, you go, 'Oh, so that's where the guitar riff is.'"

It seems that Sweet had learned this lesson well, namely this idea of commerciality and riff mixed with heaviness. *Sweet Fanny Adams* ends with a knees-up raver called 'AC-DC,' which puts a smile on what is otherwise a pretty serious record.

Dispelling for the most part, any idea that a certain band might have nicked a name from this droll Sweet anthem, Andy says, "I think we first came across them in the mid-'70s down in Australia. Somebody even reminded me that they may well have appeared on one of the big open-air shows we did in Australia around that time. And I can't believe that they would've taken their name from the track 'AC-DC' on *Sweet Fanny Adams*. I think they must have had the name before that. But it's just a hell of a coincidence, isn't it?"

The song itself is a Chinn and Chapman number, but, despite its glam gloss, it does indeed fit into the hysterical, over-driven nature of the heavier material around it, and the evolving and evolved Sweet sound in general. Andy's not surprised. "Well, as I said, it was after Mike had come to a couple of shows and seen just what the hell was going on, that he started to realise why we wanted to do things like that. So being a songwriter, you should be able to morph yourself into virtually anything. But as time went on, you could see that Mike... the songwriting side of things became a stepping stone to being a producer. Because he learned from Sweet that the one way to get a band to, shall we say, have more longevity... I think we were lucky to have songwriters and be able to write ourselves and still come through it. Because a lot of the bands they wrote for had what they had with Nicky and Mike and not much else. Because their writing was never given the space, if you know what I mean. And so, when you got to bands like Blondie, their songs were, shall we say, quite twee in places, so he grabbed something, the image, plus the songs, and he made them be the writers. So, he kind of changed the dynamic for them."

Still, in the press at the time, Andy and the guys considered "AC-DC" a weak link on the album, and even more so "Peppermint Twist," which had been included because it had been going over a storm live, as well as the fact that the guys had run out of material.

"You still want to try and find a niche," continues Scott. "This is why you've got, even today, the cults of certain bands that really and truthfully didn't do anything, but in the mind's eye of a generation were important— Joy Division for example. It means not very much to me, but I gather half of the bands that came out of that era would never have been there if it hadn't have been for a band like them. And I actually think that that's where we were. We were at a point where we had taken this loud, almost heavy metal rock to a point, that in our own country, we never would have been fully accepted, because of our starting point. And yet ten years later, in the early '80s, it was almost as if America hadn't seen glam rock from the early '70s."

"So, for me, it's so convoluted how we got the look that we got and the sound that we got. There are too many influences. I always remember Mick and I trying to say, whenever we were recording, we would put something valid for our musicianship in there as well. Regardless of, it might be a three-chord nursery rhyme, but there's got to be something, a little time signature or a drum break, or a little guitar lick where parties are going to go, 'Yeah, that's something.' And thereby a few bands in the mid to late '70s that came out which were pure and pure pop bands like Pilot and recording fantastic singles—I'm pretty sure that our sound obviously had something to do with that. I know damn well we had something to do with the fact that possibly we were there a mite too soon for the generation that followed, because Queen, just look at it now. You talk about Beatles, Queen and Abba. They are the three most covered and worked on with either tribute bands, musicals, all that. I mean, you've virtually got it there."

"And the weird thing is, although now, when I think about it, it's not so weird," reflects Andy. "We went across the water, and our actual first success was actually on the continent, rather than England. All the records charted everywhere, but we started to have big hits in Holland and Belgium and Germany, long before we started to have what you would call Top 3 monsters in England. And it's still the same today. We do a rock club/rock venue that's going to hold about 800 to 1000 in England, whereas in Europe, we just did a gig over the weekend where there were over 10,000 people with Foreigner and Nazareth. Which just shows you the complete... if you wanted a band that sat fairly comfortably in both camps, both the hit single camp and the hit album camp, especially in Germany, there was only us."

Summing up the album a few months after the fact, Brian told *Melody Maker*, "I think the next album will follow a pattern, go in a direction, maybe harder rock. Basically, I think this album shows we were trying to prove—well, I wouldn't say prove—but project what we were trying to do, put a harder, rocky feel to us. We were going great guns until I got this (points to throat). Luckily the hardest tracks had been done. You can be more adventurous with your own material. You can't be adventurous with someone else's songs."

Added Mick, "We purposely made the album diverse because we don't know yet which way Sweet are going to go. There's a variety of styles here and on the next album, you'll be able to pinpoint one. I think with most bands, the first couple of albums are feelers, finders, and once the band locks onto a particular thing, it all adds up. We were quite pleased with the way the album turned out considering we worked against all the odds to get it out. There were arguments as there always have been, and Chinn and Chapman going on holiday and saying we couldn't finish it until they came back…"

"Well, not arguments so much," qualifies Brian. "It was just that nothing fell into place very easily. First, one of them was there without the other, then the other way around, then there was restriction on studio time, so everything was against us. The more I listen to it now, the more commercial it seems. Although we are trying to free ourselves from the straitjacket of singles."

"Don't forget, to a certain extent, we were going out on a limb," says Mick. "The plan for the album was that Chinn and Chapman would have material presented to them for them to say whether it was suitable to go on the album. But we did two or three tracks and then they went on holiday, and the rest was left to us. They didn't hear all the material we were putting on, so really, we could have fallen flat on our faces. We're not really getting meaner. We're just playing it like it is. We're playing like we want to play. And there's a lot of production too."

English music weekly *Disc* gave the thumbs-up to *Sweet Fanny Adams*, FC writing that "Sweet stood to lose so much in making this album that one has to admire them simply for having the guts to do it at all. They set out to prove two things, firstly, that they could play and sing with the best of them, and secondly, that they were not totally dependent on Chinn and Chapman for hit material. If they'd failed on either count, they would've looked extremely silly, but they haven't. They made an album far, far better than I, for one, would ever have believed them capable. Apart from one old rocker ('Peppermint Twist') and two Chinn/Chapman numbers, they've written all of it. The playing is clean and unpretentious, the production almost faultless and the vocals, particularly the backup harmonies, strikingly assured. The songs themselves are all strong and catchy. There must be at least four potential hit singles contained here. The whole record shifts along at a sprightly pace, the music's got plenty of meat on it, and above all, it's fun. A very good, if not a great album."

Wrote Ron Ross in *Phonogram Record*, August '74, "Like a Frankenstein in search of true love, Sweet labour under the delusion that pop stars should be heavy musicians and cite Deep Purple and The Who as more significant sources of inspiration than hit-mongers Mike and Nicky. For a group that long suffered the same studio musician stigma that plagued the Monkees, Sweet have taken significant steps to control their own musical destiny. In trying to justify themselves as self-sufficient musicians Sweet have hit upon an alternative to the Chinn-Chapman whiz-bang singles formula that should make their stage act immediately accessible to Americans who can't get enough of that heavy metal stuff. Despite cloyingly conventional (even plagiarised) lyrics, Sweet's high clear harmonies fit their big beat arrangements like a glove and no Yank contender such as Aerosmith or Kiss comes even close to this vocal versatility. In spite of its glaring lapses, *Sweet Fanny Adams* must come close to the Sweet live and that makes me more anxious than ever to see the leather and lipstick lads perform."

Added Gary Sperrazza, "Side one of *Fanny Adams* opens with 'Set Me Free,' an Andy Scott number that fully reveals the maturity of the Sweet's arrangement circa 1974: chaotic opening with the Sweet's characteristic onslaught of solid power, then into a heavy metal blitzkrieg of speed and style. Next is 'Heartbreak Today,' sporting a gorgeous hook and Queen-like guitaring." Sperrazza later said that, "*Sweet Fanny Adams* checks into 1974 as the best heavy metal pop album of the year, with an overabundance of chilling riffs, logically effective arrangements and unmatched conciseness."

Quite incredibly, after all this seemingly effortless chart success with their singles in the UK, Sweet's first serious work of musical art, issued in April 1974, would only rise to a No.27 placement in the UK charts, albeit notching gold sales. What is even more astounding, it would be their first and last album to chart at all on home soil, as well as the only record by the band to certify gold.

CHAPTER 5:

Desolation Boulevard and Strung Up

"Ritchie Blackmore was not happy at all"

Building upon the fantastic creative high that was *Sweet Fanny Adams,* Sweet jumped right back into the crucible and emerged in November '74 with the second album for them that year, a little something called *Desolation Boulevard.*

With two weeks of writing taking place at the Hillingdon Rugby Club, Andy Scott picks up the tale, explaining the rush and the whoosh that resulted in an album not quite so boldly consistent as its predecessor. "Mike

Chapman said—after Phil Wainman had been doing the productions—I want to be given a shot. So we virtually made two albums a year apart, which is probably a little bit quicker. And he had this other idea about... he'd been to see us live, and he was trying to re-create what our live sound was, a bit more bare bones, a bit less production technique, and seeing what we had."

"And yet in the meantime, we had recorded a single with him called 'The Six Teens,' which is quite a phenomenal, big production. And so when that was slotted onto the rest of the album, which was a bit more, as I said, bare bones, it stood out like a sore thumb. That was obviously going to be the single, if they were going to choose. And from that point of view, I personally was never happy with *Desolation Boulevard*. But I liked quite a few of the songs on there, because we were trying to experiment again. And more so this time, the whole band was contributing a little bit of songwriting. I mean, there were still two or three of my own songs on there, but it was one of these, let's get everybody involved in the writing if we can."

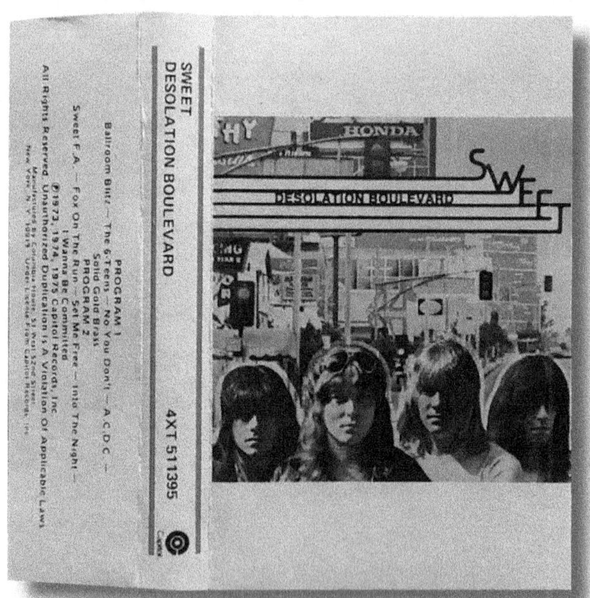

As an aside, as the band was preparing to launch "The Six Teens," Andy and Mick were busing playing music industry moguls, promoting a four-piece band out of Essex called Angel. The band was good for one single (with picture sleeve, no less), called "Good Time Fanny." The song was written by Andy and the single's two tracks were produced by Andy and Mick.

Back to the new Sweet single, mid-1974, after working on the new album, Sweet parts company with Phil Wainman, who moves on to great success with the Bay City Rollers. Sweet come out with "The Six Teens" as a UK single in late June, four months before its inclusion on *Desolation Boulevard*.

Indeed, as Andy says, the track is a huge and gorgeous production, strapped to an epic popster full up with as much ear candy as a mid-level *Give Us a Wink* classic. The acoustic guitars are steely and cool, the power chords fat and distorted, and everything else, from drums to bass to vocals, are slotted in to perfection. There are various tempos, doubled vocals, groovy yet busy drumming from Mick and even tympanis. A Chapman and Chinn composition, the song was cooked up in response to the fact that the band wanted to be seen more seriously as artists, even if Mike and Mick Tucker were at each other's throats over the thing, Tucker threatening to erase days of work on the track.

The song began life with a country western-type groove, with the artful lyrics telling the tale of six teenagers struggling with their identities back in 1968, with the story based in Hollywood. Recorded in late May '74 at Audio International in London (and engineered by Peter Coleman), the song was issued as a single in July, backed with killer proto-metal classic "Burn on the Flame," credited to the band but in truth, written by Andy and recorded at the same time.

The dynamic with "The Six Teens," according to Nicky, was that it was well and good to have chart success, but it was high time that the band combined chart success with actually being proud of their work. In parallel, the band demanded that they not be given "any more crap." Steve has said that John Mellencamp had professed admiration for the song, which can be sussed from its similarities to his big hit "Jack & Diane," from 1982's *American Fool*, when Mellencamp was still recording under the name John Cougar. Mick had been proud of two things concerning the song, one, that they pushed Mike and Nicky to try harder for something more substantial and two, once they did, Sweet dived right in and arranged it and put their skilled musical stamp all over it.

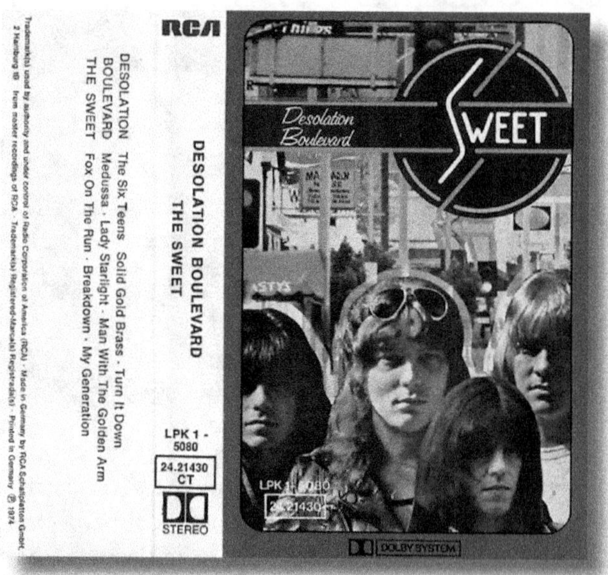

Still, the collaboration was revealing the fact that a parting of ways was at hand. The guys in the band were increasingly annoyed that Mike and Nicky seemed to be in it basically for the money, and that increasingly there was this factory feel to what they were doing, given the success at the time of singles done for Mud and Suzi Quatro.

Proclaimed Jeff Ward in a review of the track for *Melody Maker*, "Ah, it's the Kings (Queens?) of Sleaze returning with a fine bunch of mock heroics prised from the itchy hands of Chapman and Chinn, who else, of Quick Hits Ltd. Well, it seems like a change of pace for the luvvly lads—not so frantic, this one, more serious. A tale of the teens, 13 through 19: that's when it all happens but you gotta be strong to get it on. I hear tympani (drama), a touch of Moog and the stuttering guitar and slack tremolo arm of Andy Scott (should we crush the sweet hands?). Sassy Brian claims: 'This is our best single ever.' You know, he could be right. Hot damn, a surefire HIT!"

It was also Ward who got inside the heads of Nicky and Mike, getting Mike to boast in *Melody Maker*, tongue-in-cheek, that, "You can't go wrong with a Chinn and Chapman song! There ain't no crap, there ain't no chaff in Chinn and Chap! There's nobody better in the world than we are. We are the best; that's obvious. Of course we're a hit factory; we can't help it. But the kids give us the credit because they buy the records. They're buying them because they like them. You put a bad record out by The Sweet and they won't buy it, or with Suzi Quatro. Kids are not stupid, you know; they're very clever and they only want the best."

Asked by Ward specifically about The Sweet, and their assertion that they could put anything out and it would be a hit, Mike scoffs, "This is why they'd never be hit songwriters. As soon as they start talking about that sort of thing, they're out of their depth. But they've got us around, so they'll never be allowed to do it. People have to do something special to make an impression. Kids haven't changed that much. Instead of reading *Alice in Wonderland*, they now listen to Sweet or Slade. But they still have imagination: remember when you were a kid, what did you want to be or want to do?"

"I don't think we do it consciously," continues Chapman. "It's weird; you can't put it into words. We are ahead of the kids at the moment, and we've gotta make the most of it. We have to change the style of our acts progressively so they'll continue to appeal to the kids. 'Teenage Rampage' really sums it all up. From the age of two, they're buying records. Believe it or not, two-year-olds are thinking like ten-year-olds now. Kids are learning a lot quicker and the whole feeling in the country at the moment is aggression, tension, and it's having an effect on the kids. By making aggressive records, you can get the feelings out of kids and they can express themselves by dancing. I mean, we still let our feelings out. Jesus, he's 28 and I'm 26 or something, and we're still bopping around every night, going down to Tramp's and leaping about and making fools of ourselves. But my God, it ain't 'alf good for you. You wake up the next morning feeling that much better for it because there's no other way to express your feelings."

When Ward points out the regular use of the word "teenage" in many of the song titles of the day, Nicky says, "It implies immense recognition of the teenagers. I attribute it to the fact that there is a teenage movement. Teenagers are more to the forefront than they have been for many years, and also they've got a lot more money than they've had for a long time."

Adds Mike, "Each of the songs that we've mentioned concerns a teenage emotion. There's a rampage, a lament, a dream, a nervous breakdown and a love affair. So, we're dealing with teenage feelings and we are just giving the kids the chance to recognise themselves in the songs. We're just putting up a mirror where they can see themselves. Maybe we're crediting the kids with something they haven't been given credit for for a long time, like a love affair. They say, 'He can't be in love at 15,' but maybe he can be. You can have a nervous breakdown when you're a teenager. You can lament when you're a teenager. What a wonderful world it would be if everybody acted like teenagers. I don't mean the minority; I mean the majority of them, not the ones that go around beating people up, the mugs and fools. I mean the ones who are expressing themselves in discotheques, who are doing their bit at school and going on to be a welder or a panel-beater or whatever. If everybody could have that all over again… I still think like a teenager and so does Nick. We live in a fantasy world. Everybody in the pop business lives in one."

Underscoring Sweet's new slightly *less* teenage approach, the TV performance of "The Six Teens" (soon to reach No.9 in the UK) featured the band sans makeup and moving towards leathers.

"Definitely," says Steve. "I always liked leather, and it was around the time of 'Six Teens,' 'Fox on the Run.'" Asked whether it was a biker thing, Priest chuckles, "Well, we wanted it to be. I never owned a motorbike, because I would fall off it. In fact, *Bravo* magazine did a great centrepiece where they got all these choppers and sat us on them, and we said, 'Can we start them up?' And they went, 'No! The insurance won't allow us!' And that's when we all had leather." One can see the results of the shoot on a handful of the picture sleeve issues of the "Turn It Down" single produced on the continent.

And this was to represent a transition from glam into tougher rock. "Oh, absolutely. Leather and jeans, in fact. I would never wear them now, but we used to go down to Kensington Market, although by then we had people making our clothes. And we would say, 'I want this; make it,' and the rest we spent foolishly (laughs). But Status Quo were more into jeans than we were. If we wore jeans, we used to tart them up with leather patches and stuff, so it didn't look just like jeans. Because you're not supposed to look like anyone in the street."

Come November 15th, 1974, "The Six Teens" would take the pole position on the band's second album, a bold statement given its ponderous and almost progressive rock leanings. The song's lyric would be reinforced by the record's cover art, which was art directed by John Dyer and Hipgnosis, famous for their work with Pink Floyd and Led Zeppelin.

As Scott explains, "For the next one, because we knew we were going into America, with the *Desolation Boulevard* album, Ed Leffler had found a picture of the Sunset Strip on there, which was obviously completely and utterly tied up like you wouldn't believe (ed. referring to the legality of all the signs and logos on it). All they did was they edited it, because there we were, as if we are in the foreground with the Strip in the background. And when you look at it, you can see that the places that are on the Strip are next to each other, where they shouldn't be. Somebody had messed around with them. But you would never know if you've never been there."

And the title? "It was one of the lyrics in 'The Six Teens.' There is one line that goes, 'On Desolation Boulevard, they'll light the faded light.'"

The location of the shot used was adjacent to The Central, at 8852 Sunset Boulevard, West Hollywood, now the site of The Viper Room. Was the visual a sort of "Hello America," to quote Def Leppard a rock 'n' roll generation later, as it were? "I actually think that it was definitely a tip and a nod, a wink, to the fact that this was the next place we were looking to try and do something," says Andy. "I don't think we did it consciously, but it just seemed like quite a cool thing to do."

As for an additional spot of significance, let's not forget the story of music exec Rupert Perry moving from England to LA and into a building on the Sunset Strip, the iconic round office tower that housed Sweet's new record label, Capitol.

Disc—November 23, 1974 5
BACK BY POPULAR
DEMAND
BRIGHTER JOHN
DANCING
DESOLATION BOULEVARD
SWEET·THE ALBUM LPL1 5080
SWEET DATES
NOV 21 Sunderland Locarno
30 Leicester University
DEC 3 Salford University
5 Middlesbrough Town Hall
6 Hull University
7 Imperial College, London
10 Colston Hall, Bristol
11 Town Hall, Birmingham
RCA
ALSO AVAILABLE ON TAPE

After the lush, almost Latin or flamenco sounds of "The Six Teens," as Andy has alluded to, we're into the crude, early glam crunch of "Solid Gold Brass," with noisy drums, with Brian shouty, guitars mid-rangey and haranguing, everybody except Mick taking a stab at lead vocals. Of note, the version used for the US release of the album benefitted from a remix and a new guitar solo. True to character, in Sweet's world, the title of the track housed a nasty double meaning, with Steve letting on helpfully that "brass" is Cockney for prostitute.

Says Andy, further on the jarring sonic contrast of the first two songs, "Well, again, we'd done the record with Phil Wainman, the *Sweet Fanny Adams*, and it is a very professional job, everything on there. Plus we got a lot of our own material out. Mike Chapman and Nicky Chinn, I think at that moment, were not seeing eye-to-eye with each other, and hence Mike Chapman stepped forward and said, 'I know you've just done that record with Phil, but you're going to need another album in a year's time. Let me take you in. I've got a couple of great ideas'—which was 'The Six Teens' and 'Turn It Down'—'and with some of your ideas, let's record an album. But let's do it in a more live way, rather than the way that it was done with Phil.'"

"So, we went with that, but in the end, it ends up sounding rough. It doesn't quite sound like a regular Sweet record, until you get to 'The Six Teens,' for example. Then it starts to sound a bit more layered, and shall we say, a little bit more time spent over it. Whereas some of the other tracks are extremely bare bones. And in my opinion, as I said to them at the time, the guitar needs to be recorded with… we all need to record together with a bit of distance mic'ing. If that's the effect you want to go for. By keeping everything separate, you'll end up with everything smaller than it should be. You need to have a lively room if you want to go about it that way. And, as we know, the Americans picked most of *Sweet Fanny Adams* for the *Desolation Boulevard* release. And that speaks volumes."

This stab at spontaneity and performance and chemistry was all according to the stated plan of producer Chapman, who wanted to emphasise the musicianship of the band and move away from the "plastic" sound that records were demonstrating at the time. Toward that end, September '74, the band knocked off seven tracks in eight days.

Indeed, as Andy indicates, the contrast between "The Six Teens" and some of the rest of the record is noticeable right after two tracks. "Sold Gold Brass" has the complexity of the former track written into it but it's a pretty straight arrangement, with thumpy drums and really gnarly but quite dry and basic guitars. Same with "Turn It Down," a goofy but loud and proud power chord rocker more in the wheelhouse of Kiss, Nazareth and BTO—

and maybe even punk—versus the rapidly sophisticating music crew that was Sweet, certainly as they existed on the next record and the one after.

"That was inspired by Cheech and Chong," laughs Steve on "Turn It Down," referring to the classic comedy duo and the "Earache My Eye" sketch from which this is one of the punch lines—it was Mike Chapman who had been listening to them. It is here that the rough recording and rougher mix work just fine, even if the sum total of the thing is a crude and dated glam. Continues Priest, "Chapman realised that what we were meant to be doing was heavier songs, rather than the bubblegum stuff. And that's when he started writing songs like 'I Wanna Be Committed,' 'Turn It Down' and 'Hell Raiser,' for instance. It was not bubblegum."

"Turn It Down," the band's final Chapman/Chinn single, would be issued as the follow-up track to "The Six Teens," emerging in early November '74, before the launch of the album proper later in the month. Priest says it was the most fun he's ever had working on a Sweet song, although it all went for naught. In October, the BBC (specifically Robin Nash, producer of *Top of the Pops*), banned the song, killing it as a single due to the line, "For God's sake, turn it down." At No.41, it was the band's worst single showing in three years, even as it moved 70,000 copies in Germany alone.

"Quite frankly, I couldn't see anything wrong with it," Steve told *Record Mirror* at the time. "There were no naughty words in it except 'for God's sake.' But in this day and age, it shouldn't offend anyone, except the producer of *Top of the Pops*, that is, who banned us from the show. He must be living in the past. Because a couple of Sundays ago, they showed a 1915 war documentary on TV and one of the songs in the film had 'for God's sake' in it, which was changed to something like 'for Pete's sake.' I suppose it was understandable in those days, but in the corrupt society of 1974, it's a bit silly. Still, I don't think 'Turn It Down' was the best single we've ever done. In my opinion, 'Hell Raiser' was our best."

"The B-side of "Turn It Down" was "Someone Else Will," or technically "...Someone Else Will," which begins with the a capella harmony vocal line "If you don't go down on me someone else will." Chuckles Brian, "The nasty stuff's been there in the past. It's just that it's been held back! We are nasty—we are a nasty group!" After the singing the band crash in and what ensues is a bit of a leaden, mid-tempo heavy metal rocker, a bit doom, a bit funk, a bit monotone. Again though, throw this on the pile of Sweet utterances that are designed to shock, or, like their clothes, not really second-guessed at all, used more as a statement to say this whole rock 'n' roll game is preposterous and don't take yourself so seriously—after all, look at how The Sweet started.

Back to the track sequence, it's a return to the huge productions, with an "Action" and "The Six Teens" type classic called "Medusa" pomp-rocking out of yer '70s hi-fi with synths amidst pounding band, before collapsing into one of the most magical expressions of Heep-heady Sweet chemistry this side of, well, all of *Give Us a Wink*.

"That got rewritten about three times before it actually got recorded," recalls Andy, which is not surprising, given its complexity throughout. Of note, "Medusa" began life as a demo in Andy's garage (Steve called it a large dog kennel behind his house), with the song also emerging as the US B-side to "Action" a couple of years later. As bonus, "Medusa" is one of Mick Tucker's finest drum tracks, with the man's deft Ian Paice slicings and slightings on full display at the punctuated ending of every musical movement of this mystical journey.

In fact everybody's performance on this track is stellar, and as Andy says, people were starting to take notice. "In Germany, we knew we had got somewhere and we hit a vein where one year, we appeared top of what was considered the pop voting polls in *Bravo* magazine. We all won individual awards and even had best single, the best album. And also that same year, there were two magazines, one being *New Musical Express*, where we appeared above Led Zeppelin and Deep Purple in that magazine as well, 1974. There was a complete shift. Because I remember somebody telling me that Ritchie Blackmore was not happy at all. And of course, Mick Tucker, how the hell do you end up with a drummer as good as that who could play as solid as Ian Paice and John Bonham, but also have the flair and the craziness to just chuck some Keith Moon in there? I think of all of us, I have to point the finger and say he was probably the most accomplished in the band. I think I managed to fool a few people (laughs)."

Next up is passionate proto-power ballad "Lady Starlight," which would emerge in different versions as both an Andy Scott solo single as well as a track on the US edition of *Give Us a Wink*. Originally called "Save Me" (Queen irony notwithstanding), this grew from another one of Andy's garage demos. There's acoustic guitar, plus falsetto vocals from Andy mixed in with his Brian-like raggedness. Mick and Steve lock in nicely as a rhythm section, providing a perfect bed for the thoughtful chord changes, including a modulation to a brief solo section where Andy gets to show off his twin lead technique.

From ballad to weird, next it's "Man with the Golden Arm," eight minutes of jazz and hard blues and rapid-fire metal but mostly just drums, notwithstanding the hired brass section. Mick in fact performs a standard drum solo, heavy on snare work like Ian Paice, but then also does a tympani solo augmented with tubular bells. Coming out of it we get a "Fireball"-like flourish before the noisy finale.

"'Man with the Golden Arm,' that was a showcase for Mick, basically," notes Steve, regarding this track that had been part of the set since '73. "Because at the time, we would have two screens on stage behind us. In those days, unfortunately, they weren't video, they were film. And we had two cameras in synch, and they would show a video of Mick doing his solo. There were like three of him, and it went very well together, but it was hard to synch because the things would freeze and the film would burn, or you'd be a frame out. By the end of the tour, both of them were completely out of synch with each other."

Next is "Fox on the Run" but quite unlike the version that had half a million fans of Sweet in the States swooning and sending the record on which it sat to RIAA gold certification. The original UK version is a rougher, more aggressive and longer song with earthier tones and more Mick Tucker going nuts. As well, Brian sounds a little wild and raspy and really there's an extra few notes to the riff that make it less appealing—all told, the song does not reveal itself as the hit it would become.

Despite the roar of it all, even in this state, "Fox on the Run" is a showcase for lady-killer Brian more than anything. The song was issued in the UK as a single in March '75, backed with non-LP track "Miss Demeanor," a sort of bar-room pop rocker full up with all the band's syrupy charms, but just a little under-written, maybe a little too Bad Company/ BTO to live up to the standards of the top half of the songs across the band's two 1974 albums. Still there are some swell and angelic harmony vocals, and then a surprising and lengthy Uriah Heep-like shuffle section housing a pretty nutty jam that runs to the end of the song.

As for the birth of "Fox on the Run," Steve tells the story of how, totally worn-out at 2:00 AM one night, he and Andy had been working

Disc—March 15, 1975 9
SWEET SHOCK:
"FOX ON THE RUN"
RCA

on this song about groupies, and the phrase "fox on the run" came out of Steve, who adds that the earliest version of the song sounded a bit too close to "Rebel Rebel" for comfort. Curiously, Brian claims much credit for the idea, saying he got it together and literally phoned the guys to come 'round to the studio and hear what he'd come up with.

Next up is "Breakdown," one of the more obscure heavy tracks from the Sweet catalogue. Almost MC5-styled psychedelic, this one's an underrated and weirdly seldom discussed rocker with lots of intriguing riffs and shifts and musical movements—comparisons with Blue Cheer, Sir Lord Baltimore, Bang and Captain Beyond wouldn't be out of order either. The most exposure the song ever got was post-release as part of a three-song set with "Solid Gold Brass" and "Turn It Down" on a TV show called The Geordie Scene. Brian cited this one, "Solid Gold Brass" and "Fox on the Run" as his favourites on the album.

Desolation Boulevard closes with a pointless, unimaginative version of old Who chestnut "My Generation," covers being something that at the time (well, in any era, really) that was a cheap ploy and a crapshoot towards a record coughing up a hit. *Sweet Fanny Adams* had "Peppermint Twist," which very similarly marred and even scarred a perfectly proud Sweet album. Although "My Generation" peters out in a chaotic jam, one nice feature is the dual lead vocal work from Brian and Steve. A request to Townshend to appear on the track was initially answered in the affirmative, with Pete deciding against it at the last minute.

Curiously, out on the press trail, Steve found it necessary to inform Jan Iles of *Record Mirror* that although the band was at a crossroads of sort, they still had some life in them.

"We are not dead and we're not exactly alive," began Priest. "As far as we're concerned, we've got to start all over again in Britain as we're no longer a teenybopper band who appeal to six-year-olds. We're getting into a more sophisticated bag and have therefore got to prove ourselves to the older kids. Our music has become far too intricate for our fans, but we can't go on forever churning out Humpty Dumpty hits. Trouble is, these kids haven't grown up with us. So, there's really nothing we can do about it. Every band goes through changes. Look at Status Quo—they were a pop band once. You just can't dwell on the past. Anyway, that's why it's so difficult for us in Britain at the moment. But we're not dead over here, that's for sure!"

"It's only just come in the shops and it's already sold about 20,000 copies," continued Priest. "As far as we're concerned, this album and *Sweet Fanny Adams* are the only real albums we've produced. The ones before them were absolute trips. They just weren't representative of Sweet. *Desolation Boulevard* has its faults. Perhaps we went a bit overboard on the production, and we tried to do a three-piece sound without overdubbing it, which didn't come out too well. But there's no point in continuing if you reach perfection, is there? Considering it only took two weeks to do the whole shebang, I think it's bloody marvellous. On our next album, though, we want to spend more time in the studio and hopefully won't make the same mistakes."

"We've had a lot of hassles with the record company," said Steve, casting his eye across the pond. "You see, before the American label will do a deal, they must be sure you're big enough. Two rather large British bands, who shall remain nameless, lost a lot of money on their States tours, which means the record companies over there are very wary about us. I don't blame them really, because they don't want to throw their money away on a band that won't make it. Anyway, everything seems to be sorted out and we're now with Capitol Records in America. The other reason why we haven't attempted America before is because it has to be well-planned just like an invasion. The timing has got to be spot-on, and if it ain't, you've blown it. We could go over there tomorrow as someone's support band, but that would be useless because people don't come to watch the support. They're in the bar swigging back the booze until the star comes on."

Reflecting on the future, Steve says that, "We want to bring out our own singles, but before you jump the gun, Sweet isn't splitting up. We just like to do our own personal things. Like I'd really love to bring out a funky, brassy James Brown-type thing, and Andy wants to do a revamp of 'Lady Starlight,' an acoustic number on the album. Mick, well, it's a shame he didn't bring out a drum single before Cozy Powell cottoned onto it. Which leaves us with Brian. Brian's trying to learn piano and he also wants to bring out an old Everly Brothers ballad."

All that aside, fortunately, finally the US was going to get to hear what happens when Sweet put their best foot forward. April 1975, "Ballroom Blitz" is issued as a single stateside, two years after the UK got to slap their money on the counter in exchange for this irresistible slice of glammy metal mania. The US version of *Desolation Boulevard* follows in July, just in time to perk up everybody's summer.

Of the American record's ten tracks, "Set Me Free," "No You Don't," "Sweet F.A.," "AC-DC" (now "A.C.D.C.") and "Into the Night" were all lifted from *Sweet Fanny Adams*. "The Six Teens" (now "The 6-Teens"), "Fox on the Run" and "Solid Gold Brass" were from the UK *Desolation Boulevard*, and finally "I Wanna Be Committed" and fantastic smash single "Ballroom Blitz" were previously non-LP. Quite importantly, the US "Fox on the Run" was a softened and sweetened re-recording, which actually became a huge hit for the band upon issue in November of '75, along with "Ballroom Blitz," as I say, helping to send the record gold, the first and last RIAA certification the band would enjoy.

The US track list, again, as Andy says "speaks volumes" about the relative merits of *Sweet Fanny Adams* and the UK *Desolation Boulevard*, however, the US record obviously kept the title and more or less the cover art from the recent UK offering.

The re-recording of "Fox on the Run" that would be used for the US issue was conducted at Kingsway Studios (newly purchased by Ian Gillan), with engineer Louie Austin on board. To keep the vibe of the just-completed album, the band had actually asked Austin to revert from Kingsway's 24 tracks to 16, which wound up backfiring when the band got 'round to vocal overdubs. The fact that the band-penned song was a worldwide hit caused a permanent fissure in Sweet's relationship with Chapman and Chinn—Steve says he never saw Mike again until 1988, when Chapman tried to put the busted-up Sweet back together.

Explains Steve, "We had done 'The Six Teens,' which wasn't a hit, because the BBC were on strike, so we couldn't get *Top of the Pops*. And if you didn't get *Top of the Pops*, the BBC wouldn't play it, and there weren't enough independent radio stations to do the job. So we had a miss, basically. By which time Chapman had gone to Los Angeles and bought a house, in Coldwater Canyon, and Chinn decided that he didn't want him out of his sights, so he got one just up the street. I know, ludicrous, isn't it? Which left us going, 'We haven't got another single.' So, we went back into the studio and did a revised version of 'Fox on the Run,' a shorter version. And when the record company heard it, they went, 'That's the one.' So, when Chapman came back, he phoned me and said, 'Well, it doesn't look like you need us anymore.' And I went, 'No, it doesn't, does it?'"

Still, *Desolation Boulevard* was viewed as a point on a trajectory. Noted Andy at the time, speaking with *Melody Maker*, "We're still a company, but there's been a redistribution of importance and responsibility. I've always felt that I could write, but I don't think that I've been encouraged. There has been a lot of rubbish thrown around about the relationship between bands and producers, in the Chinn and Chapman situation. I think that of all the relationships, ours has been the most convincing, and when Phil Wainman was involved—I don't really want to say this—but when he was producing us, the records were better. *Sweet Fanny Adams* was produced by Phil, and for me, that's a better album than *Desolation Boulevard*, which was produced by Mike Chapman. We wanted to do *Desolation Boulevard* almost like a live album, just the three-piece, with almost no overdubs and it just did not work. There was a lot lost in the mix and Mike mixed it. Now we believe that we can produce our own material better than anyone else. We know what we want. We've been taking a lot more care over the next album. I would like to see Sweet bring out their own *Sgt. Pepper* or their own *Chicago Transit Authority*, because they are the two monster albums by those two groups. The next album will hopefully be *the* album. It could be our *Tommy* or our *Quadrophenia*."

Desolation Boulevard immediately garnered attention in the US, even with mainstream newspapers. Wrote Jon Farlowe from the *Miami News*, "Another bunch of teen ravers from over the seas, hailing from the ChinniChap 'school of instant success via formulated beat.' With their newest offering though, Sweet have left 'Little Willy' far behind and seem more interested in catching up to Noddy Holder and the boys in Slade. 'A.C.D.C.' will never be played anywhere, but don't let that stop you. This record is great if you don't take rock 'n' roll as an intellectual medium, and just content yourself with having a maximum volume good time."

Wrote *Rolling Stone*'s Gordon Fletcher in a long and favourable review, "The first side of *Desolation Boulevard* is devoted to material written by producers Mike Chapman and Nicky Chinn, five reasonably timed, concise and overwhelmingly direct assaults on the senses. The song structures are played with almost military precision with an emphasis on repeated guitar riffs and catchy hook lines. The production is designed to capture the electricity and wild energy of live performances, succeeding well in conveying a sense of explosive immediacy during the proceedings."

"Side two is devoted to The Sweet's own compositions, reinforcing their tag of 'a bubblegum Led Zeppelin.' Guitarist Andy Scott is given much more freedom in the band's lengthier, more experimental format, putting his axe into bizarre contortions à la the Yardbirds-era Jeff Beck on 'Sweet F.A.,' rifling out submachine-gun riffs on 'Set Me Free' and using intervals to create a full, forceful and effective solo on 'Into the Night.'

The Sweet has combined two divergent musical styles, the tight, restricted control of Chapman and Chinn and the guitar-based experimentalism of their own compositions, into an explosive package. *Desolation Boulevard* is decidedly English in tone, decidedly hard rock in approach, and to these years a decided success from a band with a future a mile long."

Record Mirror seemed on the fence about the album, writing in their review of the UK version back in November of '74, "*Desolation Boulevard* is quite a shock. Again, Sweet show a much more professional approach on this album. Their music is heavy without being too aggressive and fuzzy melodic without being too florid, and Andy Scott's guitar can at times be compared with the most paramount of plonkers. The popular songwriting dudes Chinn and Chapman have come up with some mind-bending muzak guaranteed to send any freak shaking their shaggy locks. 'The Six Teens,' Sweet's most adventurous single to date, is the opener, which gets the listener in a good frame of mind for what's coming next. Also featured is their new single 'Turn It Down,' with some neat guitar licks from Scott, although the song itself is very run-of-the-mill and not as instantly appealing as their usual singles. The next track, 'Medusa,' possibly the best of the bunch, opens with an Oriental piece of music accompanied by wistful harmony echo vocals from Brian and Co. The last track, a crashing crescendo courtesy of The Who's 'My Generation,' is done with panache, and music-wise is perhaps the best number of the album. Sweet have shown that they can play rowdy rock as good as the rest, but it's not a great musical breakthrough as it's all been done before."

Added the influential *Cashbox*, "Rock 'n' roll has always been a good vehicle for describing the teenage dilemma. In the case of the Sweet's *Desolation Boulevard*, the Sunset Strip glitter, limp-wrist crowd gets the band's full attention via a series of alloy-edged rock 'n' roll cuts. Andy Scott's raw lead riffs combine with Brian Connolly's frantic vocals to propel the music at the breakneck pace necessary for the effective representation of teenage mania that this record is. Highlighted on this riff-infested outing are 'Ballroom Blitz,' 'I Wanna Be Committed' and 'Fox on the Run.' *Desolation Boulevard*—harder than you'll ever be."

Besides good press, another nod to the mainstream for The Sweet in America was the fact that "Little Willy" was included on a huge-selling K-Tel compilation album in 1973 called *Fantastic: 22 Original Hits, 22 Original Stars*. This was also the record that introduced thousands of kids across North America to Focus' yodel metal (!) classic "Hocus Pocus." The Sweet stomper showed up again on a popular K-Tel sampler from 1974 called *Music Power*, which also turned budding metalheads on to Brownsville Station's "Smokin' in the Boy's Room," which enjoyed the distinction of being the first track on the album.

Revealing perhaps a silver lining and a sliver of life-extending optimism, the success of *Desolation Boulevard* stateside underscored the suspicion of the band that to keep advancing, they'd have to take America seriously as a tour market.

"By the time we were hitting America," explains Andy, "our touring in the UK was kind of coming to a... not really a halt, but we were hitting brick walls. Nobody really wanted to move us up to the big arenas like we were playing in Germany and Scandinavia. The promoters weren't coming out of the woodwork to take on bands like Sweet and Slade. Which is why we were looking elsewhere. Probably, ultimately, the biggest territories for us were mainland Europe and you're going to have to look at Australia. Plus, our forays in the beginning into America were very, very good. The first three years, '75 through to '78, it just started to dwindle a little bit. We actually became what's known as the filling in the sandwich for the last two or three years of our American... We were probably the best middle bill act on the circuit in America, between '79 and '80."

But the first trip over was in fact for *Desolation Boulevard*.

"Yes it was. They retro-released... I think they'd released 'Ballroom Blitz' at the wrong time. And so they were now looking at rushing out 'Fox on the Run,' when somebody had a bright idea and took it away, and brought it back in at the beginning, or halfway through '75, I think it was. And all of a sudden, the radio picked up on it. And so 'Fox on the Run' was held back just at the beginning of '76, which put it slightly out of synch here. But when we came over to do a couple of theatre dates... you know, we did the Santa Monica Civic Centre in Los Angeles, and then we went home. It was phenomenal, the kind of hype that it obviously had built... because they thought we were coming, and then we weren't, and then we did finally come. It was like, eh, I don't know. It worked in our favour as being a bigger deal than it probably was initially."

"But we stopped playing in Britain before '75," continues Scott. "We had about a four-year period away, three-and-a-half years, something like that, because we didn't come back and play a concert here, other than a casino on the Isle of Man and a university in Scotland. But principally, we hadn't really played in the UK for at least three years, when we came back with 'Love Is Like Oxygen' in 1978."

"Not enough, not enough," sighs Steve Priest, in closing, asked about the extent to which Sweet tried to break America. "We should've hit America in '73, and they would've gotten used to us. By the time we did come over, which was '76, we were virtually sick of touring. We'd been around the world a couple of times, and you know, as a star act, but then when it came to the States, we were virtually unknown. The songs were known, but the band wasn't. And if we had done more TV, which our manager didn't want for some reason, we would've cracked it. But again, it's timing."

Reflected Brian on the issue, in February '76, speaking with Stephen Ford from *The Times and Democrat* out of South Carolina, "We just weren't ready to do it any earlier. We had been approached by American promoters many times before, but we always turned down tour offers. We had no American agent here to represent us on tour arrangements. More important, the only single released in the US that anyone recognised as us was 'Little Willy,' which we felt didn't project the real spirit of the band. The sound of 'Fox on the Run' really portrays us now. We thought it would go well here. It's got the loud, rowdy lyrics that go well in America. The Europeans love our sound, our melodies, but they don't understand our lyrics, of course. America likes Sweet for totally different reasons than Europe. I don't know if we have the kind of music to hold up for years. We're still developing, still moving up. We should have a lot better idea of how we fare with the American audience after the release of *Give Us a Wink*. It'll probably take a few years here to tell if we're going to remain a big group."

November '75, Sweet returned with a record that in retrospect looks like career suicide, even though the album did not emerge in the US. Still, why RCA would release *Strung Up* anywhere is anyone's guess, and in a gatefold sleeve, no less.

Well, how about we let them speak for themselves? A ten-inch square insert included with the album pointed out a cock-up with the running order, but also stated: "RCA Records wish to express their pleasure in presenting *Strung Up*. The recording represents a historic stage in Sweet's career and gives a clear picture of their emergence not only as musicians, vocalists and performers, but as writers and producers and, above all, as a major force in popular music. RCA take great pride in having played a part in their career and we look forward to a long and fruitful association."

Added Tony Prince in the liner notes, "Unlike the majority of bands that enjoy success in the singles market, Sweet have avoided the temptation to put out a compilation album of their hits and when asked why, they reply: 'Until we are able to break tradition and offer something different, we really don't see the point.' I am delighted that they were true to their word, because although this double album contains a number of their multi-million-selling singles, their presentation of 50% live performance and 50% studio recordings is certainly something I have never seen done in the past. It has often been said that without Nicky Chin and Mike Chapman writing their material, and Phil Wainman producing their many hits, Sweet would never enjoy the success that they have had. I'm sure that after listening to this album, you, like myself, will disagree with the majority of their critics."

He concludes by writing, "For a band that have been accused of being 'puppets on a string,' Andy, Mick, Steve and Brian have begun to prove that they make bloody good puppeteers!"

This last point is underscored by the record's cover art, on which the four members of the band are portrayed on the front as puppeteers, with the strings carrying over to the back to reveal tinier versions of themselves as the puppets. The illustration is by Joe Petagno, famed for his work with Motörhead.

Once inside the album, first we get the live material, recorded at the Rainbow Theatre, December 21st, 1973. There are seven selections here (well, seven-and-a-half: "Burning" offers a short burst of "Someone Else Will" tucked on the end) and only opener "Hell Raiser" is one of the band's hits. Every other song, other than Mick Tucker showpiece "The Man with the Golden Arm" is one of their self-penned non-LP tracks. The delivery is heavy as hell, rough and raucous, with loads of jamming and instrumental pyrotechnics.

Elsewhere there's a version of "Rock 'n' Roll Disgrace" that is mostly jam, a tight "Need a Lot of Lovin'," a completely unravelled "Done me Wrong Alright" and one acoustic number, "You're Not Wrong for Loving Me." All told, what this is a live record in the '70s tradition, featuring loads of solos and surprise twists on theme at every turn. It's also a record one could imagine as the absolute dark side of a double live album where the rest of the material consists of the band's many hits.

But I suppose the idea here is that this album presents the hits in studio form, with the dark horses in live form. So over to the studio disc, we open with "Action," the full-on production tour de force version we'd experience on the band's next album proper, *Give Us a Wink*, albeit truncated, with a slightly different mix. As Tony Prince explains in the liner notes, although "Action" hadn't reached the heights of "Fox in the Run" for the band, it had still sold as a single an astounding one-and-a-quarter million copies across various markets around the world.

Next is the re-recorded (and vastly superior) version of the aforementioned "Fox on the Run," which had only been on the US issue of *Desolation Boulevard* to this point. This is followed by LP track "Set Me Free," the non-LP "Miss Demeanour" and to close out the side, the non-LP (in the UK) "Ballroom Blitz."

Side two of the original vinyl kicks off with "Burn on the Flame," one of the band's great non-LP metal rockers, full up with dramatic Mick Tucker flourishes plus things Queen would do. This is followed by "Sold Gold Brass," "The Six Teens," "I Wanna Be Committed" (also a first in the UK) and "Blockbuster!"

Again, *Strung Up* saw issue in the UK and across continental Europe but not stateside. Thankfully, the catalogue was about to get orderly in North America, with the action-packed US version of *Desolation Boulevard* about to be followed up by the "Action"-featuring *Give Us a Wink*, one of the great heavy metal albums of all time.

CHAPTER 6

Give Us a Wink
"Vat iz diz wink?"

Shocking that *Desolation Boulevard* didn't certify platinum in the States given how I remember, at 12 years old, Sweet mania and how intense it was around "Ballroom Blitz" and "Fox on the Run." But the most amount of critical acclaim and pure respect stateside would come from the band's first album to get issued essentially alike and intact with respect to European and North American versions.

That would be *Give Us a Wink*, a collection of mostly heavy, increasingly sophisticated, consistently edgy rockers built tall like Led Zeppelin and Queen, all told, the record emerging as a semi-underground classic for those about to rock in the '80s, an album somewhat akin to the likes of the first Montrose album from 1973 and the second Ram Jam record from 1978, yet on top of the heaviness, a kicking post to those who sniff that Queen did it classier.

But before the music, we get that odd title and the die-cut cover with the wink. It's all part and parcel of the idea that proto-metal records before the New Wave of British Heavy Metal generally didn't look heavier than REO Speedwagon albums.

"Well," laughs Andy, "the truth is, in Europe, Mick Tucker was forever asking girls, you know, if you want to come back to the room and everything. And when he used to get knocked back once in a while, which wasn't very often, his next play was, 'Well maybe you could see your way clear to giving me a wank then?' And they could never say the word wank. They always used to say, 'Vat iz diz wink?' So, after that, he used to say, 'Go on, give us a wink.'"

Adds Steve, "The *Give Us a Wink* album cover came out of a meeting with... I think by that time we were using a guy called Joe Petagno, who came up with this idea. There were two or three sleeves, I believe; the one that everybody seems to have is the one where you pull the eye through the slot, and it closes and winks at you. But the other one was, you know, the early days when you had those glasses you could get where you nodded your head up and down, they would change, and they look like your eyes were open and closed? They had stuck one of those across the eye in some territories, but it was never that successful. We all said look, it may be a little bit more complex, but as you pull this lever, the eye closing or opening is a much more credible, laughable idea. But the cover art was funny. It was just a dirty graffiti-covered wall. It was just little things. And 'give us a wink' I can't really explain. If you don't know what it means, you know what it means. Because that used to be one of our little sayings if we had picked up a little groupie: 'Give us a little hmm hmm wink; it'll only take a couple of minutes.' Hello? How deep."

An additional trivia note, the bit of graffiti on the back cover that says "are a bunch of winkers!," with nothing preceding the "are," is said to refer to Queen, the band Sweet thought was ripping them off, specifically with all those vocal harmonies.

And then with a careen and a bang, a snare crack and cymbal crash, we're into what is widely considered to be Sweet's magnum opus of an album, led by the band's magnum opus of a *song*, the esteemed "Action" (the US version flipped the side 1/side 2 sequencing, and added "Lady Starlight" as well, meaning the releases weren't exact, but close enough).

"Because we ended up producing ourselves," explains Andy, "'Action' was the one song we needed to write to get it out of our system, because we were being asked by Chinn and Chapman to stay with them. We were also being asked by our record producer, Phil Wainman, after having made, shall we say, four albums under the cosh, or three albums under the cosh, of being told what to do, we wanted some freedom. And there was another... the deal we were on with those early things, people were still kind of saying, 'Well, why would we want to change the deal?' And we were saying, 'Well, if you don't change, we're not going to sign.' It was that simple. I'm not saying that the bread and money had become the pure motivation, but when you've seen your songwriters driving around in Rollers and Mercs, and you're still scrabbling around a little bit, you start to go, 'Hang on, hang on, there's got to be a bit of parity here.' And of course, everything changed, and as soon as everything had changed and a deal was struck, an album later, the band had walked. Because now, we've got two-and-a-half years left of a record deal to try and prove something, and the first of the outings was *Give Us a Wink*."

There was also a chip on the band's collective shoulder, again, because of Queen and the success Freddie, Brian, John and Roger were having creating music in a similar manner to Sweet, namely heaviness with production craft and harmonies at both the vocal and guitar end of things. And even if many were saying, well, Queen is on another level, now up into *Give Us a Wink*, Sweet were pretty much on that same rarefied plane, even if their lyrics were, shall we say, earthier.

"Mack had a technique of mic'ing things up," says Andy, Reinhold Mack being the German engineer on the album's Munich sessions, a man soon to create a signature sound with Queen themselves. "It wasn't to everybody's taste, and when we got back to England, the engineer we ended up working with for the majority of our career, a guy called Louie Austin (later, Def Leppard, Judas Priest) in a London studio, was saying, 'God, that is huge, but the only thing I would have to say to you is, when the record company starts asking for some singles, you ain't got 'em, the way that they're mixed there.' So, we ended up having to bring... I think we ended up having to remix the whole album, but still keeping some of the techniques, but just trying to bring it back into a slightly more commercialised area, where the distinction was back, rather than this huge, you know, endless bottom end. Because that's basically what it was. Just a completely uncontrollable bottom end. I loved working with Mack, and there was a book out a couple years ago where he basically said that one of his best experiences was when we were in the studio."

"So yeah, I remember it as being a very pleasant experience," continues Scott. "Deep Purple had just been in the studio (with *Stormbringer*). Like I say, we heard about this engineer called Mack, who ended up producing Queen. And we went in there, and he had these brilliant ideas of recording things in stereo. That's why some of the drum and guitar sounds are so big. They've got twin mic'ing and out-of-phase stuff in there. When we got back to England, we had to do some new mixes for singles. For example, 'Action,' every time you put 'Action' in the middle, it disappeared, because it was all this wide stereo-placed stuff. So, we had to do a remix and virtually mono-ise it for the single. There are some drum sounds on there which I still marvel at, because I quite like the Led Zeppelin drum sound. But there are some huge drums; there's a song called 'Healer' on there, and there's a lot of looking at each other in the studio with a nod going, 'This is where we'll change.' It wasn't counting bars all the time. There was a lot of improvised stuff where, as long as you had a start and finish place, you could possibly edit it down. We were just allowing ourselves the freedom, if you like."

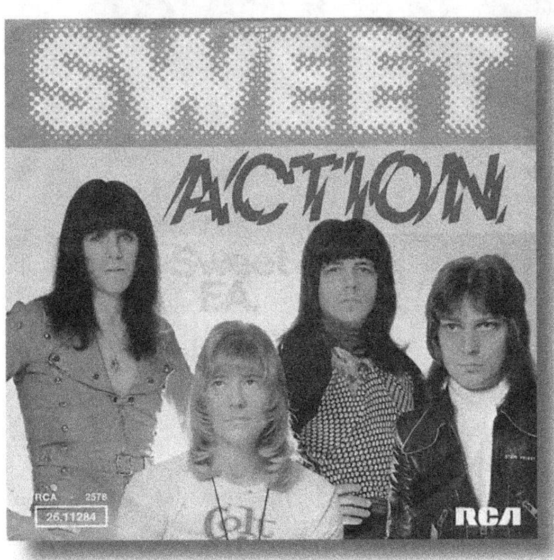

"It was the first album that we produced completely away from everybody as well," explains Andy. "Trucked ourselves off to the German studio, Musicland, which, by the way, we went straight after the Rolling Stones had done. I think they'd recorded *It's Only Rock 'n' Roll* there or something like that, and we were there just before Led Zeppelin went in there, and just before Deep Purple went in there again (commencing August 3rd, with *Come Taste the Band*). And then of course, about a year or so before Queen went in there. Like I say, Mack had some great stereo ideas, with stereo mic'ing. And the drums, it wasn't just mic'ed left and right, it was like the whole picture. We had to get rid of some of the stereo mic'ing that we'd used on the backing vocals, because they would not centre at one point. So when we got back to England, before we mixed it, we had to replace a fair amount of course, because it just didn't sound like Sweet. If you heard it in mono, half the vocals are missing. Because of like a phasing thing."

By all accounts the band liked Musicland, calling it cosy, and appreciating that the hotel was right above. Steve recalls fondly sunbathing on the roof and not so fondly discovering cocaine, having gained romantic notions about the drug from reading Aleister Crowley.

"Change of studio, for one thing," agrees Steve, asked why *Give Us a Wink* came out so mature, so full-bodied, so brimmed and rimmed 'round with confidence. "Also because of the sounds coming out, and just change of environment. We went to Spain for writing. I've no idea why. It was some sort of tax thing. If you write and record it abroad, then you can't get

Promo photo featuring Andy Scott, lower centre, as part of The Elastic Band.

Early days but already slinging the proto-metal, with B-side "Done Me Wrong All Right."

Promo shot of the band all glammed up, yet only dabblling in facepaint.

The debut album; in the beginning it was more about the singles.

Happy together. Sheet music for the Caribbean connection "Poppa Joe."

Advert for the thoughtful experimental single from 1971.

Sheet music for a classic Sweet single, which today would be classed as inappropriate cultural appropriation.

Promo photo of the band in transition from glam to nascent heavy metal. Left to right: Steve Priest, Andy Scott, Brian Connolly and Mick Tucker.

Brian, pioneer of heavy metal fashion, on the cover of Pop.

The fanny-tastic first great Sweet LP.

The North American version of *Desolation Boulevard* represented peak excitement for Sweet stateside.

Andy and Brian in action.

© Phil Mathews

Sheet music for roller-rink classic "The Ballroom Blitz."

Rosengarten, Mannheim, Germany,
April 28, 1975. © Klaus Hiltscher

Brian, Spain, 1976.
© Dick Barnatt

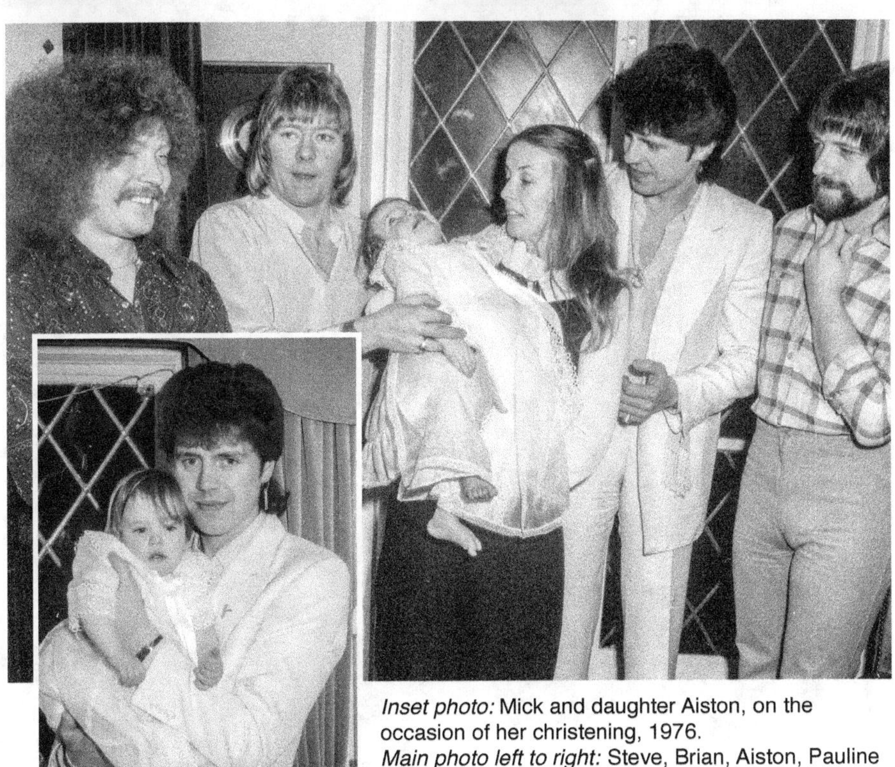

Inset photo: Mick and daughter Aiston, on the occasion of her christening, 1976.
Main photo left to right: Steve, Brian, Aiston, Pauline (died 1979), Mick and Andy. © Dick Barnatt

Japanese and French picture sleeves for "Action."

UK cassette release of *Give Us a Wink*.

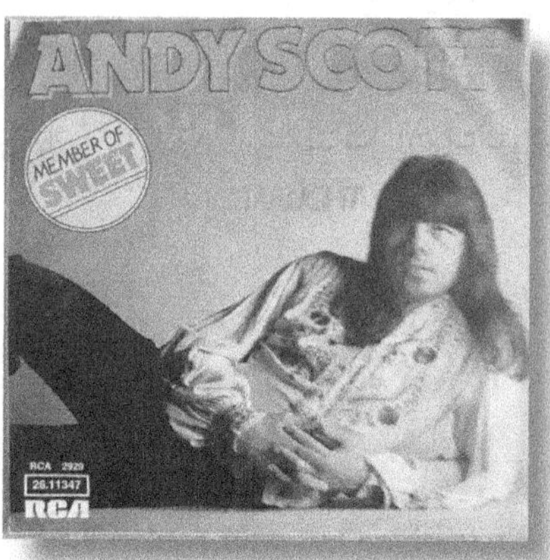

German picture sleeve for Andy´s solo single, "Where D'Ya Go."

US cover art for the 1977 album *Off the Record*.

Japanese picture sleeve for "Fever of Love."

Hammersmith Odeon, London, UK, February 24, 1978. © Phil Mathews

Late-period promo shot.

Sheet music for "Love Is Like Oxygen."

Sheet music for "California Nights."

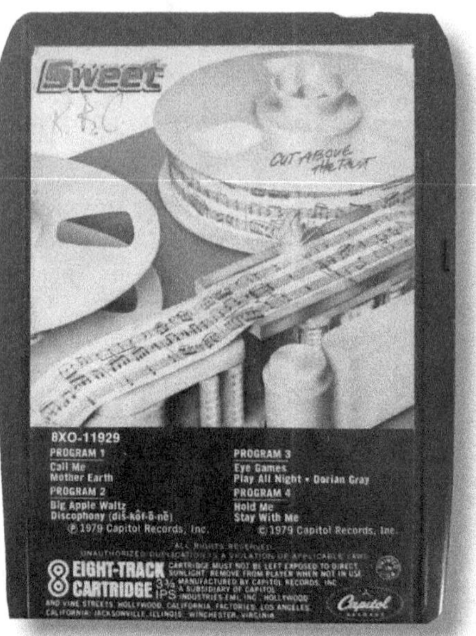

Eight-track issue of the 1979 album *Cut Above the Rest.*

Brian Connolly live with Brian Connolly´s Sweet, October 3, 1985, at Munchen Lenbach Palast, Germany. © Wolfgang Gurster

Disc—July 12, 1975 9
SWEET
'Piece of the Action'
RCA 2578
Sweet's powerful new single is
in your local record store now.
RCA
Records and Tapes

taxed in England. It didn't work, and we went to the studio in Munich, and one day I was walking… it was down underneath the Arabella Hotel, and I open this door and there's this huge hallway where they backed semis into, to unload. I just clapped and it went boom. So, then we realised that if we put some speakers in there, and fed the drums through it, and then put a couple of mics down the other end of the corridor, we got this huge echo effect, and that puts the whole album in a different light. I love that one."

Indeed, as Steve alludes to, the band went and rented a secluded home in Palma on the island of Majorca and wrote the album, mostly poolside, in a matter of ten days. En route to the writing, they recorded a live TV performance in Madrid. As Steve says, the Spanish junket was a tax dodge, as was Munich (as well, the room rates were good in the hotel above, if you were recording there), and there's a sense of all this infused into the lyrics of 'Action.' Even wider, the 'Action' lyric would be inspired by the stress experienced by the band at the time because of various managers, accountants and record companies all fighting for a share, not to mention the band itself fighting each other for songwriting credit.

"We weren't well-off," sighs Steve. "Everyone wants a piece of the action (laughs), which is why I wrote that. One of our managers had this huge office in London and I'm going, 'How come I can hardly pay for gas in my car?' Everyone was just walking away with bits of money here and there, making sure they got paid before we did. And the tax man came along and screwed us right royally. Even though we had done *Give Us a Wink* in Germany, it didn't seem to make any difference that we had done it abroad. When the tax bill came in, it was like half a million pounds. And in 1976 that's a lot of money. We were badly looked-after all the way around. I'm not going to blame everyone else and sour grapes and everything, but our affairs were not looked after very well."

The band went so far as to create a backmasked "You kiss my arse," figuring it out that if they sang "Liar, you know you believed it" just right, that it would achieve the effect. "Yes," explains Steve, "'Action' was extremely hard to put together, because we did a few backwards things in it as well, which now, of course you can do without taking the whole two-inch tape off and turning it over. But back then you had to do that. In fact, when we had done some of this backwards stuff, we erased the first verse of Brian's vocals, by turning it back over and forgetting where it was, so he had to come in. We said, 'Brian, before you leave…' 'Yes?' 'Could you do the first verse again?' And he did it, and I think he did it better than the original way he had done it. But those little things happen."

Slight variation to Steve's clapping tale above, he had explained back in the day that what happened was that someone had opened a door to the corridor from a room in which Mick had been drumming. The cannonating reverberation caused Mick to want to try to record literally in the corridor, which, once tried, turned out to be a mess. Plus, you couldn't make eye contact with Mick. A solution was found in which Mick was put back in the room but he was amplified into the corridor through two very large speakers.

"Zeppelin, definitely, had an influence on *Give Us a Wink*, for one," continues Steve, the band having just witnessed the majesty of the band at Earls Court. "Because John Paul Jones came down to watch us record, actually. In Munich. Frightened the life out of me (laughs). And yes, *Physical Graffiti* and *Houses of the Holy* were the things that really affected my little head, in that direction."

And this would be in advance of *Presence*.

"Yes, they were looking for somewhere to record. That's why they came down. Because they knew that Deep Purple had recorded there, and John Paul Jones was in Munich, and I don't know why, but he decided to come down and check it out. So, I'm working, and it just happened that John Paul Jones had come to the studio that day (ed. Steve has also said that budding rock jounro Cameron Crowe was there watching as well, resulting in the syndicated piece we've quoted from), so, frightened (laughs). I think Brian bumped into John Paul Jones in the discotheque we used to go to and invited him down. Thanks, Brian. He's a nice fella, John Paul Jones."

The album's merit badge first track, "Action," opens with what is in fact a cello riff, before crashing into its proud and regal romp to the blue blood side of "Ballroom Blitz." Like ZZ Top playing horns, a couple years later, Sweet just went and played the cellos themselves. It says so right there in the credits: celli.

"Yeah, it was supposed to be... and somebody said it was plural of cello, and I don't think it was," laughs Andy. "I always thought it was cellos. But yeah, on the song 'Action,' see, I used to play a little bit of violin in the school band when I was young, and I knew how to bow a string, if you know what I mean. So, when we were doing 'Action,' we just wanted to do something different on the beginning. In the original recording, I actually had a guitar going d-d-d-d-d-d, and I thought, we can do better than that. We tried the keyboard sequencing, and then I hit on the idea that because there were bands out there like ELO and people like that, I just said, what about trying some cellos? So in the beginning we all grabbed a cello; we had three cellos with us in the studio, but one by one each person kind of dropped out. Because quite frankly, it's better if you've got one person doing it, because it'll be... it'll sound the same. So that's all it was. And it just needed to be dropped into the track, whenever we heard it."

"There must've been half a dozen," answers Andy, asked how many cello tracks were applied. "We used slave reels, and then wide-synched them in, and I think it's what ELO must've done, and people like... well, Queen must've done it too. Because back then you're talking 16-track. I think 24-track had just sort of come into existence. I don't know whether we recorded 24-track in Munich, or if it was still 16, but whatever it was, there was lots of track-sharing, and a lot of stereo bounce-downs."

As the band finished up their roughly two weeks of recording on July 16th (with a trip back in the middle, July 9th, to record a *Top of the Pops* performance), Steve did talk to the press, indicating that they had indeed recorded 24-track in Munich, also remarking that it allowed them to record five tracks of Mick's drums for ultimate oomph. Steve had been impressed with the fact that there were few distractions there, catering was taken care of through a personal chef, and that with the hotel just above, they could record whenever they wanted, unlike the restrictions they often encountered back in England.

Bit of complication surrounding "Action," in the tradition of nothing going quite smoothly when it comes to Sweet and the synchronisation of their singles with their albums.

"When we arrived in Germany, we had already recorded 'Action' (ed. commencing May 23rd, at Audio International, engineer Louie Austin presiding, the day before the band—less Andy—saw Zeppelin at Earls Court) and it came out as a single, whilst we were recording the album, in England. But it hadn't been released anywhere else. But it was up in the charts; it was up to No.9. But I told Mack, 'Listen, by the way, we've got "Action" with us.' And he says, 'When's it coming out?' 'It's about to come out.' He said, 'Don't come in tomorrow morning. Come in at midday.

I've got an idea.' And when I came in, he cut together the new intro with the cellos on their own, and the synthesizers building, and then the band came in with that whack. It wasn't like that on the original recording, and I thought, that's bloody genius. So, it's Mack's editing that gave us the new intro, and that's the recording that was then released in Europe and America and everywhere else."

Of note, the British version of "Action" saw a second session on May 30th, a session for vocals and overdubs on June 4th, and then a final mix on June 7th, with a master of it cut at EMI London on June 10th. Brian had quipped that the song only took a day-and-a-half to write, but the recording necessarily had to take some time, given all the bits and pieces.

Asked about the shared writing credits between all members of the band on *Give Us a Wink*, as alluded to in the "Action" lyric, Andy explains that "A lot of the songwriting, not blowing my own trumpet, but it usually started with me. Along the way, there have been various sort of partnerships where me and Steve would take the reins, or me and Mick would take the reins. I remember 'Action,' for example, would be, we were trying to purpose-build 'What would we want to hear in a single? What were the ingredients?' We just tried to put everything in there like a commercial chorus, time signatures, interesting guitar parts, interesting vocal parts, the fact that it's a guitar riff that you immediately identify with. There's drum parts that are interesting. There's reverse drums in there. It's one of those moments where, look, if we're going to do this, let's bloody well do it. Let's not talk about it, let's just do it. And luckily it worked. I think at that time, the way that Mick, Steve and myself played together, it was probably one of the tightest units that you would ever find. And it shows in records like *Give Us a Wink*. I would hope that anybody, you know, delving back and now saying, it's almost 40 years ago, would go wow."

The talented Mr. Scott is also credited with synthesizers on the album. "There's not tons of keyboards on *Give Us a Wink*," says Andy, "but there is subliminal stuff. And I was so into oddball things that synthesizers really interested me. I used to have a BCS3 and a Moog, and ARP Odyssey and a 2600, and one of these Polymoogs, that was one of the early synths where you could play more than one note. I was just interested in sounds as much as anything, and it's amazing what you can do when you sit there for two or three hours in your bedroom, and although what you've got to do now is get the sound again. Because they didn't have much memory back then."

"Action" rose to No.15 in the UK charts and No.20 in the US, cracking the Top Ten in Canada and various European territories. As for the wider album, similar trends played out, with the album not charting in the UK, hitting No.27 in the US, No.9 in Germany and No.3 in Norway. But the album's set-piece, "Action," would make an impression, having now over the years been covered with some level of profile by the likes of Raven, Def Leppard and Black 'n Blue. Scorpions (calling themselves The Hunters) even did a German version of it, covering "Fox on the Run" in German as well.

"I don't think 'Action' is as instantly commercial as 'Fox on the Run,' mused Brian in late '75, speaking with *Record Mirror*. "At the moment, it's selling mainly on the chorus, which is the most commercial feature of it. But after people have heard it a few times, I think they'll appreciate its other points. With this one, I'll be quite happy if we make the top 20. With 'Fox on the Run' we set out to write a commercial single, pure and simple, and it worked. With this one, we've gone a step further and written something that's much more in Sweet's direction. Although to us, it's already a little bit dated, because we've gone on again since then. This album is 100% Sweet. We've written it, played everything on it, and we're very pleased with it. We wrote all the material in only ten days, and we were able to work very fast in the studio. Hopefully this will be the album which will really make an impression for us. There's no question of whether or not we've got a single on it. The question is which one do we put out? There are at least three possibilities. If we do make it as an albums band, we shall continue to put out singles, but as a formality rather than a necessity. They're very useful after all, because they do keep the name of the group fresh in the public's mind."

"It's a great studio," answered Connolly, on why the band chose Munich for the recording of *Give Us a Wink*. "24-track, with every facility we could possibly need. But more important, there are no distractions there. The phone doesn't ring and interrupt all the time, and there's no time wasted in travelling to and from the studio because we can live there."

"Yesterday's Rain" represents a second track—we're looking at this in terms of the US running order—of pounding yet smart proto-metal, opening with phase-shifter and offering scorching little Andy Scott licks as it lays down the law of man and woman (of the night) as practiced by the dark and doomed Brian Connolly, a hard man made that way by grim family circumstance and, increasingly now, the drink. As was periodic with Sweet, they slip in a dirty line, namely "up to my balls inside her" but because it's a so-called "album track," there's no fuss about it. And then right after, as if you cover up the earthiness, there's a gorgeous twin lead and little stabs of laboriously stacked twin vocals followed by a "voice bag" break.

Says Andy, "'I didn't come down with yesterday's rain' it was a phrase that we picked up when we were in America on tour, about a year earlier than that. And it was just one of those brilliant sayings, you know, in other words, I'm not stupid. And I thought yeah, I like that."

Reflective of the album's sophistication in general, Andy figures, "I was listening to lots of different music back then. I was listening to Return to Forever and Chick Corea, Al DiMeola, Jean-Luc Ponty, the Brecker Brothers; there was all kinds of stuff going around in my head. And some of those guitar riffs—and probably some of the time signatures—are fairly reminiscent of things like The Mahavishnu Orchestra. I'm making no bones about it. Whenever there was a moment, I would try to get something in."

"Actually, 'Yesterday's Rain,' we couldn't do everything, you know, Zeppelin-esque," reflects Steve. "We had to stick to some of our route, or we would have lost the lot. So, I don't mind. They were pretty heavy-ish poppy songs. But 'Yesterday's Rain' came from... do you remember Alias Smith and Jones, two cowboys? Burl Ives was a conniving cattle baron in one of them, and he said, 'Now listen boys, I didn't come down with yesterday's rain.' When they were trying to bamboozle him or whatever. Oh, what a great title."

Again, there's a darkness to the lyric, as if the guys are living with some degree of pushback from their womanising ways. There are repercussions to their pessimistic and even simplistic view of how things work, as the guys try for stable domesticity on one hand and then risk it all for kicks on the road. As the sexual politics remain unresolved, Andy continually throws off sharp licks over a series of chords that are thoughtful, even reflective. Vocal harmonies provide the ear candy, en route to additional solo sections.

"The song 'White Mice' is initially about... it's another word for sperm," says Andy, asked about the next track, a fast-paced rocker which features Mick Tucker artfully playing with time signatures during the elaborate solo section.

"That was hell to play," sighs Steve. "Hell. I had to take it verse by verse, or my hand would've fallen off. So that was what you call a drop-in (laughs). I can do it now, because I've got these new picks that wrap around your thumb. So, you don't have to keep hold of them. Great."

"White Mice" is a fully modern metal rocker, slightly sweetened by a deceptively melodic chorus which ultimately just comes off as creepy: gang vocals croon: "white mice, into your head, out of my head," and later, "white cat, into my head" and finally "white light, into my eyes." Frilly twin leads draw the listener back to something a bit more uptown and eventually a spirited headbang is achieved, aided by solo flourishes from Andy, who combines the best of Ritchie Blackmore and Brian May into an entity called Andy Scott. He even does some fret board tapping which wasn't a regular thing we heard much before Eddie Van Halen in 1978. It's happened but rarely and only for short bursts. Both Brian May and Judas Priest would go there, but for early 1976, this is actually one of the best examples. And demonstrating further versatility, later there's even a synth solo.

"Healer" is the first let-up on the decibels, but not on the band's striving and capability to be Zeppelin-esque on a creative tip. At 7:18, it's the longest thing on the album, but even this was edited down from a nine-minute version. But sure, this sounds like non-obvious Led Zeppelin, like something from the dark side of *Physical Graffiti* written by John Paul Jones.

Recalls Andy, "That might well have been a guitar riff that I had for quite a while. I had this idea of… You've got to remember, we're all influenced by various things, and I loved the openness of Led Zeppelin's recordings, where the guitar is just floating, you know, and there's only drums and bass—it's not overloaded with things. Which is the normal trademark of the Sweet records. It's quite layered, it's quite slick, it's got a lot of commercial bite to it. I wanted to do something that was very open and just a guitar riff, and it lends itself to it. It's hypnotic. And it wasn't until we started to play with it in the studio, with Mack, and Mack turned around, and I said, 'This needs something.' And he says, 'I've got a great innovative sort of keyboard player,' and he came in with the clavinet, and just sat there and thumped along with us, and it was absolutely amazing. There was no… It was all done with nodding of heads. It wasn't like we'll do eight bars here or ten here, you know what I mean?"

"'Healer,' that was inspired from a *Star Trek* episode," says Steve. "There was one where this guy whose ego is as big as the planet, called himself The Healer, and he used to point his hand at people and it would heal them. So I went, oh, good idea for a song." Steve has also said that the song was extremely hard to get right because of the distractions that can plague the mind when having to execute a simple plod like that. Mistakes were made, which had to be edited out. Nonetheless, the band never resorted to click tracks (until later albums), on the insistence of Mick Tucker, who quite rightly reasoned that the music would lose its organic quality.

Over to side two of the American issue, "The Lies in Your Eyes" is a popster that nonetheless pounds, featuring more than anything, the band's ethereal, almost machine-like vocal harmonies, taken to the bank a rock 'n' roll generation later by Def Leppard. At opportune moments, Andy massages in brief but polished twin leads, even quoting "Satisfaction" in one spot. At the lyric end, this one's a put-down of a lying woman, with Brian at one point threatening, "You've got a big fat mouth; watch what you say" in typical menacing Sweet fashion. There's also a reference to an earlier Sweet song with "Solid gold brass got a plastic face."

Of note, with the UK issue offering eight selections and the US issue nine, side two of the Japanese release opens with "Fox on the Run," bringing the song count of that version to ten. Otherwise, the running order matches that of the US version.

Then it's back into the crunching modern metal with "Cockroach," the heaviest song Led Zeppelin never wrote.

Laughs Andy, "Well, 'Cockroach' was... Brian was a bit of an alley cat, you know, the old night-crawler, out and about. And I can't remember how it came in, but somebody came up with a lyric, you know, 'She crawled into my bed like a cockroach.' And I thought, yeah, that's a damn good starting point. So, we just moved on from there."

"'Cockroach' was funny," adds Steve. "Well, funny. Brian has picked up this young lady, and I'd just heard the remark. His words were, 'She crawled into my bed like a cockroach.' Pardon, say that again? And it just evolved from there on."

At the outset it's just Mick drumming, and this is where we get to hear the Reinhold Mack sound in its infancy, including that signature dry snare, before he'd take it to extremes with Queen and Billy Squier. As Mack told me, "I like it open, so you—I hate to use this—but you get some air around it that you actually feel it and it's not just like somebody dropped a ball, it's got some crack to it. That is actually a very old technique; I learned it from the classical people. You don't mic the snare drum angling a microphone down towards it and using one at the bottom. I just use one on the side. I aim it at the actual shell of the drum."

More on the Zeppelin tip, what stands for a chorus on "Cockroach" sounds like what stands for a chorus on "In My Time of Dying," with double-tracked vocals that sound like a Robert Plant vocal harmony and even, at one point, the clarion shrieks from "Immigrant Song."

Moving on, "Lady Starlight" is another complicated story, living life more so—at least on the continent—as an Andy Scott solo track but already having been on the UK edition of the band's last album. It's not on the UK *Give Us a Wink*, but it's added as a ninth track on the North American version, stuck in the middle of side two.

"'Lady Starlight' was really Andy's song," affirms Steve, "although I think we all got a quarter of the writing. I have no idea why that happened. I think he wrote it about his first wife."

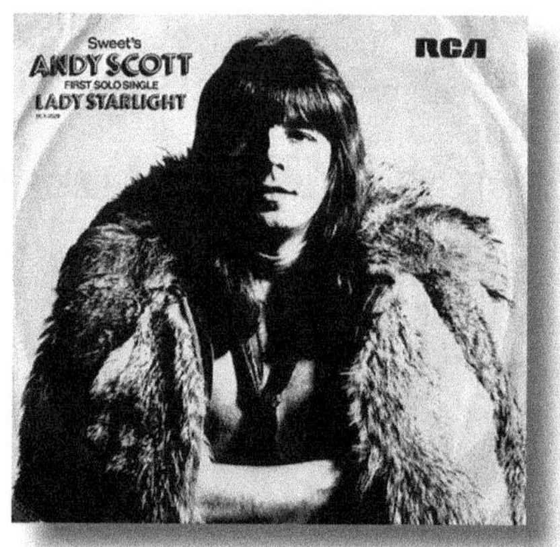

"Well, 'Lady Starlight' was on the British *Desolation Boulevard* album, originally," affirms Scott, "and Mike Chapman said this is a big hit, but he said it's not for Sweet. But he said I believe this is a massive hit. And when Sweet had one of those moments when nothing was going on, the record company decided to release it as a single, but as a solo single, because it would still keep the name in, you know, 'Andy from The Sweet; he's got a solo single out.' It did well in places like Germany and Australia and South Africa and a few other places. We did a lot of work with that in England, but it just shows you, at that time, I actually believed that the Sweet part of the career in England was at its moment when the tide turns. There is that moment in time where our career was no longer what it was in England, and we had to move on. Hence, America and Europe and other parts of the world became the major centres. No matter how much we did in England— and we did do a lot of TV and a fair amount of promotion—it didn't make an impact on the charts. So, it shows you, doesn't it?"

The song was indeed issued as a picture sleeve solo single in the UK and mainland Europe, backed with up-tempo acoustic pop number "Where D'ya Go," which is distinguished by sort of shotgun-echoing handclaps buttressed by crisp drumming from Mick Tucker. Andy sings both tracks strongly, sounding very much like Brian, lots of control, easing in and out of a worthy falsetto—that's Andy singing on the Sweet version as well.

Notes Scott of "Lady Starlight," "I got Mick to come back in the studio with me, and took the original backing track apart, and made it probably a bit more radio-friendly, added a bit of keyboards and a couple of extra guitars and vocals on there. This would have been about '75; spans the two records, I think."

Further on Mike Chapman's opinion that the song wasn't for Sweet, Andy has also said that Chapman always quite liked it but it couldn't be issued by Sweet as such because Brian wasn't singing on it. Oddly, three years later, Scorpions would put a song on their *Animal Magnetism* album called "Lady Starlight," and it too was the ballad on a record with no more of them.

Back to *Give Us a Wink*, next up was "Keep It In," a speedy technical rocker adding to the pile of tracks demonstrating Sweet's progressive, percussive heavy metal prowess. Notes Priest, "I think that was from Andy listening to Chick Corea. And that was a hell of a one to play, for me, anyway." Bass in knots to be sure, but this one's really a Mick Tucker showcase, or, more accurately a song in which the drummer really gets to have some fun, executing "Ballroom Blitz" like snare rhythms and all manner of extended fill. Steve's reference to Chick Corea is apt because there's a passage that definitely sounds like fusion. But once we get to the frantic solo section, this sounds like Judas Priest on a tear circa *Sin After Sin* or *Stained Class*.

Give Us a Wink closes with "4th of July," a curious "Solid Gold Brass"-like rocker sitting and shifting between Sweet's celebrated glam past and the newer thumping metal. Angelic vocal harmonies are everywhere, as are decorative musical licks and arrangements. It's a fitting and fun way to close an album full of fireworks. Of note, a radio edit was made for the track, although it was only launched as a single in Australia, non-picture sleeve, backed with "Restless."

"Once again, the American influence," muses Andy. "There was a piano and a guitar riff, and again when... that track was actually played by the guy who co-wrote 'Love Is Like Oxygen' with me, Trevor Griffin. He was our sound engineer, but he was quite a good little jazzer. He loved playing Fender Rhodes, and he was quite a good and interesting jazz player. And I just said to him, 'Look, have a go. Let yourself go, mate.' And after a couple of glasses of red wine, he did." Griffin had played with the likes of Gene Pitney and Australian star Normie Rowe, with his main credit being prog rockers Procession, who had started in Australia and then moved to London.

SWEET
"GIVE US A WINK!"
The latest album by Europe's
most acclaimed new band! Includes
"Action."
Capitol
NOW ON NATIONAL TOUR!

"I think there might be a few things that were never completely developed," recalls Andy, on the subject of rare demos or B-sides from the *Give Us a Wink* sessions. "But Sweet was not a band to... you know, if we had something in the can that was still, shall we say, fresh in our heads, then we didn't develop it. It would either end up on the next album as a starting point, or at the very worst, I'd try to develop it as a B-side. The only thing I have that is not developed at this last moment, is the last set of recordings that were involved with the *Identity Crisis* album, really, truthfully, which never got a full release everywhere in the world. I do actually have some tracks from there that were never developed, probably four of five."

So, there was nothing that got held over to, say, the next album, *Off the Record*. "It wasn't quite like that. There might've been a section or two; for example, the song 'Laura Lee,' there happened to be two sections. And from what I can remember now, it was two songs. And we were looking for something that wasn't just your common garden variety ballad, if you know what I mean."

In a surprisingly rare unfavourable review of a Sweet album to date, David Hancock from *Record Mirror* wrote that, "The childishly vulgar sleeve is matched by the less than subtle record it contains. But then Sweet are not a particularly stylish band. What they do aspire to these days is credibility within the rock fraternity. They are a little further along that road, though they don't deserve to be with the indulgent outing of dated harmonies and the belief that extended solos and bash-bash drumming are where it's at. They have learned how to write simple pop songs then blow them out of all proportion with the result that tracks blend into one another, exposing the worst of heavy rock music—its similarity. Only the really taut 'Action' and hypnotic 'Healer' stand repeated plays. The rest is pretentious and for people who are aware that winking makes you go deaf."

Even before the record saw issue stateside, the band was off touring, with the highlight being Sweet's second visit down under. After a 40-hour excursion, the entourage touched down for a first gig, August 9th, 1975, in New Zealand. After five shows there (along with the experience of a minor earthquake), the entourage moved over to Australia for nine shows. Underscoring the surreal nature of Sweet's career trajectory, the band were selling out large venues due to their cover of "Peppermint Twist" having been such a big hit from the previous album. There wasn't much to show for their Australian success once they left however. Having been rewarded with a bunch of gold discs on the trip, the hotel dutifully boxed them up to mail home—they were never seen again.

Asked about stage props, Steve says that "for *Give Us a Wink*, somebody made this huge eye that was on a big round support thing, and

RECORD MIRROR & DISC, FEBRUARY 21, 1976
An exciting new album from Sweet.
GIVE US A WINK
SWEET
"GIVE US A WINK!"
RS 1036
SWEET
Also available on Cassette and Cartridge.
RCA
Records and Tapes

it had an eyelid on it, and as you turned it around, the lid gradually shut—gradually. Until it was upside down, where the lid was shut, but not quite. You could still see the pupil, and it had red lines in the pupil and everything. It was horrible (laughs). But the best one of the lot, was somebody decided that they should make four marionettes, full-size marionettes, that were on stage before us, and there would be lots of smoke, and as the music built up, they all collapsed, and we came up behind them. They didn't even look like us. And they all collapsed at different times, and my one was left standing... and then just sort of toppled over. And Brian and I… we were all at the back in stitches laughing our heads off. It was never used. Oh no (laughs), we vetoed that."

Back in America, after Ed Leffler had taken a strip off of the execs at Capitol concerning their perceived lack of enthusiasm for promoting *Desolation Boulevard*, there was going to be more press this time around, in conjunction with a decent US tour, for most of January, February and March of 1976.

Don Grierson, Capitol's national merchandising manager, in May '76, countered by telling *Cash Box*, "We felt that Sweet's second LP was a smash from the moment it was delivered to us. We created two support posters featuring the album graphics. One had a strip-in area for different locales. We designed two versions of three separate radio spots—AM, FM and tour support. The first set dealt with the first LP and the tour, the second with *Give Us a Wink* and the tour. We also made a floor display dump with a lenticular eye designed to give the eye on the cover its blinking effect. We also made a mobile with the eye, belt buckles, T-shirts, sweatshirts, divider cards and sent out a massive mailing of the *Capitol Star News* devoted exclusively to the group. In short, we stayed active in the career development of the group, regardless of the fact that we had no new product coming from them for a while."

Cash Box was at the band's Santa Monica show (supported by Sammy Hagar), writing, "How sweet it was may be a cliché, however that's the way it was when the mighty quartet from England made their return to their favourite palace of rock, the Santa Monica Civic. Even though there were many similarities in their show from the last visit, the show was non-stop electrifying rock 'n' roll at its best. Brian Connolly, Steve Priest, Mick Tucker and Andy Scott who compose Sweet started to burn up the stage from the very moment their phallic cinematic short started rolling. The audience jumped to their feet as the Capitol recording artists roared on stage and performed their smash hit from last year, 'Ballroom Blitz.' What made the Sweet show so exceptional was the first-rate combination of lighting, visuals, theatrics, showmanship and musicianship which made the evening delightful. Debuting new material off their latest LP *Give Us a Wink* proved that the band has steadily improved in providing its fans with more tasty rock 'n' roll. Their latest hit single 'Action' brought joyous hoots and howls from the raucous crowd. Probably the two hottest numbers performed in their fast-moving exhilarating set were 'A.C.D.C.' and drummer Mick Tucker's audio/visual three-way drum war. The lads closed their triumphant show with 'Fox on the Run.'"

A highlight of the show was the continued use of film, to be sure, but in fact now, the use of film in Mick's drum solo. As Dan Nooger explained in *Circus*, "Just as he is gaining momentum, he stops and a film of him continuing the solo is flashed on screen behind him, flashing back and forth from film to reality in a brilliant display of power and coordination."

Explained Tucker, "I felt if I was going to do a drum solo, there were two ways to do it; either play something hard and make it look easy or play something easy and make it look hard. Whether a drum solo is good or bad, the audience feels obliged to applaud because of the physical effort involved. I thought I'd accompany myself and other percussion instruments like timbales and congas, but just putting that on tape doesn't tell the audience that you're playing them. So, we thought, we're already using film of us in these fake adverts for Guinness Stout, drinking milk and such in the intermission, so why not use films in my solo? We started with one film and now we use two. The whole thing used to be the ultimate brain-number, but now it's a lot shorter and more sophisticated. It's almost very entertaining."

Continued Mick, after explaining that he goes through a pair of sticks a night, "I play with my sticks the wrong way 'round. I hit the drums with the butt end of the stick, and though I use a 'C' stick, which is not particularly heavy, I can get a very heavy sound without throwing the tension on my drumheads out. I play so hard; I used to crack up all my cymbals. I use basically a Ludwig kit—always have—but a lot of the fittings are extra-heavy custom-made things like cymbal stands, high-hats and drum pedals."

This American campaign came after two isolated dates in September '75 on the way back from Australia. Like many rockers before and after, Sweet pulled over for a few days in Hawaii first. Unfortunately, Andy and Mick were not talking to each other after having had a big row in Australia when Andy walked off the stage ticked off that his ARP synthesizers had gone out of tune and wrecked "Fox on the Run" and "Sweet F.A." Mick wanted Andy thrown out of the band and turned on Steve and Brian when he found out nothing of the sort was about to happen. On the lighter side, despite smouldering silences in Hawaii, the guys toured Pearl Harbor and got to stay in the hotel at which Elvis filmed *Blue Hawaii*. Steve, Brian and tour manager Mick Angus also tried surfing, with neither of them managing any success at the craft.

The American tour ended on a sad note. First, at a St. Louis show, where Mick was being his usual rude rock star self and annoying the local security, Steve ripped the door off a refrigerator and a roughing up by the venue staff quickly had to be defused by Ed Leffler. The band then moved to the final gig of the campaign, playing the Santa Monica Civic Auditorium. Support was supposed to come from Back Street Crawler; however, the band's leader, ex-Free legend Paul Kossoff, dies of a drug a few days previous. Ritchie Blackmore happened to be in town, so Sweet had him guest on a cover of "All Right Now" in tribute to the diminutive Free guitarist.

Blackmore was a big influence on Sweet's guitarist Andy Scott. Explains Andy, "In the really early days when I first joined the band, we used to do 'Hush' and 'Kentucky Woman,' and we also did a version of 'Black Night'—but these were because we were playing 'popular' dance halls that wanted to hear not only our music but also some other music of the era. It was a generally accepted thing in less heavy bands, more commercial bands. We all wanted to play numbers like 'Speed King' and 'Flight of the Rat,' but we had to keep it down to the more commercial things. So much so that I could probably still play the 'Black Night' guitar solo exactly the same as it was on the record. This shows how much of an influence Ritchie was: I used to play a Stratocaster, but I also had a Gibson 335 which I used all the way through the early Sweet era."

Andy was clearly delighted, if a little surprised, to share a stage with the "Man in Black." "It was completely spontaneous. We had met him a couple of nights earlier, and the one thing that he'd said to our tour manager, who used to work for Deep Purple—a guy called Mick Angus—was, 'You'd better let me get into the gig tonight.' Because the last time we'd played Los Angeles, he hadn't been able to get into the show, because our management at that time, and record company, had virtually sold out the gig even before tickets went on sale. That's how 'in demand' that concert was. We should have done more nights there at the Santa Monica Civic that first time, but that's the way they wanted to play it. So, the second time we did it, the tickets were sold out—not so much record company stuff—by the end of the day. And one thing that Ritchie said to him (Mick Angus) was: 'I'm gonna come, and I'm gonna get in this time.' And we said: 'Of course you are!' And somebody made the joke, 'If you want to get up, put your guitar in the boot.' There was an offer to set up another stack, but I think Ritchie just said, 'Plug me into anything; I'll be all right.' And I think the only amps on my side of the stage that were available for him to plug into were the amps that I think were monitoring the synthesizers, which had a couple of horns in them, which left him with a rather loud and clear sound."

Replacing Back Street Crawler on the show was Sammy Hagar, now a solo act. Steve says that this change in the dance card might have helped hasten Sweet's decline in the US, because Ed Leffler promptly signed on as Sammy's manager, and later got into a nasty lawsuit with Capitol over Sammy's contract.

In conjunction with the band playing the States, reviews of *Give Us a Wink* came rolling in.

Wrote Gerry Barker, from the *Fort Worth Star - Telegram*, in advance of the band's March 1976 concert date in the area, "If you weren't convinced of their power by the first album, *Desolation Boulevard*, or its two singles, 'Ballroom Blitz' and 'Fox on the Run' (which got very limited area airplay), this new effort should make you a believer. The combined efforts of Brian Connolly, Mick Tucker, Andy Scott and Steve Priest are nothing short of dynamite, starting with the first cut on side one, 'Action,' also the group's latest single. 'Action' kicks off with a *Rollerball*-style organ intro that quickly blossoms into an ear-drenching crescendo of guitar, drums and vocals and everything in-between. Through nine tracks, they offer some of the most vigorous guitar work to be heard in years as their songs pulsate, grow, explode and regenerate within limits that approach psychedelic proportions. Special mention might go to 'Yesterday's Rain' and 'Healer' (featuring a drumbeat that will rip your headphones), a piece of macho rock called 'The Lies in Your Eyes' and a boiling 'Keep It In.' 'Lady Starlight' is the lone ballad try here, and it succeeds despite an overall lack of vocal strength on this type of song. If indeed the live show bests their albums, the walls of McFarlin Auditorium might need to be reinforced just in case."

Seconded David C. Scott from the *Dayton Daily News*, "Sweet's lead song rather sums up the group's entry into rock's highly competitive marketplace—everyone wants a piece of the 'Action.' The British foursome's sound is very much like that of countrymen Queen. Vocal harmonies share the spotlight with energetic instrumentation and electronic trickery. The result is very tight and enthusiastic, if not completely original. Since a myriad of musically inclined young persons have proven the pop consumers' capacity for new groups serving up somewhat similar sounds is seemingly endless, Sweet obviously feel there's enough 'action' left for them. Capitol has done its share too, by providing a colourful die-cut, two-part album jacket and some very excellent technical production.

So, if you're receptive to still another variation on hard rock's basic guitar and percussion progressions, Sweet will deliver. Whether or not *Give Us a Wink* contains any chart success depends largely on the current mood of the FM jocks. With enough airplay, several cuts could endear themselves to enough listeners."

"The band's first self-written and self-produced effort is uneven," wrote Robert Hilburn on the *Los Angeles Times*, "but its best moment suggest the English quartet is fully capable of standing on its own. Not only has the Sweet come up with a bit of punk rock abandon in 'Action' (already a hit in England and in much of Europe) that matches the better moments of the Chinn-Chapman days, but it also offers some other tracks (notably 'Yesterday's Rain' and 'Fourth of July') that touch effectively upon a slightly broader teenage rock mould. The Sweet's strength is in simple, tough, tenacious songs that involve the repetition of catchy, often surly or challenging phrases ('I didn't come down with yesterday's rain/ You're foolin' nobody' from 'Yesterday's Rain') that are delivered in a high-pitched, urgent vocal style. The purpose of the backing music is to simply reinforce the intensity of the vocal."

"While *Give Us a Wink* shows that the quartet can come up with the phrases, put together the harmonies and provide energetic backing, the album's weaker moments (many of them traceable to an apparent attempt to achieve a slightly 'heavier' musical stance) raise questions about the group's production abilities. The biggest problem in the album is the band's failure to know when to end a particular track. All too often the group weakens a song's impact by allowing it to continue well beyond its natural length. As a discipline factor, the band might do well to set a limit of three or three-and-a-half minutes per song. Or it might see if Shadow Morton— who did such a good job on the second Dolls album—has some free time. Either way, the Sweet—which is now on its first US tour—proves it has a place in the post Chinn/Chapman world."

Then there's this review from Hackensack, New Jersey's *The Record*, which would have given the guys fits. "The material on *Give Us a Wink* picks up right where songs like 'Fox on the Run' left off. The sound and feeling of the album is in exactly the same vein as that single. For this album, the members of the group have also diversified their talents as instrumentalists. To the guitar-bass-drums-voice line-up, they've added a voice bag, cello, synthesizers, phasers and a string machine. To some extent, the new style copies some of England's most successful bands. The song 'Action,' for example, is a faithful copy of Queen, right down to Brian Connolly's lead vocals. For some groups this would be a fault, but for a band that is predominantly singles-oriented, it is a help, since it gives the fans something to grab hold of. It is easy to hear, on the basis of *Give Us a Wink*, that The Sweet have settled into the American Top 40 charts for a long stay."

"Sweet's dependence on straight-ahead heavy metal chording gives way to a counterbalance of depth on *Give Us a Wink*," noted industry standard *Cash Box*. "Well defined synthesizer passages mark the layers of hard while subtle cello shadings accent the shrillness of the punk-tainted vocals. The overall feel of the album is as subtle as a train wreck while not grating on tender ear fibre. AM enshrinement is assured while longer cuts stand an FM chance. Top cuts include 'The Lies in Your Eyes,' 'Action,' 'Cockroach' and 'Yesterday's Rain.'"

Good to see Sweet get serious consideration in *Creem* as well, Detroit's high-concept mag for hipsters. Wrote Richard Riegel in his review, "Though it's less design than fateful coincidence, the Sweet have mastered the Beatles' old trick of adopting every worthwhile contemporary musical influence and channelling them all back into an unshakably bourgeois centre, thereby winning over the greatest number of fans in the shortest possible time. Thus, Sweet's classical metal riffs and hooks, played with clean precision. Timely hints of jet-set S&M and bisexuality, always secondary to the pure aggression of the music. Four pub-crawling closet skinheads in matching shags and platforms. From 'Little Willy' to 'Fox on the Run,' both in the Top Ten. The list of contradictions the Sweet have mastered (and transcended) is endless and suggests something of their formidable reserves of r'n'r energy."

"*Give Us a Wink* lives up to either side of *Desolation Boulevard* (take your pick), with impressive performance, production and composition throughout. Many of the songs depict a universe as tumultuous as Connolly's pub-depths prophesied. 'Action,' 'Lies in Your Eyes' and 'Yesterday's Rain,' among others, reinforce the misogynist stance of 'Fox on the Run:'

the usual Sweet protagonist enjoys an I'll-abuse-you-before-you-can-abuse-me relation with all the young ladies of both sexes. 'Cockroach,' indeed, contain some of the meanest invective uttered since the real punks departed for that great circle jerk in the sky: 'You crawled into my bed like a cockroach… but I love you.' Mick Jagger didn't think of *that*, even after A.L. Oldham had buggered him! Nope, a nod's never been as good as a wink. Get Sweet's *Give Us a Wink* now, and tune into the best British Invasion since Slade hocked their spellers to buy guitars."

Finally, from Berkeley, California, we have Evan Hosie, who optimistically writes, "Very few groups actually make it in America, and Sweet, a young punk English group is coming closer than most. Now, they write their own material—'Fox on the Run' was the first—and are trying to lose the reputation as just a singles band and the 'teenybopper' stigma. Someone once termed their music 'bubblegum Led Zeppelin' and it's an apt description. Just listen to 'Cockroach' on the new disc, *Give Us a Wink*. They attack their music with the same heavy metal style and Brian Connolly half-screams over the top like a spirited but less versatile Robert Plant. Mick Tucker, Andy Scott and Steve Priest add the high harmonies and keep a snarling rhythm section. With *Desolation Boulevard* and *Give Us a Wink* doing well, they shouldn't have any trouble establishing themselves as a legitimate hard rock band. None of the 'kid stuff,' rather 'teen stuff' for these boys. They're off to blitz the world, starting with America, and with their high rock 'n' roll and three strong albums, they just might get the sweet success they're after."

Cracking and original album as it is, *Give Us a Wink* didn't exactly find the band conquering the Top 40 charts stateside or back home. The biggest disappointment would have been that it didn't achieve RIAA gold, while its predecessor, *Desolation Boulevard*, did. As well, it must have been a disappointment that the band wasn't making it with songs they wrote and essentially produced themselves.

"I think that *Give Us a Wink* was particularly well received in America," sums up Scott. "But you have to remember, in America, *Desolation Boulevard* was the backbone of *Sweet Fanny Adams* with a couple of tracks from our *Desolation Boulevard*, and a couple of the singles, such as 'Fox on the Run' and 'Ballroom Blitz,' which were added to it. America, I'm afraid, got almost like a greatest hits package for the first album. In the UK, by the time other people were jumping on this bandwagon, '75, it had long gone, as far as people like Slade and us, and a few other bands—we were moving on. By that time, '75, '76, we were starting to have success in America, and luckily the Americans had nothing to totally draw on, when we started to go over there in the mid-'70s. So, we were treated like a British rock band.

And thank God for that, because by that time we were wearing that mixture of dressed-up leather with all the studs and the high boots and silvers and metallic leathers. So, we must have looked a bit like that when we arrived and played our first show in Los Angeles."

So, there was weird and confused timing in the States, and then a sort of missed opportunity in the UK. Like many British hard rock bands, there was a sense from the fans that Sweet had forsaken the home territory, and as Andy explains, maybe they did.

"We could not play... we did not play in England between the end of, well, '75, '76, '77, we did no shows in England. Not until 'Love Is Like Oxygen' in '78. We did the Hammersmith Odeon, I think it was then, and when I talk to my agent now, he says that at the time, he wasn't the main decision-maker. He said when he knew that the Hammersmith Odeon wanted us to play there, he said we should do at least two nights. The one night sold out in a matter of a couple of days, and we probably could've done three nights there. There was that kind of demand for tickets. So, we only did the one night, and as we know, it's one of those historic gigs that should've been filmed, should've been recorded, but it wasn't."

Indeed, quite astoundingly, Sweet's last spate of dates on home soil had been in December 1974, with a single Isle of Man show in July '75. The next one would be the Hammersmith date of which Andy speaks, February 24th, 1978.

"I would love to find out if it is," wonders Steve, on the supposition that *Give Us a Wink* probably is technically gold in the US by this point. "I know it was 400,000 at one point, and that was years ago. I know it's still selling, slowly; that and *Desolation* have been steadily selling for years. But they don't give you gold records anymore because it's too expensive."

"I think we were probably a little bit early for the moment," reflects Scott on the changing times and Sweet's jumbled place in them. "And quite frankly, you'd already handed a few Sweets out in the very early '70s, and it's not as if you could come out with something absolutely new, because they'd seen the transition from being that sort of bubblegummy pop band into this fairly gnarly, snarly, you know, rock/pop band. And I think bands like Status Quo definitely helped the odd band change their spots, as it were, the leopard changing its spots, but I really can't see that many. Once you've established yourself, especially in England, it's a hard slipstream to get out of once you're in there."

"But I think when we got into America, there was a lot of change going on. More so than was probably realised at that time. Because I remember our manager turning around to us and saying, 'I don't want you doing a lot of TV or having a lot of film. I want to create a kind of, "There's this English band; now you've gotta go and see them.'" I understood the idea, but that's why there's a complete lack of footage of what we really did there, because it was the first two tours, '75 through '77, where we established what we were. But quite frankly, the acceptance of the slightly later albums like *Off the Record...* I think *Level Headed* did okay, but the acceptance of the later albums, I think the triggers missed somewhere along the line, because we'd wound up being the most used middle bill. We called ourselves the sandwich, the filler."

"Anyway, I'm glad you like the record and think like that," Andy tells me, in reaction to the idea that in many ways, *Give Us a Wink*, even if it didn't outsell *Desolation Boulevard*, established Sweet's stateside critical acclaim once and for all. "Because it was only really on mainland Europe that I thought it had any real success, and actually Canada! Yes, we did have a good record of success there where you are, it's true. So, it wasn't a failure, but it wasn't considered the right kind of successful follow-up to the *Desolation Boulevard* album in America, because I think it was possibly a bit too much of a change for the record company. Yet, for me, at that moment, that was the defining, shall we say, musical moment for Sweet."

CHAPTER 7

Off the Record

"The most monumental crew-versus-band pea-shooter fight"

As Sweet were back in mainland Europe—Denmark, Sweden, Germany—serving the markets that supported them best, May '76, the band got word that *Desolation Boulevard* had been certified gold in the US. This was followed by an extensive Japanese tour in August before the band got down to business in October working on a follow-up to the critically acclaimed *Give Us a Wink*, moderately successful in the marketplace of hard rock ideas due a thrilling roller-coaster ride called "Action."

"In Japan we were huge," chuckles Steve, "until Ed Leffler started having a go about Pearl Harbor. Our manager at the time started arguing with the promoter about Pearl Harbor. And I went, 'I'm walking away from this one.' This should not be discussed in Japan. Well, it didn't do us any good, because the promoter would never have us back. We played in the Seychelles once; it's in the Indian Ocean, right on the equator. We played there because it was the 200th anniversary of the British stealing it from the French. The silly thing about that is their money was the rupee, and it had the Queen's face on the right-hand side and if you turn the rupee note sideways, it spelled 'sex.' I had loads of them. We just went, yeah, that's funny. And somebody spotted it. And then of course the ten rupee note, which was worth about two or three pounds, all of a sudden went up to a few thousand, for collectors. And I had a bloody pocketful (laughs)."

Nat Freedland wrote a piece in *Billboard*, September '76, about Sweet's success in Japan, with Ed Leffler stating that the band was told they were getting the biggest flat guarantee (i.e. guaranteed pay) for a band's first tour of Japan. Booked were nine sold-out shows, based on record sales that had jumped from a thousand units a week to 5,000 units a week.

Freedland pointed out that Leffler had just become a solo manager, breaking away from his previous partnership (Katz/Gallin/Leffler) and was now managing on his own the likes of Sweet, Steve Harley and Cockney Rebel, Juice Newton, Silver Spur and Sammy Hagar.

Mused Leffler, "I think that clients that are more oriented towards creating music, rather than winning MOR show business success, are nicer people with less ego and are more open to management advice. I'll be happy if I never see another Las Vegas showroom again."

As for Sweet, "The first thing I told them they'd have to do if they wanted me to manage them is to not release any singles in the US for the next 18 months. Although the group was a big success in England and much of Europe, recognised as a fine all-around rock band, it was known to the general US music public only for 'Little Willy,' a bubblegum novelty that completely misrepresented what Sweet is really capable of. There was a brief backlash against big English groups at the time, especially on the singles level. The kind of music which was succeeding as No.1 singles in England was not what AM programmers wanted here."

"We more or less broke even," continued a hopeful Leffler, on a US tour that was not well attended. "Capitol came through with outstanding label support, so it started building an American concert following. And its stage performance improved tremendously. The group has never done a long road tour before. In Europe, you play ten dates in one region and go home. What Sweet learned on the US tour is what made it go over so big in Japan."

Back from exotic lands, the album we come to discuss this chapter is an unjustly quite ignored long-player in the band's history called *Off the Record*, which arrived in April '77 on the racks with an amusing and enigmatic wrapper that shows close up, in illustration form, just what happens when needle hits groove. The gatefold and back cover continued the weirdly lonely and forlorn theme, and save for a fuzzy, crappy live shot of the band, no real connection is made. Makes sense, because by this point, that starry, magical relationship anybody with a heart could feel while listening to "Ballroom Blitz" would rapidly wane, until lead singer Brian Connolly leaves the band two records later, pushed, essentially, because he couldn't sing anymore.

And the artist responsible for the sleeve? "Norman Goodman," says Steve Priest. "He did the *Level Headed* one too. It's really pop art; I like it. He was the engineer at the studio we were recording at, so he just brought his ideas in, and that one looked good to me. I don't believe the painting was any bigger than the album cover. In fact, it was the same size. I used to have a poster of it."

"*Desolation Boulevard* was the easiest to record; we did it in ten days," continues Priest, by way of a sort of two-year ramp-up to the under-rated Sweet classic that is *Off the Record*. "We knew all the songs, so we just went in there and played them and sang them; it was very easy. We couldn't believe it and we said, 'Oh, we finished it.' We'd only been there the better part of a week (laughs). Laborious? That would be *Cut Above the Rest*, which seemed to go on for eons. We just couldn't... I don't know, it was after Brian had left and there were things going on in the band that were not good. You know, it was just everyone was at each other's throats. It was, 'I don't like that, even though you do.' That sort of thing."

"But by the time of *Off the Record*, I suppose we were still getting along fine. It was a pretty laid-back atmosphere. In fact, we used to have peashooter fights at one point, just because we had run out of ideas or something. And they were apparently picking peas out of everywhere for years afterwards.

Audio International; that's where we did our first songs (ed. the credits cite two locales: Audio International and Kingsway Recorders). And Nicky Chinn loved the place. He had this superstition about, if we don't do it in the same studio, you know, it won't be a hit. Which is a lot of horse bollocks (laughs)."

But other than the credit "Arranged and Produced by SWEET for Chinebridge Ltd.," those two cats were nowhere to be seen on *Off the Record*. All songs were credited simply to the four guys in the band, just like on the last record, even though out of the four, it was Andy that was carrying the heaviest load. In fact, Steve says that Mike, Nicky and Phil Wainman still got paid as the producers, even though the band had to do it themselves. What's worse, use of the studio was expensive because the guys wound up writing most the material in the studio, fuelled by cocaine or what the guys called "Old Charley," which more often than not just threw the guys into a state of confusion.

Adds Scott, "In the Monty Python scheme of things, that is the contractual obligation album, where we still had an album that needed to be released through RCA and everybody knew that we'd got this new deal with Polydor. Now at this time there was no 'Love Is Like Oxygen;' the track and the song hadn't been written. And when we went in to do the *Off the Record* recordings, we still had two or three tracks from the previous album, *Give Us a Wink*, which I think we managed to rework a couple of them. But we still needed therefore to write a couple of handfuls of songs for an album that might not get the justification that it deserves, but you can't think like that."

"And I remember sitting in the studio and thinking it's such a shame that this album probably won't see the light of day in the right way. Probably what should have happened is that some deals should have been struck whereby we didn't have to make that album. But I'm glad we did because we had probably the most monumental crew-versus-band pea-shooter fight over a weekend. And the guy who owns the studio called us all into his office on the Monday, and he said, 'I'm either going to throw you out of the studio now, or you're going to… all of you are going to come in and help clean it up because my cleaners are refusing.' And so, we did, and the engineers, they'd lift out modules on the desk and they started to find peas from pea-shooter fights in the modules and everywhere. So, Monday was a huge, huge cleanup, and then everybody got back to some serious work after that."

Asked to clarify on the carry-overs from *Give Us a Wink*, Andy explains that "They would have been riffs; they would have been ideas. There wouldn't have been a complete song. We wouldn't have been able to pick and say, well, that didn't make the cut. I know that the more I read about Led Zeppelin, they'd resurrect backing tracks from two or three years previous and bring them forward onto *Houses of the Holy* and things like that. This is the way I perceive it. We were never quite like that. Everything that we did got used. We very rarely had things in the pipeline."

The result of the pea-shooter wars indeed turned out to be worth the violence. *Off the Record* is an accomplished collection, even if *Give Us a Wink* might be considered closer to a conceptual masterpiece, at least on the sonic side. Diving in, *Off the Record* opens with "Fever of Love," and immediately one notices the album's modest sound.

To qualify, we'll be examining the track selection and track order of this record as it pertains to the US issue. The differences are as follows: "Fever of Love" has a different intro than the UK issue (galloping solo guitar in the US, while the UK reverse fades straight into the full band playing), "Live for Today" is offered in clean version on the US copy ("gone too far far far" instead of "gone too fucking far") and "Stairway to the Stars" is an additional song on the US version. As well, the track sequence is slightly shuffled over and above the UK configuration.

Back to "Fever of Love," even though this is a bit of a galloping rocker, it's definitely poppy, even a little... disco. Still, you gotta love that Brian Connolly roar, along with the band's trademark angelic harmonies. Worn by the stomping on his throat years ago plus the drink, his voice speaks of experience come the ascending pre-chorus and climactic chorus. Here he evokes Roger Daltrey before him and Robin Zander from Cheap Trick, a contemporary that would shortly leap-frog Sweet to stardom with a similar rock and pop alloy to that of the masters of UK glam. All told, "Fever of Love" is a gorgeous example of Sweet doing what they do best, namely serving up complex melodies seeded somewhere back with the Beatles, now rendered with a fusion of guitars and synths, and always interesting up top given the vocal shapes thrown. The end result is a buzzing urban disco song, exciting and downtown, speaking of possibility for the night before the booze and coke kick in.

"I don't know exactly what fired that one up," says Steve. "I think it's probably from the song 'Fever;' you know, 'She gives me fever.' And it was just brought into a modern idiom. It's one of my favourite Sweet songs, actually. The production on *Off the Record* was different. It was a lot cleaner than *Give Us a Wink*. I love *Wink*'s production because it's huge. We were lucky because we were doing it at the Arabella Hotel, or the studio underneath the hotel, and there was this huge place out the back of the studio where these big semis came in to unload stuff for the hotel. So, we closed off the doors, put a couple of 18-inch speakers down one end of this huge hall, mic'ed it up, and then sent the drums through it. And they just sounded huge! But yeah, Audio International was a lot cleaner and neater than that."

"Fever of Love" was issued as a single, essentially everywhere but America, backed with non-LP track "A Distinct Lack of Ancient," a sort of funky but heavy instrumental, almost jazz fusion of disposition.

If "Fever of Love" was an auspicious start, "Lost Angels" put things right. Even though this isn't all that hard-charging of a rocker, it's a real charmer in the Sweet catalogue—a demo version actually finds it slower and thumpier from Mick's end, with a little more of an organic, unpolished sound. But what an uplifting and even challenging song: it's got more parts than it feels like, it's got acoustic guitar, synthesizer, sinewy twin leads and a multitude of altitudes, including a gorgeous culmination. And the harmonies on this one are thin in the ether to the point of inhuman. Twin with Journey's "City of Angels" for a sublime and reclining soundtrack to... a top-down cruise through the City of Angels? Seriously, the parts build and build toward the heroic, somewhat like Thin Lizzy of the era, but the language and the tooling is all Sweet.

"'Lost Angels,' we released as a single," notes Steve. "Which was a great song. I don't know if it's a great single, but it's a great song." In fact, both "Lost Angels" and "Fever of Love" would be released as singles in advance of the launch of the album proper, which came in March '77. The advance of "Fever of Love" was a UK-only issue, which was soon followed by the US-only version of the single to coincide with the album's release, with a different B-side. "Funk It Up (David's Song)" and "Stairway to the Stars" would also be launched, making it four singles from the album and none of them a hit.

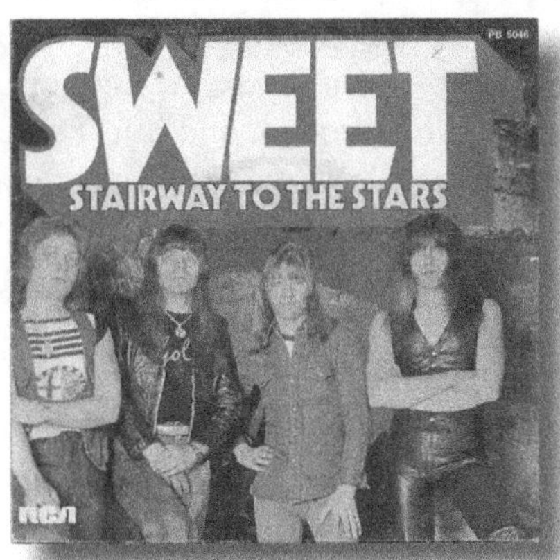

Next up was "Midnight to Daylight," a solid and chugging metal rocker, albeit one easily missed given the gauzy, bass-challenged production on the record. "'Midnight to Daylight'… 'the things I say at midnight, I'm not going to say them at daylight,'" laughs a particularly irreligious Priest. "You've taken a girl back to the room and say anything she wants to hear, but of course, when it comes to the cold light of dawn, it's, 'Did I say that?'"

This one's structured like a shuffling, doomy Sweet rocker from a few years back. Add that harmonica in (played by Steve) and it becomes oddly Sabbatherian—compare with the harmonica solo section on *Never Say Die*'s "Swinging the Chain."

But again, there are those helium-high vocal harmonies… "The basic concept of the band was to have really heavy backing, heavy guitars and drums, but three- or four-part harmony," notes Steve, who of course also sang lead vocals from time to time (and then took over once Brian was edged out of the picture). "Actually, I went to a website in England, and somebody's got a list of all the songs I've sung and I was quite surprised (laughs). There weren't that many big, big ones, but only one… 'California Nights' was a hit here, which I sang back in '78. And I sang another one called 'Call Me,' which was a hit in Germany and around. And for sure, when it comes to backing vocals, I'm on every one. Oh yeah, that was part of our thing. Myself, Mick Tucker and Andy Scott would sing three-part around Brian, with no problem. We always knew what our parts were before we even worked them out."

After an odd spot of near psychedelic folk called "Laura Lee" (Steve: "That was done in two parts. I don't know where that came from, actually, and I wrote it! It's an incredibly romantic song"), the band storms back for the truly Sabbath-like stomp of "Windy City," of which Priest quips, "'Windy City' was because we toured America in '76, and went to Chicago, and for some reason it stuck in my head. It was absolutely freezing. It was pretty run-down where the auditorium was, so there were a lot of homeless people lying around, and it just stuck in my head. And all of a sudden, one day I went, 'I want to write a song about Windy City.' And I wrote most of the lyrics for it too. In terms of that riff, I don't know. Andy started playing that and I went, 'Yes, that'll do!' (laughs)."

Love the fret noise on this one, as well as the manly roar of Connolly, proving himself here to be one of the great unsung vocalists of precious mid-years metal. A massive commotion of a jam stretches this one to a hefty 7:27, and alas, we come to the end of side one with what will stand as the album's heaviest track, even if the closing half of side two puts its fists up valiantly.

Side two starts, nonetheless, with a rocker called "Stairway to the Stars," gorgeously glammy, fully fun and dripping with pop hooks, a bit Stonesy in verse construct. Again, this constitutes a tenth track on the US Capitol Records issue versus the nine on offer on the UK RCA issue. On home soil and across mainland Europe, RCA held the track back to issue as a single, following up (in a general sense, with all territories not treated identically) "Fever of Love" and Lost Angels," none of which bothered the charts to any great extent. The B-side to "Stairway to the Stars" was a non-LP track called "Why Don't You Do It to Me," a stomping pomp rocker covering all the Sweet bases, including crude, lascivious lyrics.

This one's followed by another great Queen-like rocker strafed with elaborate Brian May-like textures over quickly paced chugging chords. Andy's solo is testimony to his tone and taste, the only drawback to this track being its levity-undermining chorus.

Recalls Steve, "'Live for Today,' that was just a 'need no politicians' party rocker. It was just before the days of punk, in fact. And we got our foot in the door (laughs). In fact, we did a show in London in 1978, and everyone was absolutely amazed that most of the kids there were dressed as punks. And I went, 'You're kidding.' And they said, 'Go and have a look.' So obviously I did eventually, when I went on stage. There were so many Mohicans and tartans and rings in noses in everyone and they were all going nuts! So, I was quite pleased with it. I think it's because we were looked upon as punks. Most people were dreadfully scared of us, to have us on a show. And the women interviewers… we were very gentlemanly, but do you remember Alison Steele? She interviewed us once and went, 'I think I'm supposed to be frightened.' And I'm going, 'No, don't worry, we won't kill you.'"

Ask Andy Scott about punk, and he recalls, "I remember Mick Tucker and I standing in a queue, for a specially invited audience for a show that The Who were doing, in Brixton, in south London. We tried to work out how we were going to get tickets, and they said, 'No, no, the whole audience is invited,' and we stood there alongside The Damned, with Rat Scabies, and Rat was all over us, saying, 'Fantastic, I'm so glad to have met you.' And then he got down on his hands and put his hands on his knees and played the intro to 'Ballroom Blitz.' And then Mick said, 'That's not quite how it goes.' And he said to Mick Tucker, 'That's how I do it, mate.'"

I asked Rat what he thought of Sweet and the glam craze in general. "Oh, quite a lot," answers Scabies. "It was socially unacceptable to the mainstream. You know, all those Genesis fans didn't like Sweet or T. Rex or anything. But when you're learning to play, you pick up a guitar and you can learn 'Get It On' in a few seconds, and you can learn 'Ballroom Blitz.' They're not complicated songs but they sound great and they *are* great. I always loved the drums on 'Ballroom Blitz.' I always thought they were cool. Mick was like Ian Paice. If you do listen to the B-sides of their singles, they wanted to be a heavy metal band, and they wanted to be taken seriously. And it was really ironic, because they were quite far down the credibility chain compared to, say, Iron Maiden. So, it was quite odd. Heavy metal fans turned their back on them so much, because they were such a blatant pop band."

Indeed, Rat performs a complex bass drum and snare drum pattern on the "Ballroom Blitz" cover The Damned did in 1979, used as the B-side to their "I Just Can't Be Happy Today" single. On the Sweet classic, Lemmy from Motörhead guests on bass. The band's near "piss-take" has been reissued many times, becoming pretty much their most popular and known cover version.

But generally, Andy figures punks didn't align too regularly with the likes of Sweet. "No, not in my experience. I used to go to gigs a lot, because

I ended up producing a few bands that were considered a little bit punky, and they always had a soft spot for me. Especially in the early '80s as well with the New Romantics. Steve Strange had a club in Camden, and I used to go along there in a pair of jeans and just an ordinary jacket and a T-shirt on underneath, and there would be all these really weird people dressed up in eastern saris and all the weird and wonderful clothes, and all I used to do is lob up to the VIP bar at the top and have a couple of drinks and meet a couple of people. It's never really been a problem. I think music transcends that."

Back to the Sweet cabal, at this point relations in the band weren't too far gone, but in general terms, Steve does cop to turmoil, as well as the band's aforementioned reputation. "We used to drink too much, so that's always a good way of arguing. Mick and Andy used to argue a lot. I used to stand back and say, 'What the hell are you arguing about now?!' I would say, 'Oh, what's the point? You're arguing about nothing.' Those two used to really get into it (laughs). But it was a chemistry. When it was good, it was very, very good; when it was bad, it was awful."

The atmosphere around the band wasn't helped by the fact that for most their career, Sweet were savaged by the critics. Including on their records tracks like the next one, a bit of a lark called 'Funk It Up (David's Song),' surely wouldn't help matters. Indeed, this one was a disco joke.

Says Steve, "'Funk It Up' was having a go again at one of our managers, David Walker, since deceased. He loved disco music, so it was having a go at him. You know, David's song. David was dancing… he was always dancing (laughs)." Walker died of a heart attack at the age of 57, after attending a birthday party for his 18-year-old son.

"But yeah, fair enough, the album as a whole is slightly more poppy, if you like; it's not quite as heavy as *Give Us a Wink*, because, I don't know, here we go again… the record company can't hear a single on there, that hit single syndrome. 'Well don't hear one then—just release it.' Of course, they don't do that. So yeah, it was a bit more controlled and a bit less heavy than *Give Us a Wink*. But the songs on there were brilliant."

"I never used to read critics," continues Steve, reacting to the assertion that the scribblers could always find something to grouse about, while glossing over such stunning material as "No You Don't," "Cockroach," "Action," "Set Me Free," "Sweet F.A." or this record's crushing next track, "Hard Times," which could have been a Zeppelin metal classic, had it shown up on *Physical Graffiti*. "Mick and Andy did, and they used to always get upset, and then start writing or producing the way the critics wanted. And it's like, 'No, no, no. Have you got any... you need some strong gonads, dear. Ignore them! And write the way you really believe we should be doing.' I knew that the critics were having a go, but as long as they're spelling the name right… But sure, when Queen came along, for some unknown reason—it's timing I'm sure—they were accepted doing exactly the same thing that we were doing. They had strong backing guitars, and three- or four-part harmonies."

As regards "Hard Times," "That was a redo of 'Action,' if you like. It was just having a go at management. We were virtually getting paid nothing. And all the managers had these offices in the West End of London, in Beverly Hills and all that, and we're going, 'Excuse me, I'm having trouble paying the mortgage.'"

I asked Steve, given the inscrutable songwriting credits, who was writing what here. "Usually, if we got together to write an album, the majority of the people that were in the room when the song was born got the credit (laughs). Basically, which is fair enough. Somebody may have come up with one word and you go, 'Aha!' Something stupid, but that's the way it always happened. And most of the time it was me and Andy. I used to sit with him. Andy would fart around playing chords, or with a lyric, and I'd go, 'I've got an idea.' And then I would hum it to him, and he would play it."

As to whether Priest considered himself more of bass player than a songwriter, he figures, "Whichever I'm doing at the time. I mean, yeah, I'm a bass player. I can play guitar, but only in the quiet of my chambers (laughs). I can play keyboards to a point, but I'm basically a bass player. I always like to write songs for somebody who can play guitar. I can hum a tune or give them an idea and they can figure it out. Instead of me getting a book of chords out and going, 'Oh, I think that will fit.' Which is what the Beatles did, actually."

Off the Record ends with "She Gimme Lovin'," a classy speedy rocker almost no one ever talks about when considering Sweet classics, even though they should (spot the phase-shifter). Laughs Steve, "That one's a killer to play, I mean hard. And yeah, lyrically, that one explains itself, really." Additionally, note the Deep Purple "Fireball" homage courtesy of Mick Tucker, who deserves a lot more praise in the pantheon of percussion than he usually is offered.

"He would do a 20-minute drum solo," marvelled Steve, on Mick, "and then go into 'Set Me Free.' I never knew how he did it. And as a rhythm section, we were totally nut and bolt. Once we were together, it was locked tight. His kit was pretty big. It was double bass drum, and I think he had five tom toms, three on the drums and two on the floor—he might've had more than that."

With respect to stage props this time around, Steve says a few quickly come to mind. "For 'Windy City' we had these revolving three-sided columns at the back of the stage, and they had different fronts on them, for different songs, and one of them, of course was skyscrapers. But they had to turn them around, and that was a frightening event, because they were about 15-feet high, so as they turned them, they're all wobbling away, and I'm surprised they didn't fall over."

To sum up, *Off the Record* is an album that is actually quite a bit heavier than its reputation, with, really, only two of its ten tracks falling squarely outside of hard rock, and a good four—even five—of them stone metal sledges. But alas, no single, which just exacerbated the lack of funds pouring in, or at least, trickling down to the four guys who deserved the spoils.

"Hard comparison to the one that came previously," answers Andy to offer a personal summation of the *Off the Record* album, "because people thought we had written far too much for the *Give Us a Wink* album. But that's not really true. There was an album, and we knew that Polydor wanted to sign us, but there was one album that was left to be delivered to RCA. So, we ended up, because of the problem with Brian, and inasmuch as anything, recording two albums almost back-to-back. We had a world tour with *Give Us a Wink*, but as soon as that was over, we were back in. So, we were writing and doing things on tour."

"And the one thing everybody was saying to us was, 'Don't make another heavy metal album.' Which compromised the situation, because coming off *Give Us a Wink* and all the other stuff, our heads were full of ideas, that that's the kind of album we should be making. So, I guess the only way I think about it is, it's full of compromise. It was a very pleasant album to make, because we were back in London and it was recorded very quickly. But I can't say that it was as well accomplished as *Give Us a Wink*."

"But still," continues Scott, "who was it, BMG released the first five albums as a group of albums. They should have made it a box set, but they released them all individually, so it made a Sweet logo down the spine of the CDs, when you put them on the shelf. And quite frankly, the cut and the quality of *Off the Record*, finalised master, the remastering, it almost stands out, because the recording quality is incredible. It's very good. So, it's made the songs come to life a bit more for me, because I quite dismissed it. But remember, I hadn't heard it for years. And somebody sends you a bunch of CD pressing masters for approval, and the one that leaps out… and I haven't even done the sleeve notes for that one, so the first thing I said was, 'I didn't believe it when I heard this album, because I hadn't heard it for years,' and that's how my sleeve notes start for it."

In fact, *Off the Record* has been reissued three times. The 1990 version adds three tracks, "A Distinct Lack of Ancient, "Stairway to the Stars" and

"Why Don't You Do It to Me," while the 1999 issue just adds the two non-LP B-sides. A 2005 reissue, however, includes these three, plus the disco mix of "Funk It Up (David's Song)," and extended version of "Midnight to Daylight," a demo version of "Lost Angels" and alternate versions of "She Gimme Lovin'" and "Hard Times."

Wrote Steve Freedman of *The Muncie Star* in his review of *Off the Record*, "Steve Priest, Andy Scott, Brian Connolly and Mick Tucker are at it again as the fourth Sweet LP is more of a whirling dervish than either *Give Us a Wink, Sweet* or *Desolation Boulevard*. The predilection to rock is gratifying with every roll in place. A pounding backbeat serves as a conduit for emphatic vocals and an overall cohesiveness. The writing of songs and album direction was a collaboration among all band members and this togetherness proves most admirable. Careful planning and a large amount of time obviously went into *Off the Record* and you know something, Baretta? You can take that to the bank!"

"Despite its name, there's nothing sugary about Sweet," warned the *Sydney Morning Herald*, in a review tied to a promotional giveaway of 50 copies of *Off the Record*. "Its specialty is solid, thumping rock 'n' roll and distinctive high-pitched vocals. *Off the Record*, written and produced by Sweet, has it belting away at the same tried and true formula. Such tracks as 'Fever of Love' and 'Lost Angels' have that sledgehammer drumbeat, snarling guitars and sizzling synthesizers. 'Midnight to Daylight' delivers simple lyrics with a straight-between-the-eyes punch. 'Windy City' rages along merrily until a clever change of pace, then finishes like a hurricane. 'Laura Lee' is the closest Sweet comes to a ballad, and for something a little different, 'Funk It Up' is a reasonable disco facsimile."

But Charles Bogle from *Circus* makes a good point, pointing to a lack of a single. "Off the record, indeed!," he writes. "If these guys keep this nonsense up, next they'll find themselves off the record player! A couple of Top Ten singles, a gold album and a vacation of a year or so, Sweet have come up with a perfectly produced album that offers a lot of high-energy stuff done in their totally identifiable style. Unfortunately, what the LP doesn't offer is one tune worth remembering. Sweet actually manage to chase their tail for two sides without moving at all. They do aimless disco ('Funk It Up'), take a stab at catchy melodies ('Stairway to the Stars'), and turn out their quota of the usual drum-infested, harmony-laden, foot-tapping sounds ('Fever of Love,' 'Windy City'). But for some strange reason, they don't come up with one real song. A lot of almosts but coming closest never accounted for much except in the realm of horseshoes. Sad to say that *Off the Record* lives up to its name. This one is as hummable as a Kraftwerk album."

And he has a point. As much as the deep fans of the last three records admired the album for its inherent and exquisite Sweet-ness, from an artist-and-repertoire point of view or from a radio programmer's point of view, you don't come away remembering these songs as having given you a great big hug, something the band managed repeatedly in the past, both with Mike and Nicky and without.

Still, there was some success, even in America. As a recap, Steve explains that "*Desolation* went gold, *Give Us a Wink*, I think, went gold, but as Capitol's disappeared now, nobody's counted it. But yeah, *Give Us a Wink* sold steadily after it was released. I know it went up to like 460,000, and that was in the first few weeks, and then it gradually kept selling for a long time, so I'm sure it's gone gold now. And *Level Headed* sold very consistently as well. They keep selling. There's a new audience each year."

But as discussed, Sweet were well on their own by this point, and yes, as Priest says, flourishing creatively and even selling records. But somehow, vaguely, they were losing the public relations battle. Could this be down to management woes? As well, Chapman and Chinn were long gone...

"Yes, they were well behind us by then," says Steve. "We had done *Give Us a Wink* before that without them. Nor did we get paid for production either. They did. That's why Chinebridge Ltd. is listed as a production credit. They had nothing to do with it."

And as we've discussed, lack of touring in America—especially in the formative years—along with odd billings, has got to be pegged as part of the cause of the band's declining fortunes at this point, beginning with the album at hand. "We did tour Germany for *Off the Record*, but I don't know why we didn't tour America. Something went haywire and I can't remember what it was. The timing was wrong, or the money was wrong… something was wrong. The previous year, in '76, we came over as headliners, which was an absolute stupid mistake. We should have been doing TV shows etc., and getting out in front of a huge audience, a bigger audience than just headlining. I mean some of it worked. We were on… what's his name, 'All By Myself,' Eric Carmen; his record was No.1 at the time and he was supporting us, so that didn't do any harm. It got bums on the seats. But it was a lot of hard work for very little. And then in '77, we didn't do anything. In '78 we came back with Bob Seger and toured with him which was very successful. That's when we had *Level Headed* out, which was even poppier, a little too poppy for me, but it was good. So, we were filling half a hall and his lot was filling the rest. We had sold-out gigs, when we were on stage, which is always good."

"Yes, they put Eric Carmen as our opening act," chuckles Andy. "But I can see why they did it. He was absolutely brilliant. But carting an absolutely white grand piano around and screwing a pickup onto it every night, and then spending time with tuners in places like the Aragon Theatre in Chicago was a bloody nightmare!"

CHAPTER 8

Level Headed

"We've grown tired of that type of music now"

Conjuring *Off the Record* in the studio didn't prove to represent any sort of magic touch, so come time for a follow-up, Sweet decided to do what Black Sabbath and Deep Purple before them did, and cart off two hours to the west to drafty and haunted Clearwell Castle in the Forest of Dean for a writing session.

The band spent 28 days there on the material that would comprise *Level Headed*, sometimes working, sometimes playing cricket and soccer, but always drinking, sometimes down at the local pub, formally named The Allpool but known to all the locals as The Whorepool. In fact, the guys were said to have downed 300 bottles of wine, yet somehow in all this Brian was singled out for ostracization due to his advancing alcoholism. The result is that band relations became increasingly surly, with Brian staying in a distant part of the castle to the other guys. At one point the increasingly isolated Connolly returned from a visit home with a shotgun and proceeded to take shots from his window at the birds flying by; only trouble is the rest of the band were down below playing cricket.

Then it was off the Chateau d'Herouville in France, again at great expense to record in a romantic but not altogether practical setting—there was no air-conditioning, and Steve pointed out that you might be able to hear birds chirping on some of the songs because they had to record with the windows open. This was followed by more work at Kingsway Studios, with Louie Austin engineering at both locations.

Level Headed, issued in January of 1978, would be the band's first album through Polydor Records, after manager David Walker and his company Handle Artists had negotiated a new deal reported to be worth £750,000. So, the band wouldn't be on RCA anymore back home, but in the States, distribution would continue through Capitol like nothing happened. The new sound was being framed as a sort of classical-infused pop, akin to what Electric Light Orchestra were doing. There would be strings and acoustic guitars, but actually not a lot of synthesizers.

As Steve told Chris Charlesworth, for a large feature in *Circus*, "We've been playing the same sort of music for the past two or three years and we decided that people must be getting fed up with it and so were we. We decided to go away for a month before recording this album, and to write our music in a completely different atmosphere from ever before. We wanted to find some mellow surroundings. We used a 30-piece orchestra on a couple of tracks, and it was the first time we'd ever worked with an orchestra; it was a beautiful experience. We even used a fellow playing old English instruments, things like crumhorns, and that was a strange thing for us too. We figured, as I say, that we'd been doing the same thing for so long that the risk was worth taking. The single is already high on the English charts and the album went in at No.69 last week. Usually, we have a hard time getting into the album charts in our own country."

Addressing the vocals, Priest explained to Chris that, "We've used harmonies before, but this time it's very different. We're trying to be a bit more subtle and musical than ever before. I sang a couple of tracks on earlier albums, but I haven't sung with the group a lot. With this album, it just happened that we used more voices. I just fancied singing 'California Nights' so I went in and sang it. No one seemed to object."

Having had it pointed out to him that what they were unleashing on the public was a record that was the direct opposite of the punk rock in vogue at the time, Steve figures, "People are fed up with the new wave anyway. And it could be a good thing. We haven't gone into the top 100 with an album for three years in England. So that must say something. Every other band that is on television in England is a new wave band. And they're all copying each other by looking exactly the same. The tour and album will have been worth waiting for. Because we put a lot more care and attention into it."

"We're really excited," noted Brian Connolly, speaking with Andy Secher, jumping on the task of selling the new album to Americans. "We've been waiting to come to the States for quite a while now. We feel very comfortable and very secure with our new music, and we feel ready to prove to America that we're a great band. Our music definitely comes first.

A few years ago we were very concerned with our image, but now we are only interested in making good rock music. We're trying to show that a band can still rock while producing satisfying songs. Here we are, big stars everywhere else, and doing little in the biggest rock market in the world. It's quite frustrating, but I think this new tour we're doing will change all that."

"We're not just a singles band," added Steve, who had been accurately saying as much for three record cycles now. "We've proven ourselves in a variety of rock styles and we found it rewarding to know that our fans have accepted the more melodic sound that we've used on the new album. Our image has become secondary to the music now. Even making money has to take a backseat to our artistic happiness. Many bands today use stage theatrics and strange costumes to hide their musical deficiencies, but we want our abilities to emerge without the restrictions of the old days."

Most pointedly, Andy offered that, "We all loved heavy metal bands like Led Zeppelin and Deep Purple. We wanted to try and get some of their sound into our music. The fans who had enjoyed our early records had grown up a little, and they seemed happy to accept our hard rock sound. But we've grown tired of that type of music now, and that's why *Level Headed* has more melody and instrumental subtlety on it."

Speaking again with Andy Secher, but now for *Super Rock* magazine, Andy Scott expanded further on this concept, and the resulting shocker of an album.

"On *Level Headed* we've made a conscious effort to radically alter our sound. We seemed to be falling into a musical rut on *Off the Record* and were becoming quite dissatisfied with the direction our music was going. I think we realised all at once that there was a big difference between making music that would sell and making music that was artistically fulfilling. Our fans seemed very happy with our hard rock sound, but we were not. We all agreed that we had to make an adjustment in the texture of our sound and we decided to make our lyrics and song construction the most important part of our music. I think this change is quite evident on the new album, and the entire band is very satisfied with the results on *Level Headed*."

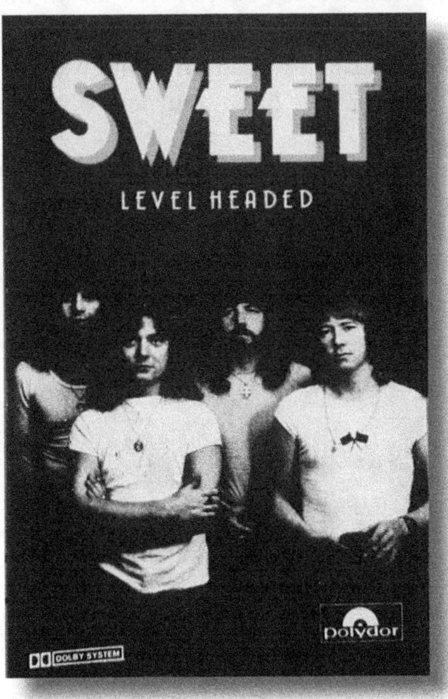

"It's not so much that Sweet has changed their musical ideals as much as we have changed our philosophy towards the whole rock scene," continued a thoughtful Scott. "We have been around for quite a while now, and we have gone through a number of rather startling changes as far as our music is concerned. In the past we always seemed to be chasing after some huge chunk of money that was being dangled in front of us, and this stood in the way of our artistic growth. Today, however, we feel our main priority must be to make music that will please us first and the record company and the fans next. This is by no means a put-down of our fans. It's just a simple realisation that you can survive in the music business just so long before you feel forced to take control of your own destiny and do exactly what you want in terms of song production. With some of our earlier music, it seemed as if we were 'machines,' where a song idea would be fed in, and a finished product would emerge. This quite obviously is not satisfying in terms of your musical growth and creativity."

"We have always been content with our music, yet in the past we have had a sneaking suspicion that many people were not taking us seriously. Our last few albums have increasingly wandered away from the musical ideals we set for ourselves when we did *Desolation Boulevard. Give Us a Wink*, for instance, was designed almost exclusively for musical 'heads,' people into guitar and strong rhythms, while *Off the Record* seemed to wander about. It was a disappointing album for us. We realised about halfway through that album that we had really gotten away from our main purpose as songwriters and musicians. We decided to re-examine ourselves and completely alter our sound. On *Level Headed*, we have returned to writing songs instead of just producing music."

For an album cover back in the UK and across Europe, Polydor went with a very level-headed look, sticking a black-and-white photo of the band on the front, and swoopy, hand-written album credits on the back. Inside the gatefold was a nifty illustration that reprised the idea used for *Off the Record*—there we got a close-up of what happens when needle hits the groove, and here it's the intimate workings of a cassette deck. Capitol in the US and Canada (and Japan) flipped it, putting the heads-and-capstans picture across the front and back and the photo on the inside of the gate. On that shot, the band look sombre, almost tired, eschewing any vestiges of glam in their white T-shirts, the only decoration being neck chains with medallions on each of the guys.

THERE'S NO MISTAKIN'
Love is like oxogen
Love is like oxigen
ove is like oxy
ve is like
Polydor
POLYDOR REFORM SCHOOL
SWEET

The American issue of *Level Headed* featured the same ten songs as the official UK edition, but in a different running order, which is how we will break down the record. Opening the Capitol offering is "California Nights," a geographical hello courtesy of a band from far away, although Sweet were making some inroads on the west coast, due in no small part to their strong association with Capitol at this juncture. As a portent of things to come, it's Steve Priest that is singing this one, issued as a single no less, the record's second and last, in July of '78.

In the official promotional video for the song, Brian is alongside the bassist, playing acoustic guitar and providing backups. Interspersed are shots of the Sunset Strip, but mostly it's the band playing, Mick looking hard but playing soft, Andy turning in a clean and twangy guitar solo like some sort of Avocado Mafia strummer from Laurel Canyon—indeed he looks pretty pleased with himself. Outside of this section, there's also faintly disco-like "chicken scratch" rhythm guitar, a twin lead and constant and vigorous sawing away on an acoustic. At the lyric end, we learn that Miami "ain't no place to be," because girls from New York—and Vegas, amusingly—are converging upon the Strip to chase their dreams of love and dancing and stardom. All told, this one takes us all the way back to "Co-Co" and "Poppa Joe," to Key West and Jimmy Buffet, basically.

"California Nights" was issued as a single backed with the non-LP "Show Me the Way," which is an up-tempo pop song, laced with a bit of guitar with the distortion pedal on and shouty vocals from Brian. Still, the beat is perky, and the primary instrumentation is vigorously strummed acoustic guitar, despite late in the action, Andy turning in a full-on electric guitar solo.

Next is "Silverbird" and Brian is back, singing on another spirited popster, this one about flying home to the one true love (after all the senseless shagging on the road for which Sweet were notorious). Andy turns in another nice twin lead, but this one is all about the irresistible chorus—it should have been floated as a single, maybe without the false ending, although here we get another guitar solo and a Mick Tucker waking up and vamping a bit, his parts laden with a novel echo effect.

The shock at the soft Sweet continues with "Dream On," a piano and strings ballad that sounds like the Beatles crossed with Queen—in other words, Electric Light Orchestra, who became a philosophical touchstone for the band during this phase. This one is written by Andy who also sings it, with Sweet demonstrating across the first three tracks on the album that they have three strong lead vocalists who also operate within the same orbit with respect to the characteristics of their voices.

Andy sings "Fountain" as well, another pure pop song dominated by acoustic guitars. But at least there's drums, not to mention harpsichord, taking this one proggy, a direction underscored by fairly sombre melodies, some twin leads, slide guitar, synths and an ambitious art rock instrumental section. Putting the song right over the top is a solo harpsichord closing sequence, the perfect dramatic flourish for what is to come.

"Love Is Like Oxygen" is the song that saved Sweet to fight another day. Despite the cocaine ravaging the band, and despite Brian slipping away into oblivion from the drink, all of the excesses of the band's bacchanal as

A NEW LEVEL FOR SWEET....
HEAR WHERE
ROCK IS HEADED
Capitol
RECORDS
SWEET
LEVEL HEADED
START
STOP
© 1976 CAPITOL RECORDS, INC.

well as the fanciness of the castle and the chateau… that's all there on this expensive-sounding but sublime track about getting too high or dying… from love, of course.

There's a point in the first verse where Brian mutters, "There's a rumour goin' 'round the town that you don't want me around," that resonates with the deteriorating situation in the band, and it's set to mournful music, which in fact describes the entire song, if one can accept an up-tempo version of morose.

Notes soon-to-be Sweet keyboardist Gary Moberley, asked about the magic of the track, "It's got different pieces in it. It's got the slow section and then there's a riff and then it goes into the chorus, and I think it's just well put-together. Andy was kind of doing the production at that stage."

Further trivia… Andy admits to being influenced by a Hall & Oates song called "Grounds for Separation" that includes the musing, "But isn't it a bit like oxygen, 'cause too much will make you high, but not enough will make you die." But Andy isn't the sole writer of this song. He's co-written it with one Trevor Griffin, who was part of the industry first with bands but also as an engineer and even a roadie—Griffin had also provided the piano solo on "Healer" from *Give Us a Wink*.

Recalls Scott, referencing two years back, "By that time, the relationship with RCA had waned slightly, and I guess Polydor were just waiting to see what we were going to release with RCA, and what we were going to end up giving them. Well, I hadn't finished 'Love Is Like Oxygen;' otherwise that might have ended up on *Give Us a Wink*, or it would have been on *Off the Record*. That was an idea that my sound engineer, one of our road managers, was toying with, and I remember in the studio just throwing stuff around with him when nobody else was about, and just formulating the way some of the chords were mixed together. 'If I play this guitar riff against those piano chords, what would happen?' And as I said, it was a work in progress."

As the track winds up, Andy fulfils his mission pertaining to writing a song like complicated Sweet but using soft rock parts. After some more very ELO- and 10CC-like flourishes, there's a short disco vamp to close things out, a part that was edited out for the single version. The alluring number was a top ten fit in half a dozen territories, attaining the bottom rung of that status in the all-important markets of America, the UK and the band's mainland stronghold, Germany, or again, as it was known then, West Germany. The track was nominated for an Ivor Novello Award, honouring UK songwriting, but lost out to Gerry Rafferty's massive concurrent hit "Baker Street," actually a wistful, sort of dark pop song coming from a somewhat similar place, fatigue with the industry and just weariness with the rock 'n' roll game in general. Like Brian, Rafferty would also die from the drink but not for many, many years.

The single issue of "Love Is Like Oxygen" featured as its B-side the non-LP "Cover Girl," a sort of heavy pop rocker that hearkens back to the psychedelic '60s crossed with Gary Glitter, with, as a bonus, a bass line straight reminiscent of classic Paul McCartney.

Over to side two of the original vinyl and we hear Renaissance-type harpsichord giving way to Brian singing over acoustic guitar and piano, before the band kicks in for the full-volume chorus. "Anthem No. I (Lady of the Lake)" was inspired by the idyllic surroundings of the French chateau at which the band were recording. Helping place the song appropriately upscale is a gratuitous string arrangement, which goes full classical eventually, executed in tandem with the returning harpsichord. Brian brings back his storied vibrato and sings this earnest song with utmost formality.

Next is "Strong Love" which is a sort of New York nightclub disco song, featuring brass and woodwind arrangements (courtesy of Ronny Asprey and Richard Harvey) that remind one of Andy's hero Frank Zappa at his most behaved. Placing it squarely in disco is Andy's chicken-scratch guitar, Steve's disco bass clichés prominent in the mix, and then up top, Brian's high register "love of my life" vocals.

"Lettres D'Amour" is another one that was inspired by the band's French sojourn, with Steve joking that at the music end, Andy was indeed listening to a lot of Hall & Oates and considering himself a worthy proponent of blue-eyed soul music. Ultimate this is merely another shockingly light ballad on Sweet's new album, played to a lush and surging 3/4 waltz beat, guest female vocals courtesy of Stevie Vann Lange, a session singer best known as lead vocalist of Night, who issued a self-titled album in '79 and *Long Distance* in 1980 before calling it quits—Stevie was the first wife of soon to be famous producer Robert "Mutt" Lange, with both of them being of African origin (Zambia for Stevie, South Africa for Mutt) and then emigrating to the UK.

"Anthem No. II" is a mere 58 seconds of Geoffrey Westley-arranged classical strings—we've now been taken back to the early days of Sweet when they didn't play their own records!

Level Headed closes with "Air on 'A' Tape Loop," a curious number that sounds very much like classic Pink Floyd. Recorded at Kingsway, Steve and Mick played for about 20 seconds to get down a sober and hypnotic bass and drums gallop, which was then looped to create the six-minute song. Up top, Andy offers his best David Gilmour licks while also impersonating Rick Wright (or Alan Parsons). There's a passage with an overdubbed bunch of African-style drumming from Mick, some creepy

Floyd-like "synthesizer voice" mumbling from Steve, but mostly at the vocal end, it's just "Alpha Beta Gamma Delta" over and over again until the music fades and we're just left with winter wind, the band presumably "snowblind" by this point.

And that was it for *Level Headed*, the same ten tracks on all issues but in shuffled order, with future reissues, in '91, '97 and 2005 variously catching up on the single edits of "Love Is Like Oxygen" and "California Nights," and including the two non-LP B-sides.

Out in the marketplace, fans were perplexed, and the record got no traction, save for its smash single, which recalled the novelty days of yore for the band. Indeed "Love Is Like Oxygen" is clearly the most ambitious song on *Level Headed*, and sounds nothing like the rest of the comparatively delicate record, even if it's ten kinds of delicate itself. As far as fans of classic Sweet were concerned, the band was committing commercial suicide, checking out of the scene very deliberately, almost aggressively.

But this of course allowed the hard rock haters to say something nice about the band. Wrote Steve Wosahla from the *Messenger-Press*, "*Level Headed* not only marks a step in Sweet's mental maturity, but in a musical framework as well. In using an orchestra, Sweet emerges with a previously unheard virtuosity. The material is also more accessible on American terms with a definitive mainstream flow and a surprisingly great deal of sophistication to match. Both the single and 'California Nights' are especially ideal songs for the late '70s."

"Well done, Sweet," commends John Shearlaw from the UK's celebrated *Record Mirror*. "Picking the commercial view—and the lads, remember, have just moved to a new record company—this album is the one that will reunite the aims and ideals of the group with the tastes and whims of the British record buying public. In short—and let the surprise be contained no longer—*Level Headed* will be enormously successful. I think. In long, though, there are still a few barriers to overcome before the former barons of bubblegum can claim that this is a *Rumours* of their very own. But the circle has turned, and the present face of Sweet is very acceptable indeed."

"Not that the others weren't," continues Shearlaw. "After a dazzling career delivering perfect pop, one which inevitably contained a built-in detonator (although 'Teenage Rampage' or any one of those singles remain classic and undimmed), they moved to mastery of pop heavy metal. *Off the Record* from last year illustrated a superb and exciting control in their new pasture. And it sank like a stone. Now a rethink, advancing maturity or maybe just an attempt to earn an honest penny— who's worrying?— has resulted in *Level Headed*. 'Love Is Like Oxygen' is just the start. 'Strong

Love' is Sweet funk. 'California Nights' is plugging freeway Sweet, 'Fountain' is Jeff Lynne Sweet and that's without 'Anthems I and II'—snappy Sweet rock opuses—and the lovelorn Sweet of 'Letters D'Amour.' Cool, calm and collected in a crisis. A clever 'rock' album. Very definitely of the first order. They'll get away with it. I think."

The album's brief review in *Billboard* read as follows: "This may well be the album that will launch Sweet in the US. From the opening good-time rocker to the end, this album is well-crafted, energetic, freewheeling rock. The four-man English rockers alternate lead vocalists so that the chances for vocal repetition are slim. Even the lengthy instrumental breaks are fluid and maintain a fervent drive that gains in power more than it slackens. Many tunes are reflective of Pink Floyd with their eerie textures and ethereal rock sound. The generous but not excessive synthesizer interplay among guitars, bass, keyboards, horns and strings keeps the instrumentals as vibrant as the vocals." *Billboard* then goes on to recommend "California Nights," "Love Is Like Oxygen," "Dream On" and "Air on 'A' Tape Loop" as the best songs on the album.

Record Mirror also sent Robin Smith out to report on what the new-look Sweet were going to sound like live, with Smith writing that, "The metamorphosis is complete, Sweet aren't looking silly anymore, the old posing is gone. Remember the limp-wristed Brian Connolly? He looks good these days, Rod Stewart substitute for the girls. Everything from the sound to the lighting was very creditable. They played a few of the oldies, but even these have lost the old bubblegum feel that used to make you cringe. 'Ballroom Blitz' was almost along Deep Purple lines, structured from the pumping bass. 'Fox on the Run' was a foot-banging stomp-along that developed into a chant. Yes, you can take the band seriously at last, especially with the rendition of J.J. Cale's 'Cocaine.' The set borrowed extensively from *Level Headed*, 'California Nights' being accompanied by watery scenes of a coastline. Surprisingly, 'Love Is Like Oxygen' was delivered early on in the set, handled with as much care as the single. But the impetus wasn't lost. After that the band went on to create fresh excitement. The chemistry is there. I haven't seen them since their teeny-bop days, silly costumes on *Top of the Pops*, etc. The effect now is shattering. The wait, to quote a well-worn cliché, has been worth it."

Over in America, Sweet were now three records into a sales decline past the enthusiasm sent their way because of *Desolation Boulevard*. Andy tried to put a brave face on the band's slippage from headline status but couldn't hide his discontent, telling Steve Wosahla, "It's an interesting package. But it's not Seger or Foghat as a support act. It's not as if we're a new band either. We've been together for ten years. There's a lot of interest purely by talking to agents and promoters. You know that there's a new sort of vibe about us being on the bill. We've never had to play support to anybody before. All of us have done it at some time in previous groups but we've never had to be a guest on anybody else's bill. I think it's been good to do that. It's shown character beyond the ego, because there were egos. We could have never opened two years ago before *Level Headed*. It got to a certain stage where a 60-foot stage wasn't big enough. We all had working stage space, but there ain't no working stage space now. It's like working on tables, but we're still managing to get over energy like we did in '72."

"For the first time," continues Scott, "instead of using tapes of synthesizers and acoustic guitars and dry ice and smoke bombs and revolving balls that you spin light off of, we've got rid of all that and we've added new musicians for the live performance: a guitar player, Nico Ramsden, and keyboard player, Gary Moberley."

"Well, they needed somebody to go on the road and play the keyboards, because there's a lot of keyboards on that album," explains Moberley, recalling his time with Sweet. Gary, an Australian, would build an enormous session and live resume, including work with Elton John and The Bee Gees, not to mention obscure NWOBHM act AIIZ, who had a single produced by… Andy Scott.

"So, they interviewed people," continues Moberley, "and I went down to the management office in Mayfair to meet them. And in comes Mick Tucker with a David Bowie haircut and gold drumsticks and a fur coat (laughs). And I thought, 'Cool. This is definitely rock 'n' roll. I think I'll have some of this.' So, then I met the other guys and we went down the pub, at midday. At 11 o'clock that night, Brian or one of them came up and said, 'You've got the gig.' And I said, 'Really? I haven't played a note.' 'Well, you can keep up with the drinking' (laughs)."

"So yeah, this is after 11 hours in the pub. Anyway, it turns out that they'd seen me on *The Old Grey Whistle Test* with John Miles, who I went to Canada with, strangely enough. He had an album out called *Rebel* and a big hit called 'Music.' We toured Canada with John, and I was with John at the time, so I left him to join the Sweet. And then we toured everywhere, really, Canada, America, all throughout Europe. A massive tour of Europe."

Things were going downhill with Brian, however. Andy and Steve had taken over more of the lead vocals, with Brian being too drunk to perform. Indeed, one night in Birmingham, Alabama, a rep from Capitol had come out to see the band and Connolly was legless, having to be dragged off after one song, resulting in a tongue-lashing from manager Ed Leffler, who also had pulled a surprise visit.

"The difficulty is that I didn't see it coming," recalls Andy. "But there had been talk amongst people, about Brian's wayward ways, and not showing up to meetings and being a little bit, luckily, not too drunk, but drunk enough at gigs and things. It wasn't until later, in 1978, when we were on the tour supporting 'Love Is Like Oxygen,' that it all came to a head, when our manager came to a gig. He rung me up and said, 'I'm hearing a couple of funny reports here.' I said, 'Mate, I'm not the one to talk about this. I don't really want to get involved in inner-band politics, but when the show suffers, something has to happen.' And he said, 'I don't want you to tell anybody, but I'm going to come to the show in Birmingham, Alabama.'"

"And he arrived—we were supporting Bob Seger, I think it was—and he arrived at the gig, didn't say anything, we went on stage, and within the first song, this is the worst I'd ever seen Brian. He did not know where he was. The next thing I knew, two people had rushed onstage and removed Brian, and Steve and myself ended up finishing the show as vocalists, and luckily we had a keyboard player with us, Gary Moberley, so it wasn't as if we were going to be missing any instruments, you know what I mean? Brian played a bit of a keyboard here and there. And I'm afraid there was still a lot of shouting going on when we came off stage 45, 50 minutes later. I knew then that something was going to have to give. The band basically came off the road for a few months, to see if there was anything to be resolved here. I thought it was resolved. He went to a therapist; he went to rehab, as they call them now, and I really thought that, well, at least we were going down the road of repair, rather than destruction. But I'm afraid it was very short-lived."

Additionally, the band had taken to covering J.J. Cale's "Cocaine" live, which served as a nightly reminder that the rest of the guys weren't exactly operating with a full deck anymore either. After another bad night for Brian in Atlanta, Andy was calling for his head, while suggesting to the guys that they should hire Ronnie James Dio, who had just split from Rainbow— Andy in fact confirms that he definitely had brought up the possibility with Ronnie.

The US tour took the band from April through early July, supporting the aforementioned Bob Seger and Foghat, but the guys also played with REO Speedwagon, Cheap Trick, Uriah Heep and Rush. Brian's last gig with the band would take place on July 9th, 1978, in Jacksonville, Florida, where Sweet would be playing with Alice Cooper.

"If there's any kind of hype, I'll blow it out," warned Andy, not wanting the pressure of living up to high expectations with this rendition of the band. "I don't want to know about any of that. There was a lot of hype before we came here the last time and we've totally laid back and purposely said to people, 'Do not say the things you said the last time.'"

"In 1972 it was like 14- to 16-year-old girls. Now it's like, 20-year-old guys who want to talk to the band. I don't mind the change. I'd rather be playing to blokes who know what they're listening to rather than girls who all they're interested in is trying to get in your bed. In Europe, the average age of our audience is between the ages of 17 and 25. They're slightly younger when you get into Scandinavia, but that's the average age at the moment. I think Seger's is even older than that. But I don't mind playing to old men as long as they clap their hands. I enjoy playing here, but I don't like some of the conditions we've been playing under. I don't want to be an opening act, and I don't think anybody else in the band does either. If the conditions don't change, if we can't get over this opening act bit in the next 18 months, yeah, we'll leave America."

"I hope you don't take this the wrong way, but we don't need America," concludes Scott. "The way I feel about America is that if America needed us, fine. There's been lots of bands in America and a couple of British bands as well who seem to have taken what we've had. I'm not mentioning names, but I can hear it in the songs. The bands know themselves as well. I've met them."

A NEW LEVEL FOR SWEET...
HEAR WHERE ROCK IS HEADED
Capitol RECORDS
SWEET
LEVEL HEADED
© 1978 CAPITOL RECORDS, INC.

CHAPTER 9

Cut Above the Rest
"Would you like to have a go with Ronnie Dio?"

And then there were three.

If Sweet would have still been in the spotlight, it's hard to imagine that they would have risked turning in their next record lopped off by a member, presenting themselves as a trio, without their front man and lead vocalist Brian Connolly.

And yet, given the singing skills of Andy, Steve and Mick, on record at least, Sweet didn't miss a beat.

"When we started to record the next album," explains Andy, "which was *Cut Above the Rest*, we all knew. We had one of our managers saying, 'Brian is complaining that the songs are not in his keys.' And we'd just say, 'Well, they're the same keys that we've been doing everything in all the way through the years.' You know, a guitar player always plays in E, D and B. He doesn't want to play in C and F and G. It's not really a guitar key, if you know what I mean. It's more like a country, easy listening key, a piano player's key. So, we were trying to just say, well, we can try detuning. But some of the riffs are what they are. Having said that, there's a lot of heavy metal bands that tune down to flattened D all the time. So, they're not having to sing in those original keys, where you need to hit top B and E from time to time. But I realised that Brian's voice was shot when we were doing the *Level Headed* album, because when you listen to that album, there's a lot of vocals on there from Steve and I, because we were the ones who could hit the notes."

It doesn't end well for Brian, but, says Andy, his sad decline might have been predicted early on. "When I first met Brian—and he was the one I started to hang out with—I realised that if I kept up with him, I wouldn't last long. He was… well, he was a hell-raiser. You would go out for an evening... I never knew where the hell I was going to end up. And I needed a little bit of stability in my thoughts and the way I needed to go. He was a fantastic front man, and I think part and parcel of where he lost his way was in the areas of, you try and be this person that maybe you're not. His drinking, I think, possibly stemmed from the fact that maybe—it's been put to me quite a few times—but maybe the rest of us, Mick, Steve and myself, were leaving him behind in a musical direction. And when we started to go to America, I think he felt out of his depth. Because it was on those tours of America when we were away for six months, where you don't see him on the days off so much, and as long as he's not pissed on stage, you get by. But when you start to see some stuff that you don't want to see appearing on stage, that's when you have to think about things."

"In my opinion, it was the worst thing we ever did," says Andy, referring to Connolly's ouster from the band. "But if we hadn't done it, I don't know if the band would have continued anyway. His removal… because we all thought by saying to him, 'You've got to go, mate,' it would've been the shock that would've brought him back. But it didn't."

"I didn't realise that Brian hated Andy," adds Steve, "and well, it's normal in every band that the lead guitarist hates the singer and vice versa. You know, 'I'm the star.' 'Yeah, right. Sure, you are.' (laughs). So, there was some animosity between the two of them, but I didn't realise how deep it was—and it was. I mean, Brian was a great front man. Yeah, he was the star, definitely."

"I don't think at that moment there was a better-looking guy fronting a band," continues Andy, trying to grapple with Connolly's appeal. "Once again, seize the moment. He also had one of those voices that no matter what you could give him to sing, you knew it was Brian. It was not that imitative. He grabbed it and went for it. I actually think that some of the change for him from shall we say more pop to rock, caused more damage in his vocal range than the rest of us. Because you had singers like Gillan and Robert Plant and various others out there, and he was not like a Whitesnake, the kind of singers who came later with the soulful thing. He was definitely a Roger Daltrey, an Ian Gillan. But he didn't have the range of Gillan, which is why every time you hear a high squeal or shout, that's usually me, on the recordings, because that's my range. I think that that was certainly a lot of the reason why on some of the later recordings, you hear more rasp than tune. It's definitely down to that, I think."

"Andy wanted Brian out of the band, basically," continues Priest. "It was sometime in '78, and Brian had a dreadful gig where he was completely out of it and blah blah blah. So, we sat him down and said, 'Look, if you don't sort yourself out, you're out. We can't go on like this.' He said okay, and he did. He was fine from then on. But he hadn't got his studio confidence together. Now for some reason Andy decided that we had to go back in the studio, even though we hadn't finished the American tour. And 'California Nights' was just about to enter the charts, with me singing. So we went back into the studio, and as I said, Brian hadn't quite gotten his full confidence together yet, and I think Andy decided that he didn't want him in the band. And Brian said, 'I'm fed up with yelling songs. I'm going to do my own stuff.' And he left. He wasn't exactly sacked like a lot of people said. He made up his mind to go, and he left. He was perfectly sober then, but he hadn't really gotten his voice back yet to where he wanted it. Everything was in too high a key for him."

"We all liked singing," reflects Andy, "but Steve put himself forward at that moment. Although after Brian left, Steve proposed, 'Would you like to have a go with Ronnie Dio? Things like this. But then Steve basically said, look, we've been doing it as a three-piece because we've been carrying Brian for a year or two anyway. Why would we want to bring somebody else into the mix? And I just thought, well, if you don't bring something new in, it's going to be the same thing. But I was more than willing to give it a try. I think to a degree it worked, but neither of us have that kind of commercial voice that you immediately go, 'Oh, that's Sweet.' That was the main difference. Even though I had been—and Steve had been—ghosting Brian on some recordings for a little while, we're not Brian, you know?"

Asked to clarify this idea of "ghosting" Brian, Andy explains that "If we were living in the digital age back then, Brian could have sung everything and we'd have made it work. Because there are studio tricks. Never believe what you hear anymore because, you can make somebody who can't really sing that well, sing. And if it was just a little bit of tuning, a little bit of timing, you can bring that in. And a lot of the time it was things like that with Brian, towards the end. It was the looseness of the voice, the idea that it wasn't that tight controlled situation. So, there were times, especially in our harmony block where he's not even there, you know?"

"When I first joined and I first met Brian, he was the obvious guy who did everything," continues Andy, on the subject of Brian and drink. "He drove the van. He would go and have a meeting on a backstairs with an agent who would give us some gigs. He would be the guy fronting us and talking to people, doing any kind of interview. He was acting virtually like a manager anyway. And I sometimes think back now and look at that. He loved all that. He loved the full-on… and he was brilliant at it; he was really good at it. Now, could you imagine, you've now had half a dozen hit records and you're no longer the person doing all of that because you can't. You can't be seen to be doing that because you're the lead singer in a band called Sweet that was starting to tour all over the world. And no, you can't go and have a pint with the agent and he's going to give you, you know, the next month's worth of work that we've got at whatever it is, 30 quid, 40 quid a gig. 'No, you're now the lead singer. We'll tell you when an interview is needed, we'll tell you where you need to be. We need to get on a plane here.'"

"When you get to the other end, you've got two days to kill of doing nothing except maybe drink," continues Scott. "And I've honestly… I've sat there and I've tried to work out what might've been the best way for Brian. And it probably wouldn't have been having loads of hit records. It would have been Brian still being the go-getter, the trouble-shooter… when we changed the van, we started to get some money in. We'd had one or two hit records and the van we were travelling in was awful. Nicky Chinn put up some money and said, 'Until the first royalty check comes in…' and Brian had said, 'Oh, I know where I can get us the right kind of van, this company who, when the vans are two years old and they've done quite a few miles, they 'out' them to the business. They're still very usable and very good.'"

"But he knew where to go down near the airport," chuckles Andy. "And somebody would put a partition across the back to split the back to the front and put some aircraft seats in. So, all of a sudden, we now have a van, like all the professional bands. And if it hadn't been for Brian, it wouldn't have happened. And these are the kinds of nuts and bolts things every band must have. For me, the music is my part in Sweet. And for Brian, it was the organisational skills and the sociability, to be the guy who can talk things up."

"I think once you take that away from somebody like that, the whole dynamic changes. Left to your own devices, as I said, you fly to America, you're not doing anything for the first two days because you fly in, you might do a press conference, but you're not really needed for at least 48 hours because the gear is going to be at the first rehearsal or gig or whatever. And in that first two days, maybe you sit in your room and you have a couple of bourbons and you quite like it and you carry on. I don't know; that's not what I did. I certainly wouldn't want to make any kind of judgements or excuses for any of it, but it's a very sad story when you break it all down."

Rehearsals for *Cut Above the Rest* took place at Clearwell Castle. Amidst a blizzard of cocaine, Brian, still part of the circus, had with him a new girlfriend called Melissa, who had to be temporarily stored at the local hotel when Brian's wife Marilyn briefly visited. Connolly had contracted a sexually transmitted disease (STD) from this Melissa, who had also given it to another unnamed member of the Clearwell contingent. Meanwhile Steve's marriage with Pat was on the rocks as he began seriously falling for his new girlfriend Maureen, who he would later marry.

With respect to cutting Brian, Andy says that "The decision was made after we'd done the preliminary recordings down at the castle, with the mobile. When we actually got down to it, we realised that instead of having this gypsy nomadic lifestyle, it was all going to have to come into a proper recording studio and have it dissected. I think we ended up being 48-tracking on a few of the things and you can't be doing that on a mobile. And we brought back the arranger, the keyboard player for 'Love Is Like Oxygen,' Geoff Westley. He came back in to do a few bits and pieces for us."

Westley is credited with "pianos and arrangements" but Gary Moberley is participating as well, credited with pianos on "Call Me," "Stay with Me" and "Dorian Gray." Finally, along this tack, is veteran Eddie Hardin, who is credited with the ARP 2600 solo on "Discophony."

Recalls Moberley, "That was all done in London, basically. But we were rehearsing at Clearwell Castle, which was quite interesting. We had the Rolling Stones Mobile studio, to try and write stuff. We were in the basement trying to think up material, having these medieval dinners. So, we would have to stop. But we mic'ed up the women's toilet for a laugh (laughs). Never mind. I think there was a ghost there. Steve said something about a ghost. We didn't record there though. But if they came up with something they would be able to keep it. They tried all sorts of stuff, to get performances out of people. Over to the studio (Townhouse, in Shepherds Bush), there was a stone room, at the studio, which was built for the place so they could get a vibe on the drums, a live sound. Mick had a lot to do with that. He was very serious about his sound. He would spend ages, a day or two, just getting his drum sounds, before he'd start playing. Of course, they don't do that anymore. The engineers will come up and try to change your sound, because it's easier or whatever. But there was a time when there was loads of money for recording. Back then it was just a much healthier time for experiments. But this room, I can't remember, but possibly Sweet were the first ones in to use it and Mick had something to do with it. He was a good drummer; he always remembered what he played on the record. Good singer too—they were all good singers."

Interestingly, Brian was still part of the band at Clearwell, except that, as Steve has indicated, although the guys were working up all sorts of music, by the time they'd left, Brian hadn't done any singing whatsoever. What's more, it would turn out that the guys would use practically nothing that they had recorded on the Mobile, making the visit (in Rolls-Royces and the like) an expensive excuse to snort coke and play soccer. Soon both Steve and Andy would leave their wives and end up together in a rented house (along with Andy's new girlfriend, Alice) in Princes Gate Muse in London and continue writing for the new album. When Maureen was finally able to visit, Steve proposed to her.

At Townhouse, Brian's closest ally Mick was given the job of trying to get onto tape a decent performance out of Brian and hours were spent trying to make it work, with Andy and Brian nearly coming to blows before Brian would exit the picture, November 2nd, 1978. Things would be kept quiet until February 23rd of the following year, when it was announced by band manager David Walker that Brian had left to pursue a solo career as a country rock artist.

Before we look at *Cut Above the Rest*—and the work of these good singers—first we see the album cover. Over here in Canada and the US (plus in the UK), what we got was a Norman Goodman illustration that extended the run established on *Off the Record* and *Level Headed* in terms of a close-up look at audio equipment. But this time around it's more than that. The image is of a spool of audio tape, customised to show actual musical notation. The old-school cutting process is pictured in action, with the latest edit indeed being a "cut above the rest," i.e. a splice just beyond a musical rest. The razor blade (which also hints at cocaine use) is rendered embossed, as is the Sweet logo in the upper left. Eminent photographer Dick Barnatt is back to shoot a picture of the band for the inner sleeve, capturing the guys sitting at the desk, smiling as Mick presumably reaches across to turn up his drums (Dick also shot the band for the gatefold of *Level Headed*).

In mainland Europe, the front cover art was a horrendous "woodcut" image of the band, all told an awful image and, to boot, one that hammered home the point that Brian was gone—Steve says the band considered changing the name of the band to STP. What's more, the posed shot demonstrated that the guys were men out of time, struggling with their hairstyles in a punk age just like they would struggle with their sound, not playing punk, not rocking out. If anything was to be remembered, they were mounting a vague protest against disco, while offering no deliberate alternative in its stead.

Weirdly, perhaps demonstrating the band's state of irrelevance at home, *Cut Above the Rest* was issued in March of 1979 in North America but only in October of that year in the UK. Into the record, the album opens with a vampy power pop number. "Call Me," written by Andy, is somewhat flamenco of disposition, taking us back to the band's very earliest hits. There's a synth solo, a modulation, but in actuality, a pretty decent chorus. Mick hated the song, calling it "pop pap."

"Play All Night," however, is classic Sweet, heavy, layered with futuristic Queen-tilted guitars and pounded hard by Mick underneath multi-tracked vocals. Construct-wise, it's one of these songs that opens with a run at the chorus, which makes perfect sense given how catchy and articulated the lyric is. It would turn out to be a bit of a flash in the pan, but "Play All Night" is an enthusiastic nod to Sweet's exciting and electric past, most pertinently solid and strong at the vocal end, proving that the guys could get the job done without Brian.

Still, there's a version of this sung by Brian and he does a perfectly good job on it. Smart management would have done more to get Brian cleaned up, perhaps installing him in some kind of rehab situation. Hearing "Play All Night" with Brian proves that the guys were at least 10% along to getting the album done with Brian. Knocking out ten more songs with Brian singing acceptably, or even six or seven more, would have been a smart move, after which the album could have been issued with all the parts in place, and then Brian could have been taken care of. How long, really, would it have taken to get half a dozen more Connolly vocals on tape?

Next is "Big Apple Waltz," which is just that, a rote waltz track, accomplished enough and indicative of the band's tilt toward the likes of 10CC, Electric Light Orchestra and Queen—Andy's solo is indeed evocative of Brian May. The band's limited skill as producers lets them down on this one. It's boxy and Mick is too loud, especially given his stiff performance on the track. This one was written by Steve, inspired by his new affair with Maureen. "Call Me" was slated as the first single from the album (trimmed by a minute to remove an offensive bit) and "Big Apple Waltz" was the second, with neither making much of a dent. "Big Apple Waltz" is sung by Steve, which makes sense given the lyric, but Andy had taken a shot at it too. This was par for the course on *Cut Above the Rest*—without Brian around, the guys were trying everything to get the optimal vocal down.

Technically speaking, the production credit on the record indeed goes to the band, but the heavy lifting would have been done by Louis Austin, who in fact dials in nicely the album's next track, "Dorian Gray." This one is Sweet courting power pop like the pros they are, and like the veterans of pioneering the form that they are. This is a gem of an unsung Sweet song, and again, very utilitarian like a smash Queen hit—all told, "Dorian Gray" might have turned things around for Sweet had the label recognised its subtle charms.

Closing side one is the band's last decent US hit, "Discophony (dis-kof-o-ne)," which is also essentially only their third hit across this record and the previous two, taking in "Love Is Like Oxygen" and "Action." And this would be the least successful of the three, although like those, it's a tour de force of parts, always interesting, and just all 'round well done with lots of meat on the bone at six minutes long.

Reflects Andy on "Discophony," "I could see that being where The Sweet were headed for the future. I mean, the one thing that used to always make me laugh—and I knew that we'd hit a vein—was when Frank Zappa released 'Dancin' Fool' at the same time as we released 'Discophony' and the DJs in America used to start playing them back to back. There were radio stations that were still trying to promote rock, because, if you remember, there was this rock versus disco thing going on towards the end of the '70s in America. They hadn't really had the punk thing. And I just think that 'Dancin' Fool' and 'Discophony' each had their messages. They both sound like disco tracks but they've got a message in them."

"And Frank was an influence. I would travel to go and see Frank Zappa, wherever we were in the world. If he was in Germany and we had a day off, then I would make sure that I could go and see one of his gigs. I was starting to move into a different area at that point. I would go and see people like Jean-Luc Ponty and the Brecker Brothers and Return to Forever, the sort of jazz/rock crossover bands. It's difficult to perceive now that that was where my head was going, especially with a band like Sweet. But you can hear some of the influences in there if you know what I mean."

"There was some good stuff on that album," muses Gary Moberley, who gets a co-write on the track with Andy and Steve. "That song was very anti-dance and anti-disco and sort of wants to be heavy. It's a statement, isn't it? There's quite a few where I started off the tracks. I'd start playing something and Andy would chime in on it. I was a session musician, proficient, studied music, had the art of knowing what works. And when I first came to do session work with Andy, I was into people like Jan Hammer. Andy said, 'That's great; keep that for your own album. I need four notes' (laughs). But that song is great; they came up with those harmonies for the lyrics, which at the time was really unusual. But yes, that song is a statement."

And of course, it's Steve that sings this late-period Sweet classic, sounding, frankly, enough like Brian that many a potential Sweet fan wouldn't notice that Brian had been sidelined.

"After 'Love Is Like Oxygen,' I think they'd had enough of Brian in the studio," remarks Moberley. "They couldn't get what they wanted. I don't want to criticise Brian. The guy needed help, and I didn't do anything. I don't think anybody did. To actually help him with his problem. It's very sad, in the end, because people were latching onto him at the end of his career, when he obviously couldn't function properly. And they were putting him out there at different venues, pushed him out the front so they could get gigs. I think that's horrible. And if that's what you have to do, then you're not really a musician, are you? If you can't earn a living without doing something like that. People were ridiculing him and it's all very sad, really. But, yeah, I don't think Brian knew his father. So, there were a lot of issues. He felt, ostracised, etc."

"So, Brian left or whatever and they continued on. They were going to go out as a three-piece Sweet, but they ditched that, kept Sweet and carried on. But once Brian left, they had lost a lot of momentum. Because, him being the front man, there wasn't anybody to replace him, really. Brian was a very lonely guy. He didn't have any friends, and he didn't have any friends in the band, really. Everybody was into their own thing, and I guess they didn't… I mean, you've got to realise, they were millionaires in their 20s. And that kind of thing can either ruin your life or make it. If you're sensible and invest, fine, but if you just keep the rock 'n' roll life 24 hours a day, there are consequences if you do that."

Back to *Cut Above the Rest* and over to side two of the original vinyl, next is "Eye Games," a gorgeous bit of pop confection that thematically carries on from "Discophony," opening with the lyric, "In the discos and the bars, they're playing eye games." Under two minutes long and credited to Andy and engineer Louis Austin, the track is essentially folk with a bit of a Hawaiian music flair to it. The only percussion on the arrangement comes in the form of a few well-placed handclaps. Augmenting the warm campfire acoustic framing of the song are some inviting and subtly complex vocal harmonies. The end effect is a sympathetic song about human connection, the polar opposite of the aggression and cynicism of "Discophony."

But again, at the vocal end, this is bold, signature Sweet, no apologies, a showcase of singing despite the remaining three having lost their singer. I stressed with Andy that it was pretty remarkable how similar the melange of voices that could come from these three guys could sound like Brian. "Well, yeah, yes, okay, to a degree," muses Scott. "But remember, we'd been doing the backgrounds. I'd been doing all the wallpaper vocals on all the recordings for years. So, if we didn't know how to put vocal harmonies together and know the complexities within by then, then I'm in the wrong job."

"Mother Earth" is somewhat of a prog number, again indicative of Andy's shifting tastes in music, with Andy taking the lead vocal as well. Steve fondly recalls that the opening lyric was inspired by his new love Maureen, and that the line helped kick off the track, which Andy had been working on outdoors with an acoustic guitar. All told, "Mother Earth" is a hefty achievement, coming off like heavy ELO with a memorable ascending synth line that sounds like classic Styx. The song was fully demoed at Clearwell and was quite close at that point to what they had cut as a final version. Besides the Styx-like synths from Andy and the ELO falsettos of the chorus, there are parts of this complicated song that sound like Genesis and even the John Paul Jones end of Led Zeppelin.

On his increasing interest in synthesizers, Andy says that "They were extremely new in the early '70s and of course me being the guitar player, and me being the one who's more interested in, should we say sounds as it were, of course I'm going to be the one who is going to get his hands on synthesizers. I remember, years ago I spoke to Pete Townshend and he was going down the route of the Avatars, where each string of a guitar was set up to a synthesized module. But it was very, very complicated and it depended on how hard you hit the string as to what you got and all that stuff. Whereas what I was trying to do was more simplistic. I was more than happy when Roland rolls out this and refines that. And then there was the Casio. Essentially this meant that somebody had done all the homework for

Page 56
NEW MUSICAL EXPRESS
March 3rd, 1979
'CALL ME'
The new single from SWEET
DISTURB
DISTURB
Polydor
POSP 36
It takes the waiting out of wanting.

me. I was able to get to grips with the playing rather than the technology."

"I loved my ARPs and you can hear them all over the Sweet records," continues Scott. "But it's just one of those things. The main thing about all of that is when you're in the studio and you get a sound, you've got to get the tape on the machine and get it recorded now because it will not be there tomorrow, no matter how much you think it will. I haven't touched anything—it won't be the same. I learned that very early on. I've read all kinds of studio blogs from various people, including Abba, when they did songs like 'Does Your Mother Know,' getting that pulsed synth sound, which I think ended up having to be played because there was no generator of that kind of pulse, and if so, not long enough. They were like in 16th-note or eighth-note sections, you know? So, once they got the sound, they had this huge super-synth delivered and he was looking for a sound and he got it, and they hadn't even thought about recording the song at that time. But he knew that if he didn't get that sound down now, it would probably never come back. So, they recorded something like, maybe ten minutes of loose synth sounds, just so that they had something to work from."

"It's stuff like that I could appreciate. I was into these experimental guys like Tomita and, well, Wendy Carlos, who started out… I think she was transgender in the end. You know, the one who did the soundtrack for *Clockwork Orange* and things like this. 'Cause now you're talking about before anybody else had synthesizers that were sound generators that were being harnessed into the music business. But it was natural that we were going to go there, because once we'd had a couple of hits with 'Fox on the Run' and 'Action,' the logical step after 'Love Is Like Oxygen' is to be a band that is probably going to be more in the Genesis and Yes camp than in the glam rock area of the early '70s, and that's where 'Mother Earth' comes from."

Which, again, always posed a challenge.

"Right, because if it starts with the synthesizer then it's going to be a hard nut to crack, generally. The Sweet tracks started out as… we tried not to play to a click track. This is the other problem. If you want to start using generated pulses and synth sounds, everything that you heard before, like some of the latest stuff in the '70s, things like 'Fox on the Run' and 'Action,' they were not done to click tracks. The synths that you hear that you think are clocked in time with the track or were synched, no, they were played. They are not computer-generated. We wanted the sound, but we didn't have the means to clock it and make it work—it was played."

"So, you tend to rewind the tape and start dropping it in again, just to make sure that it's in time again. That's the way that it was done. I think 'Baba O'Reilly,' for example, was an experiment in Pete Townsend's home studio. And I just think he had lots of it recorded, and once again, no click, but the generator was the… because the ARP would generate a pulse, but you had to be there to control the notes that it was going to play and how it was going to play it. So, what came first, the chicken or the egg? In areas like that. You just have to go with what you have."

"I had many good friends who were fantastic keyboard players who, like some of those early funk records that you hear that have got like a bass on them— that's played by somebody. And, once you get your head around that, what came later was fantastic, the way the computers would join everything up with those great pop records by bands like Pet Shop Boys, for example, with nothing played really. Everything's generated from a box somewhat, but still, they're fantastic pop records."

Back to *Cut Above the Rest*, next is "Hold Me," a slow and dour ballad from Andy, first acoustic, then full band, with more innovative synthesizer sounds. Keeping with the prog narrative, there's an up-tempo section near the end that sounds like a completely different song. Again, there's stark and stabbing synths, very much like Styx, followed by a gorgeous wash of twin leads more Queen-like than what Andy would normally do.

Closing the record is "Stay with Me," on which the band create a drum-dominated din evocative of *Give Us a Wink*. Still, with the synths and the acoustic guitar at the verse, not to mention the Boston-like melodies, it's clear that even when attempting to rock out, Sweet has moved on, yanked this way by the band's musical director, Andy Scott. All told, it's a curious end to the record, part party-rocking, given the hint of boogie to the thing, and part prog, from the profusion of sections.

Cut Above the Rest wasn't much talked about in the press, nor did the guys do many interviews for it. *Cash Box* chimed in however, opining that, "With last year's 'Love Is Like Oxygen' and the album from which it was culled, Sweet finally, after too many years, became an AOR force to be reckoned with. *Cut Above the Rest* will, in no uncertain terms, sustain this momentum beautifully. Though now a trio, following the departure of Brian Connolly from the lead vocal position, Sweet carries on with no let-up in vocal quality and instrumental flair. AOR formats have already made the album second most added of the week."

Unfortunately, the record would be the last to chart for Sweet in the US, managing a No.151 placement on Billboard. In the band's West German stronghold, the band could only manage a No.49 showing, this after *Level Headed* had reached No.15, *Off the Record* had reached No.11 and the preceding three had all broken the top ten.

Gamely talking the album up, Andy had told *Cash Box* in March, "I think *Cut Above the Rest* is an extension of the more refined direction we took with our last LP. But there's plenty of rock 'n' roll energy and rhythms on the LP, and there's a more spontaneous, lively feel to the album." When asked why Connolly left the group, Scott replied, "Brian had been moving in a different creative direction with his songwriting during the past few years. In addition, he has lost interest in touring, and Mick, Steve and I feel that touring is essential to supporting our albums."

On that front, the band executed a brief US campaign, beginning June 9th, 1979 at the Palladium in New York and finishing up July 2nd at Norman, Oklahoma. Steve says that this Palladium gig was the only time Sweet had ever played New York, and that they argued with Journey over who should headline the show. June 23rd, the band played San Antonio (Sweet were supporting Cheap Trick by this point), with Steve in agony from sunburn—he had lazed by the pool all day with Maureen while the others went to check out the Alamo.

Steve famously griped about touring and essentially, soon it would be his refusal to do so that would quash this already reduced version of the band. Reflects Andy, "Mick, Steve and myself were a bit of a force when I first joined and then all through that first half of the '70s. It reminded me of The Who or Led Zeppelin, where you've got a bass player, a drummer and a guitar player who knit together well—that's what it reminded me of. But I think as time went on, Steve wasn't enjoying it as much as Mick and I was. So, by the time we started touring America, Steve wasn't having the time that Mick and I were having. And I think some of that shows up in the playing or the fact that you're not that interested, that you're quite happy for somebody to tell you what to play: 'I think you should play that here.'"

"Look, we're all a little different. If we were all the same, then it would be a boring world, wouldn't it? But I just remember him saying to me when Mick and I were reforming the band in the mid '80s, he eventually came out with the immortal words, 'Look, I bloody hated touring that first time 'round.' And he said, 'The last time when I came over to England, when we were recording the last album, I hated the idea of being back in the UK.' I said, 'Well, Mick and I want to carry on.' And he said, 'Well, I prefer if you didn't, but I can't join you.' And I said, 'Well, without you it will be different.' But I was very lucky to find a bass player with a similar range of voice, in Mal McNulty. But it was never going to be the same when you do these reformations, unless you strike lucky, like Fleetwood Mac did with Buckingham and Nicks and all of a sudden you've got something that is so irrepressible."

Still, at the time, Gary Moberley didn't see any complaints from Steve about being on the road.

"Steve was a very nice guy. I liked him a lot but he kept himself to himself very much. But he certainly seemed to be having a good time, if you know what I mean. And so, I didn't know that he was unhappy with anything, or not that I noticed. On the first tour, I noticed that Brian was feeling isolated and quite unhappy and, as I say, I regret that I didn't give him more time to try and help him with his situation. I had him at my place a couple times. He used to come over during the day. We had barbecues and things. But things got a little out of hand. I had a BB gun (a type of air gun designed to shoot metallic spherical projectiles called BBs), which we used to shoot the cans off the back fence. And unfortunately, Brian says, 'Oh, yeah, I'm good at this.' So, he spun the gun and shot himself in the balls. It was like a pistol BB gun. And then he started shooting at the cans, and the BBs come back and just missed my mum's head by about two inches. So, we thought, hmm, time to go now (laughs). So, we all went inside and hid from him."

"But I never really joined Sweet," reflects Gary. "I never joined a band because I don't want to get stuck in other people's personalities. But I can play all kinds of music. I'm a person that can adapt and morph into any kind of music and Sweet was quite heavy. John Miles, which is a different thing, is what I left to join The Sweet, so I could get more experience in heavier bands. And then I went back to lighter bands with the Bee Gees and people like that. I'm getting on a bit now, so I don't want to be travelling great distances. But I had a band, which we used to tour Europe, quite a bit, which is like the original Jukebox Heroes, which was guys from different bands. I played music from the bands they played with. So, we had Steve (Whalley) from Slade, and the drummer from Smokie and we had all different people in this. And one of the guys from the Bay City Rollers. It was all different music and all different people. At the moment I'm writing music which is kind of spiritual, from 400 years ago, and I'm putting synthesizers and things around it."

Indeed, this is a far cry from the travelling circus that was Sweet. But on that subject, asked about Mick Tucker, Gary offers a slice of life with Mick on tour.

"Mick was a great drummer, very underrated. He was up there with Cozy Powell and people like that. But he was certainly a character He used to come around the studio and say, 'Any more beers? Any more beers?' So, we put that on a loop. When he'd come in, you'd have this loop going all the time, saying 'Any more beers? Any more beers?' Plus, he was very unorthodox in his dress and everything."

"The whole tour was filled with anecdotes," continues Moberley. "We were in some place in the south of America, the southern States, and we went to this club, and he walks into this bar and goes, 'Fucking rednecks' (laughs). And he's got on a fur coat and a pink suit and pelican-skin pointed shoes. Gold drumsticks. Consequently, a fight broke out and so I left with a girlfriend at the time with a Trans Am. Because they follow you around America once they latch onto you. But first I see is Martin, the roadie, trying to stop Mick from getting his head punched in. So, Martin was copping all the punches instead."

"But Mick was quite a character. Another night, we were leaving somewhere, a club or something, and I couldn't remember the name of the hotel. So, he jumps in the limo and I jump in the other side. And he says, 'Get out of my limo.' And I said, 'Mick, I don't even know where I am, mate. What's the name of the hotel?' So, he said, 'Get out of my limo.' He was just a bit wired, if you know what I mean. So, I thumped him, dragged him out and thumped him. He went, 'Ah.' I said, 'You know, you're getting too big for your boots, mate. I'm a musician as well.' And from then, he put his hand out and went, 'Mates, then? We're mates, aren't we?' We shook hands and got on great after that.' He was just being obnoxious, and I wouldn't have it. I mean, he was out of it. But you don't say that to an Australian (laughs)."

I asked Gary if Mick was much of a fighter. "Mick was very tall, yeah, but he wasn't really a fighter, no. I liked Mick. He was a man's man. He had an ego, but when you're travelling around the world like that, with no roots, nothing stable, all you can do is get pissed and get out of it on whatever you can get a hold of. And that's a recipe for ruination if you don't stop it when you get home. The fact of the matter is, when you get that successful so young, it can either ruin you or make you. It can ruin you as a person because normality goes out the window. You need to stabilise yourself. I used to go into a clinic for two weeks, to dry out, and then I'd come out and say, 'I'm never doing that again.' And then you go back on the road. Yeah, I liked Mick a lot."

"And it was a fantastic experience. Playing with Kiss was funny, because we went backstage, of course, and we see this guy ejecting his tongue. It's a wonder he didn't throw up on it. I liked Cheap Trick too; they were just a good rock 'n' roll band. And we supported Bob Seger as well because his big album was out. And with Sweet, it was never, 'You do this and we're doing that.' If they flew first class, I was there with them. They treated me very well. I'd like that to be mentioned, if you can—they always treated me the same as themselves."

"Even like, one day they mucked up the booking with the plane. And the tour manager was there, and he said, 'Look, we've got a gig tonight for $100,000. If you don't get us there, we're gonna sue you. We booked this flight three months ago.' They seem to do that in America. They'll take bookings and then take other bookings for the same thing. Next thing, we're all flying off in a Lear jet. There were experiences like that."

Citing another fond memory, Gary says that "When my mother came over to see me, 'Love Is Like Oxygen' had taken off. We were just on the last week of the American tour, and they had to extend it. They said, 'Oh, we're gonna do it' and I said, 'I can't do it; my mum's flying over from Australia to see me. She's saved up for years.' And they said, 'Well, so how long is she there for?' I said, 'Ten days.' And they said, 'All right, we'll fly you back on the Concorde. You see your mum and we'll fly you back and meet you at the gig.' That was an experience, the old Concorde. It's like getting out of a taxi; quite a small plane, really. And when it goes to the different machs, it's like going in top gear in the car. You don't feel it; it's just like a bump and it takes it to the next stage. It was fabulous. All free drinks and free food, everything—fabulous, great experience."

"But Mick wasn't well," says Gary, in closing, on the beginning of the end. "He didn't have his strength. So, he stopped. When Andy wanted to pursue it without Brian, even then Mick wanted to leave the band as it was and not do anymore, just leave at their height. Mick was down the pub every day. You can't be doing that. Simple as that. But it's your own decision. I mean, that was the lifestyle. It's your choice, isn't it?"

CHAPTER 10

Waters Edge

"I can see why it didn't excite the public"

Sweet stayed in North America after the American *Cut Above the Rest* campaign to record their next album at Eastern Sound in Toronto. Steve had a brother who lived there and his wife-to-be Maureen lived in New York and was able to fly up and visit regularly—Steve would in fact soon move to New York, living with Maureen in her tiny apartment there for the next couple of years. Back in England, Priest's broken home would get sold given that he would no longer be able to cover the mortgage after the band was hit with a £500,000 tax bill—Pat and his daughter Lisa would have to move.

"We had a great time," says Gary, on the trip to Toronto. "Yonge Street, the main street there, we were always down there off and about, because it was a good active street and there were loads of bands. Pretty sure I actually saw Ronnie Hawkins, The Band, around that time, which is one of my favourite bands, because they were different. They couldn't come out of England, The Band. It was impossible for them to come out of England. It's just so American. Yeah, we had a good time, and we were all naughty boys, and we did the album there."

"I'd say this was the first real album where we were out on our own, out on a limb," reflects Andy. "Brian… we stopped at the *Cut Above the Rest* album when Brian was still there, and it got finished without him. And it was never the same. There were some things on *Cut Above the Rest* that were incredible, like 'Mother Earth' and 'Discophony,' but, the new record, I know that Steve didn't want to come back to the UK. You had the guys in the UK who wanted us to record in the UK so they can keep an eye on us basically. And then I know that our American manager, he said, logistically you can't record in America because it'll just end up costing too much. There was something in somebody's wisdom at that moment in time that if we recorded it in America, it wouldn't work, but if it would be in Canada, not a problem. So, we all relocated to Canada and spent a month, six weeks, living there, going in and out of the studio, Eastern Sound where Rush and Ian Thomas had recorded. And the album that we came up with, *Waters Edge*, I think some of the songs are quite innovative and really good."

The album was finished in late 1979, after which tragedy struck, December 26th of that year. Mick's wife Pauline had been taking strong tranquilizers to treat her depression. As Steve has stated, the story goes that she was on a regimen of two of these a day, and had forgotten she had taken her daily dose, took two more and died in the bathtub, only to be discovered by a frantic Mick when he returned from drinking at the pub.

As Andy remembers it, "When we finished that last studio album, Mick had a dreadful thing happen, where over a Christmas, he found his wife in the bath, with his two-year-old daughter running around the house. It was, well, misadventure, you know; there were a couple of sleeping pills involved and some wine and stuff. There was a little bit of everything going on. I don't think anybody got to the bottom of the why-fors and where-fors and what had happened. Would you ask somebody, 'Why would you do that?' you know? Would you ever really sit down, even with your best mate, because he doesn't know why she did it. There's no point in talking about it, is there?"

Life went on and *Waters Edge* would be released, in the UK and Europe, in August of 1980. Canada and the States got completely different cover art and the title *VI*, referring to the fact that it was the band's sixth record for Capitol. The North American issue would contain the same ten songs, but with a different running order.

Opening both versions was "Sixties Man," a cover, and a song slated as a single in both the UK and US. It seems that manager Dave Walker also managed Pip Williams, and thus worked to get a song of his onto the record to make a little extra cash. This is also why, according to Steve, there are two songs by Ray McRiner on the album, and why McRiner was added to the band as support live guitarist.

Andy's version of events is a little different, and a bit more artistically oriented. "When we got back to England, Pip Williams, the guy who was producing Status Quo, had written this song called 'Sixties Man.' And when I heard that song, I said, that's a great song. He said, 'Well, I'm still waiting to hear back from Quo, whether that's going to be on the next album and potentially a single.' And I said, 'Well, if I say we would do that and you come and produce it…' And all of a sudden, strings were pulled and we ended up recording that track. It just shows you where we were going. I'm not saying we were rudderless, but we weren't as focused as we possibly should have been. Because as I say, Steve was now spending more and more time in the States. Recording in Canada was not ideal, but he was living in New York, and it was not the same as having to come back to London and staying in a hotel or come and stay with me or whatever. And we also had a songwriter with us who was the second guitar player when we were touring, a guy called Ray, Raymond McRiner. He wrote 'Too Much Talking.'"

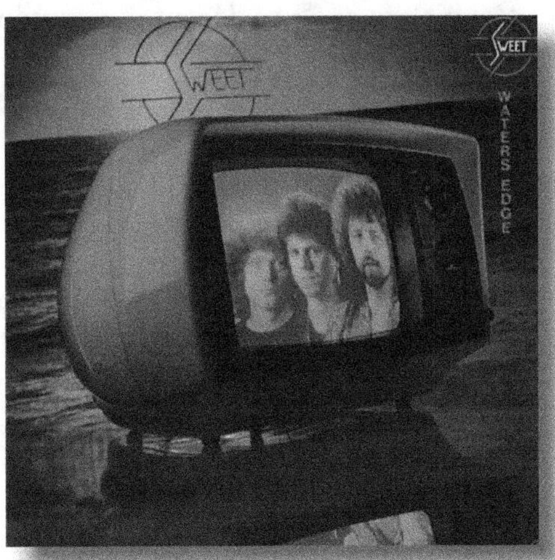

"Pip produced 'Sixties Man,'" recalls Gary. "Some people like it, but Steve hated it. But then again, what did we have at that time to compare it with? People are trying to get hit records. And basically, I don't think they were that… They wanted to spread their wings and do what they wanted to do. Which, right or wrong, takes a lot of fortitude, doesn't it? A lot of self-belief."

Moberley—credited as sole guest musician on the back cover, nearly a member, in terms of the text placement and point size—features prominently on the track, playing synthesizers, while the band execute the sprightly, almost power pop tune.

As Gary says, this one came from a whole different session, back in England, with the band working at Kingsway Recorders and Marquee Studios in London. The sequenced synth pattern sounds like something Devo might do, but it's massaged in fairly deeply behind Andy's vigorously strummed acoustic guitars, Mick's four-on-the-floor drumming, Steve's lead vocal and fairly prominent vocal harmonies, which are actually rougher than usual, oddly un-Sweet-like. Ultimately, despite the musical architecture of this one not sounding particularly '60s, it still wasn't particularly wise of Sweet to express what was essentially a proclamation of has-been status and leaping a whole already-passed decade to boot.

A basic production video was made of "Sixties Man," featuring a pulsating jellyfish super-imposed behind the band as trio. Weirdly, when the guys are montaged, Mick hogs the screen, with Steve crowded out to the right. Plus, there's shots of Mick's deft bass drum foot spliced in regularly for little apparent reason, along with his snare, his high-hat and close-ups of his face, the end effect saying, "Look at this band's drummer, please."

Next—we're following the European running order here— is 'Getting in the Mood for Love' which is another decent power pop song, a bit like The Records or Bram Tchaikovsky with a hint of 1979's Mod revival to it. It's not heavy Sweet nor is it the occasionally proggy Sweet of the last two albums. Rather, it's a modern twist on the rocking pop the band pioneered way back, bonus being the squarely heavy metal guitar solo from Andy.

"Tell the Truth" is also pert pop, but tilted a bit toward the band's ELO and Styx directive. "That's the one with the fast piano riff in it," recalls Gary, who gets a writing credit on this one, along with Andy and Steve. "I started playing that (sings the circular riff), and started working around that, which is not the easiest thing to play—it was fast. I was trying to give myself something difficult to do, really, but obviously, it made the guitar part work. A lot of that song was done sitting around a piano."

"He would keep the spirits up; let's put it that way," chuckles Andy, asked about Gary. "He was a great keyboard player. And it was natural that we were going to take him with us because even though he didn't actually play on the *Level Headed* album, he was brought in for all the touring. So, most of the keyboards after *Level Headed,* it was him on the recording. I mean, 'Tell the Truth' is a lovely track. He had an idea for a song, and I had an idea for a song, and it was fun. It's one of those moments in time where you go, that bit will fit with that bit. So, it's two songs that have been welded together."

Next is "Own Up," which is called "Own Up, Take a Look at Yourself" on *VI*. Presumably the shorter title is to distinguish the song from the completely different Sweet song from 1974 with the exact same title! And to make sure we are well and confused, the chorus indeed goes "Own up, take a look at yourself" over and over again, in harmony, atop a tribal Mick Tucker bash. And indeed, even if it's a completely different song, it's fully retro in its no-nonsense hard rock arrangement. Unfortunately, the connective riff (the heaviest part) is a bit uninspired, as is the verse melody and the somewhat Gary Glitter-y chorus. Still, this is Sweet trying to revisit their past, Mick pounding away, and Andy turning in a meaty slide lead, always musical, lyrical even, to the extent that guitar parts can be deemed as such.

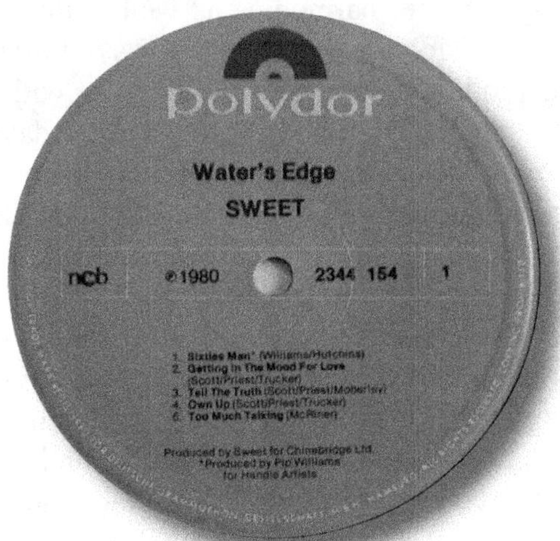

"Too Much Talking," with lead vocal by Andy, is the first of the Ray McRiner compositions on the album, and it's a good fit, given its tough power pop pulse and beat, again Sweet coming off like a slightly new wave and English version of Cheap Trick. The highlight is Andy's guitar solo, where he gets heavily electric over a pretty rocking backing rhythm before we're back into the FM radio-friendly chorus refrain.

Over to side two and the tough pop continues with an up-tempo yet bluesy shuffle called "Thank You for Loving Me." The fact that it's a shuffle isn't the only Uriah Heep-like thing about this one. There's also the lead lick, the barrelhouse piano, the Hammond, the modulation and the highlight of the track, the dramatic, tribal and heavy pre-chorus. Mick even sounds like Lee Kerslake on this one. Late in the sequence Andy peels off another brief and gorgeously composed twin lead that recalls Brian May. The only let-down of the track is its sing-songy chorus—and the production.

We haven't addressed this yet, but all told, *Waters Edge* is muddy and noisy, as well as compressed into a middle range. This helps achieve a punky, power pop vibe, but one can't help but wish for a sharper, clearer rendering of the various smart performances of the guys all over the album. Cheap Trick records are like this too, and one might surmise that the idea was to make a record that sounded good on radio, always the excuse for squashing the sound away from rich bass on one end and sizzling highs at the other.

"At Midnight" is yet another potential single on this record of near misses. It's fairly heavy, it's disco, it's Cheap Trick power pop and it's classic Sweet all at once. Andy's vocal is one of the better ones on this record where much less of it sounds like Brian Connolly compared to the last. There are ample Sweet harmonies as well, with the biggest nod to modernity being Gary Moberley's proto-MTV synthesizer pulses. At the drum end, Mick is plodding along four-on-the-floor with much of it being tom-tom-dominated, a ploy the band took to the top in days of yore. There's a nice break as well, which leads to a modulation. Still, "At midnight, I'm going to love you/I'm going to make you mine at midnight" gets old pretty fast.

Next up is the record's title track, another one of these songs that sounds like it could have been a hit a couple years later, with the rise of the likes of .38 Special, Bryan Adams and John Cougar in the wake of MTV. "Waters Edge" sounds like "midwest rock," modern Kansas, Shooting Star, Night Ranger, Survivor, even Molly Hatchet and Blackfoot trying to update. This is achieved by the halting, rock-solid beat from a conspiring Mick and Steve, Gary's various keyboard embellishments, and even Andy's regal, composed leads, everything in place except a strong front man presence. Steve in particular took the lyric deep to heart, given its mournful examination of moving on and literally moving out, in dramatic fashion from the UK and his few connections left there, to a new life with Maureen in America.

"Hot Shot Gambler" sounds almost like Sweet's attempt to show up Brian and his supposed oncoming career as a country rocker. The track is essentially Sweet's attempt at southern rock, enthusiastically strummed guitars and some nice rootsy licks from Andy along this road indicative of his versatility.

In essence, this sounds like a Nazareth experiment down a similar dusty road, or something April Wine might write. The song works perfectly as a set-up for the record's closing track, "Give the Lady Some Respect," which is advice all the guys in Sweet could have heeded more carefully throughout their lives of relationship regrets. Despite the "lies in your eyes" watching Steve dole out this kind of advice, the music represents a second round of poppy boogie rock in a row to close out this curious record.

The song was issued as a single in the UK and Germany backed with the non-LP "Tall Girls," which perpetuates this theme of the band having lots to offer but arriving too early—this is essentially a solid (albeit early days) hair metal song, just recorded by the wrong band at the wrong time, with an arrangement that would have needed updating to compete in 1983 or 1984.

In fact, the B-side to "Sixties Man," also non-LP, "Oh Yeah," could have fit on a Twisted Sister or Quiet Riot as well. But this one is 100% pure heavy metal, a bit "Windy City," a bit Helix, somewhat doomy like Alice Cooper at his hair metal heaviest. This is Sweet having a go, as it were, getting down and dirty in the gutter, going against their true natures now three records away from the metal, although one must figure that Mick Tucker was enjoying the hell out of this one.

But that was it for *Waters Edge*, an album frustratingly forward-thinking and utilitarian, with hit potential but a little rough at the sonic end. Andy, every thoughtful, later called the album "armchair rock," and telling the author, "Looking back, that album looks a little bit like an eaten mess. It's not the kind of album that you go, 'Yeah, I can see that.' You know, you can see all these different influences. I can see why it didn't excite the public."

Wrote the eminent Dante Bonutto in his review of the album for *Record Mirror*, "If, like me, you've always thought Sweet were a much-underrated outfit and that Chinn–Chapman numbers like 'Hell Raiser' and 'Ballroom Blitz' were actual classics, *Waters Edge* should add considerable grist to your mill. Simply, it's a stunner, proving that even without the tight-trousered charm of Brian Connolly, the band are still masters of the bubblegum art. Only now there's no makeup, no trace of the overt sexuality/vulgarity that had them banned by Mecca in the early '70s, just a concentration on the music and a balancing of their delightfully trashy commercialism with a sparkling synth-dominated approach that makes for a quite irresistible package."

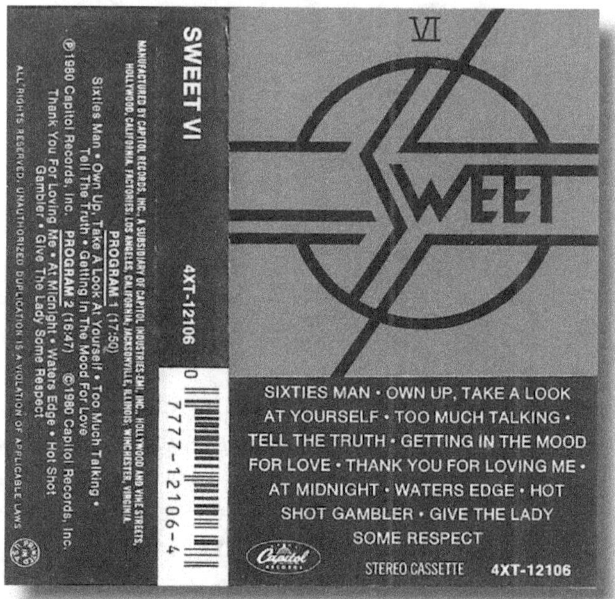

"The first three numbers, 'Sixties Man,' 'Getting in the Mood for Love' and 'Tell the Truth,' show this new style perfectly, with the Queen-ish harmonies and guitar/synth interplay of the latter quite outstanding. And then it's back to more familiar territory for 'Own Up' and 'Too Much Talking,' with Andy Scott's guitar growling and riffing like on those great heavy metal B-sides of yore. In fact, the only below-par number is 'Hot Shot Gambler,' the lyrics and subject matter of which are a little too mindlessly 'Wig-Wam Bam'-like, even for my taste. But overall, *Waters Edge* is a fine return to form. It's beautifully produced, expertly played and instantly memorable. Sweet, but never sickly."

Bonutto nails the balance near perfectly, if not hoping and projecting that's there's more heaviness here than there really is. But yes, the tracks assertively pushed at us across *Waters Edge* are energetic, propulsive, couched in the language of guitar and with more than a nod to Sweet tropes from the golden period, even if it's the more basic and glammy of the band's early '70s pop choruses that seem to be celebrated here. The point is, *Waters Edge* marks a shift away from the symphonic pop and prog of the last two records into this sort of modern Quo, Foghat, Kansas and Nazareth zone, marked by these old bands making a statement that they won't cede radio to the new (and new wave) breed, even if the ploy wouldn't much work for any of them.

"I don't think there was a single on that album," Steve told Rob Patterson from the *Scrantonian Tribune*, dismissive only three months after the release of the record. "The tracks weren't 'radio' tracks—any of them. There were great songs on it, maybe some of our best songs. But they were either too long or contained naughty words. And I don't think we could go out and play without taking all the proper lights and sound, and we just can't afford to do that until we have another hit song. We'll just keep at it until we get that. We've had hits before, with all kinds of songs, and I think we'll have 'em again."

Asked about Brian, Priest indicated that, "He was more interested in doing stuff that was very country-styled, which is not at all what Sweet is. We knew that it just wouldn't work."

Sweet played the Lyceum in London in January 1981—a then unknown Duran Duran was slated to support but then subsequently pulled out. Already Sweet had a couple of new songs in the set, with "Identity Crisis," sung boisterously by Steve, showing much promise. This was followed by a short UK tour in March, with the original three-quarters classic line-up Sweet playing their last show March 20th at Glasgow University.

Steve cites the low point being the show in Nottingham, on March 7th. He and Andy had gotten fairly pissed at the bar before the gig, and in front of a strong crowd of 1500, Andy walked off the stage after having a plastic beaker being thrown at him. Given that there weren't even keyboards at this point, Steve and Mick had to keep the large crowd entertained for 20 minutes before "Her Royal Highness" (as Priest puts it) could be coaxed back to finish the gig.

BLOCKBUSTER!

CHAPTER 11

Identity Crisis
"Why would I want another ten years of lies?"

Sweet would be good for one more album before shuffling off stage, although few would be aware that *Waters Edge* indeed had a follow-up—*Identity Crisis* was issued in Germany and Mexico only, with the Mexican edition showing the song titles in Spanish. This means no UK version and no North American version, and not that it would have mattered much, given the album's horrid cover art.

The songs for *Identity Crisis* were written by Steve and Andy between boozing sessions at Andy's house. Recording took place, as Steve puts it, "in a shitty little studio on North London" with much cocaine and bickering fuelling the sessions. By this point Steve had been put up in Chelsea Cloisters, which he describes as a retirement residence. From here he took the "tube" to the studio, having gotten used to the subway from his time in New York City. Steve's attitude at this point was that what the guys put down on tape hardly mattered given that the record deal Dave Walker came up with meant that there would be no UK or American issue of the album.

Still, despite reduced circumstances, the music enclosed kicked up a bit of a fuss, the guys demonstrating that even under greatly diminished circumstances and the drama of their personal lives they could rise to the challenge and be counted on for a modicum of quality.

Released in October 1982, *Identity Crisis* opens with its feisty title track, a hard rocker that is tight and economical, arranged with discipline and maybe even too much of it. This near punk proficiency continues with "New Shoes" and "Two into One," which amusingly combines Cars-like new wave quirkiness with hard rock chugging and a prog rock hiccup in the verse.

"The band was imploding a bit by the time we got through *Identity Crisis*, hence the song 'Identity Crisis,'" reflects Andy. "There were some good things on both of those albums, and you can hear that we are moving back towards Hammond organ and piano rather than synthesizers on both of those albums, because we realised that we were still fantastic live, that we had a great live band. And the last thing we wanted to become embroiled in forever was not being able to possibly reproduce what we played on the records. With Zeppelin, you make a track like 'Kashmir,' you want to be able on stage to recreate that. And somehow, they did. It was the same feeling within our band—you want to start getting back to your roots, and I think that's what happened."

"And I love 'New Shoes,'" continues Andy. "I'm glad you brought that one up. Mick Tucker had his own amp and Stratocaster. I used to go around his house and we used to have a little jam, and he came up with this idea of, 'I've got myself some new shoes to walk away from my blues' and he had the idea of a little blues riff. I said, well, if you turn it around a little bit and you make it more like—should we say—something like Paul Kossoff might have played rather than just like a standard blues… So, it went sort of circular. And from nothing came this fantastic song. And then, of course, you start getting into some of the studio tricks with the slowed-down voices and things like that."

"Love Is the Cure" continues along the spare and direct line thus far established, this power trio version of Sweet most definitely coming up with simple, hard rocking arrangements that would be no problem live.

But it sounds like Andy would have wanted to dress things up a bit more. "Yes, well, the disappointment with *Identity Crisis* was we had management who needed to deliver an album to get the last tranche of money. And this is what it comes down to sometimes. I'm in the studio, I'm not ready to mix, but I'm told you must provide listenable mixes. So, the record company… just so that we can release the money and everybody's then contractually obliged, you'll have time to do a proper remix when the album is going to be released properly. Well, that never happened. The things that I delivered are the ones that got released that don't have all the final overdubs on them that don't have—should we say—the final mix. It's what I would call good demos. If you had demos like that, you'd be very pleased."

"And that's when I realised that I didn't want a manager ever again, because I realised that I'd had ten years of lies. Why would I want another ten years of lies? So that's the main difference. Plus, as I said, the band was imploding. Steve was moving to America, and we were never going to be the same again."

"It Makes Me Wonder" finds the band back in this sort of guitar-based arty new wave direction, like heavy Gary Numan or obscure Cars. This one's all about atmosphere, with dark new wave chords placed upon a boxy four-on-the-floor from Mick. Come chorus time, there's this nerdy "Why, why, why" refrain to go along with the titular musing. The second chorus is even more mechanistic (and maybe even militaristic) than the verses, again, the likes of Devo being evoked, especially with the extra window dressing of a synth break.

Next is plodding hard rocker "Falling in Love." Not sure what Andy is referring to here, but he told me, "Killer guitar in that one. It's just a shame that the song wasn't as good as the guitar riff on 'Falling in Love.' You know, that is straight out of the Ritchie Blackmore school of guitar riffing, and I really wished it would have been welded onto something a lot better than that particular song."

Again, the arrangements are kept simple and tight, this one being all about chugging guitars. "Louis was very meticulous," says Andy, asked about engineer Louis Austin. "He was the one who would make notes. And he wasn't exactly musical, but he knew what a song needed. Also, we would have things blasting into the red if we were left to our own devices, and he made sure that the sound sounded like it was blasting into the red but wasn't about to jump the needle. It wasn't about to jump off the record. He was, at that time, invaluable to just be the mediator, the guy who would make sure that everything got done."

Next is "I Wish You Would," a cover of a song by blues harmonica man Billy Boy Arnold. Sweet work the song up into a punchy number but all told, it's traditional rock 'n' roll sent up like Gary Glitter (save for the headbanging guitar solo section and subsequent punky break), an ill fit to the modern American feel of the rest of the album.

Identity Crisis closes with "Strange Girl," which finds Sweet back in that odd FM-friendly American heartland rock zone at the chorus, and for the verses, addressing, again, American new wave, almost like light Ramones. Mick is once again utilising a robotic four-on-the-floor style, the end result being a song that fits well with the cohesive yet not particularly Sweet-like direction of the album.

Not that any of this would matter—Sweet, in the Andy, Steve and Mick configuration, would never play live again. Soon Steve would marry Maureen, with the couple continuing to live in New York until a move would take them to the West Coast.

EPILOGUE

"We've been slapped in the face a few times, but we're still here"

If you think you'd seen Sweet trip an' fall to every sad rock 'n' roll cliché already through their career, then hang onto your hats, because the long, sad goodbye throughout the '80s and beyond would bring many more examples of ridiculousness, some of it amusing (three competing versions of the band) and some of it just tragic (three band members passing on).

As Sweet (proper) was throwing in the towel, England was going through the New Wave of British Heavy Metal. Sweet were regarded as part of the old wave and thus Andy had a good name about town with the younger bands and was in the running for various producer gigs, having proven that he knows his way around a board.

Asked if he recalls much praise from the new metal acts for what Sweet had brought to the genre, really from '74 through '77, Andy says, "There's been quite a fair bit of it. I did actually have Iron Maiden in the recording studio, early days. And I used to talk to Nikki Sixx for example, in the early hours of the morning. Somehow, he got a hold of my phone number and he would call me up and basically say, 'I've got a band; come over and produce us.' He eventually sent me some tapes. Quite honestly, I don't want to be derogatory, because I never am, but I thought they needed a hell of a lot of work before they even should have been making demos. It was very, very primitive. But you could see that they had something because all of a sudden, a picture of them appeared about six months later in an English magazine, and I looked at them and they certainly looked the part. Now all you've got to do is get them to play the part."

As regards Maiden, "My managers in France at that time knew their manager, and I got on well with Rod (Smallwood), and he said, 'Look, take them into the studio.' Because originally, he wanted to replace just the drums. Because the original singer, Paul Di'Anno, actually had a stomach problem. And they said, 'Can you just replace the drums on this particular track?' It was 'Running Free.' And I said, 'The tempo is awful. You know, the tempo rides. If you could find a drummer...' Well, they said, 'We've got

Clive Burr, who is joining, if you want to have a go…' And I said, 'Well, we need to make a copy of the tape, if that's the way we're going to go, or we can start from the beginning and then see about drafting his voice across onto a better backing track. You know, we could try that.'"

"So, they went along with that," continues Andy, "and I thought we were making a very, very credible backing track, over a weekend. We also did a track called 'Transylvania,' which I think ended up on one of their EPs or LPs or B-sides or something. And the singer still couldn't sing, and they said that they would get back to me. I was in the same studio with another band about two weeks later, and all of a sudden somebody said, 'Iron Maiden are on *Top of the Pops*.' And there they are, with the demo, miming to the demo of 'Running Free.' Somebody at the record company said, 'We need to get this out now.' They were starting to happen. And it shows you, sometimes, never mind the quality; you can feel the attitude and it's the way forward. I didn't think so at the time, but I do now. Sometimes I think people have missed the boat by trying to get—shall we say—something a little bit more correct, rather than just going with your gut instinct."

"Anyway, there were quite a lot of bands that came in through my hands. Some changed their names down the line. There were a few of the New Wave of British Heavy Metal bands, but none of the ones that really broke through. I produced a band called Weapon, and I got to know the guys. Because remember, it was all so incestuous back then. People would be in a band for five minutes and then they would join Praying Mantis, for example. Or the guitarist from Tygers of Pan Tang would join this band. This was going on all the time. There was another band I was going to get involved with called Angel Witch. There were a lot around that time. But where I had my best success was in places like Germany and Scandinavia. There was one band in Scandinavia called Sha-Boom, where we had a lot of hit singles and a couple of big albums over in Sweden."

"But it was always on a shoestring. The record companies that were around… I mean, Iron Maiden were very lucky; they managed to get a deal with EMI. But there were a lot of smaller labels that were floating around, and everything was being done on a budget. It may have looked a little bit more than it was, if you know what I mean."

Asked about how close it got with Angel Witch, Andy chuckles, "I got to know them and once was given a lift home by the bass player, Kevin Riddles. There was a club on the river in Putney, and you would usually end up there three in the morning, and I had to get back to somewhere like St. John's Wood or Primrose Hill, South London, and he would say, 'Are you coming with us, Andy? Get in the back of the van.' And there he was, taxiing around those that needed to be gotten home."

Andy produced a couple of singles for AIIZ, namely "No Fun After Midnight" and "I'm the One Who Loves You," this being the band notable for coughing up drummer Simon Wright to AC/DC. Scott would also issue a few solo singles, but soon he'd be forming a new version of Sweet, with Mick Tucker on drums, Mal McNulty (from Weapon) on bass, Paul Mario Day (More, Wildfire) on vocals, and Grand Prix's Phil Lanzon on keyboards, the latter soon to find fame and decades of stability as part of

Uriah Heep. Brian would form his own version of the band, called The New Sweet, but his drinking had worsened, and the band was a non-starter, managing only a few gigs.

"I used to meet up with him," says Andy, asked about getting back together with Mick. "And in fact, I still kept him in touch with the business by a couple of albums that I was producing, when somebody needed a drummer, here and there. I would still call him up and say, 'Come on, come down to the studio.' So, there was always probably going to be a moment when the phone call came, when he would then either say yes or no. Yes, I'll come and play or no I won't. So, when the opportunity came, and I bumped into the agent at the end of '84, I rang Mick up. I actually went over to his house after that, and we sat down and I said, 'Well, he's telling me there's lots of work out there. It's up to you whether you want to do it or not.' And when he said yes, I knew that we were up and running then."

In 1982, Argent's John Verity produced a solo single for Brian, issued on Carrere. Verity was associated with the French label, also producing Saxon's debut album for the imprint. Brian's single paired an A-side called "Hypnotised," written by Joe Lynn Turner, with a Connolly number called "Fade Away."

"I did love Brian," laughs John. "You couldn't help it. He was one of those guys that you just became attached to really quickly. I don't know what it was. It was something about Brian. But he was a nightmare to work with. I mean, I put a band together behind him and we had great players. But getting Brian to focus long enough to do stuff was not easy. Drink was a big part of it; there's no way getting away from it. That was the big problem. And his management were trying to manage it, and it wasn't really working."

"His problem was really bad in the recording situation," continues Verity. "He was unreliable and he would turn up pissed, which obviously you don't want. But he turned up pissed with a smile on his face, so you couldn't really get angry with Brian (laughs). It was funny. There were a lot of people who really cared about Brian and really wanted to get him on his feet again, but he was his own worst enemy. I don't think anybody would mind me saying that."

As for playing live, "We did a tour with Pat Benatar over here in England which was fairly successful, and across Europe, and Brian was actually okay. He pulled himself together on that. I was in that band, but I couldn't stay doing it because I was doing my own thing as well. I did Brian straight after I recorded *Interrupted Journey*, I think, so it would've all jumbled into one. But with Brian, there was no pulling out or anything. I mean, the material that we chose was carefully chosen around Brian's vocal range and everything so he was fine. But with him, there was a lot of back-of-the-throat gravelly stuff, which is not good for your throat, really."

Andy's version of the band would play fairly regularly, even finding their way to Australia and New Zealand. A performance conducted in February '86 would result in the *Live at the Marquee* album, issued on double vinyl and CD in 1989 in Germany and on CD in America the following year. The live material consists of the expected Sweet hits but there are three new studio originals plus a cover of the Holland/Dozier/Holland classic "Reach Out… (I'll Be There)." The new material found the band making a play for hair metal greatness, but, if the live video performance of "Jump the Fence" is any indication, well, here's another leap into the realm of ridiculousness. The guys look preposterous, awkwardly glammed up, equal parts nascent LA hair metal, NWOBHM band gone pop, Duran Duran New Romantic and, last quarter, a revisitation of the visual abortions Sweet and Slade presented of their ridiculous selves in the early '70s.

Paul Mario Day would latch onto an Australian girl from the band's visit down under and eventually move there, resulting in Mal McNulty taking over lead vocals. Jeff Brown takes over on bass and Steve Mann joins on guitar. Meanwhile, in 1988, an attempt is made by Mike Chapman to get the band back together. He summons them to LA and as the guys are getting off the plane, lagging is Brian, who looks like a hobbling old man. They go to a studio and attempt to record "Action" and "Ballroom Blitz" but it's of no use—Brian is too far gone. The previous year resulted in what would be Brian's last recording, a song called "Sharontina" that he did with pre-Andy Sweet guitarist Frank Torpey. This would later emerge on Torpey's *Sweeter* album, from 1998.

In 1990, Andy's and Mick's version of the band tours America and Canada pretty extensively, in support of *Live at the Marquee.*

In advance of a show in Vancouver, BC, Mick tells Tom Harrison, "The album is enabling us to tour. We're here with a view to getting a major label deal. We base our set around the *Desolation Boulevard* album, but as the tour progresses, I'm beginning to realise how many hardcore fans there are out there asking for an amazing number of diverse songs, including 'Little Willy' which the band hasn't done in 18 years."

Looking back, Tucker tells Tom, "To be honest, when we started slapping the makeup on, it was done with tongue in cheek and for only a few records, because we had no idea how big the band was going to be. We spent several years trying to consolidate ourselves as a bona fide rock band. I'm glad that when we finally came over to America, we were perceived as a rock band. I think one thing the set us apart from the other bands Chinn and Chapman produced was that we were all good musicians. What I always wanted was a band—like Cream with Eric Clapton or Led Zeppelin—of good musicians with its own songs. We made our statement, and we influenced a lot of bands. Now we'd like some of our dignity returned."

Also in 1990, Brian's version of Sweet flies to Australia for a tour but Brian is checked into hospital upon arrival and misses the first gig, although he plays subsequent shows. Also, this year, the classic Sweet line-up is reunited once again, but only for the promotion of a Sweet documentary film. The following year we get another Andy Scott solo single along with the news that Mick Tucker is leaving Sweet—Mick plays his last show on May 5th, in Lochau, Austria.

Things are looking up come 1992. After fighting with Brian over the

Sweet name, Brian's thing becomes Brian Connolly's Sweet and Andy has to rename his band Andy Scott's Sweet, the latter producing a studio album of nine new originals and a cover of Australian band The Angels' warm and woodsy "Am I Ever Gonna See Your Face Again." The album is called *"A"* and is issued on LP and CD by SPV in Germany. The band consists of Andy, along with Mal McNulty on lead vocals, Steve Mann on guitar and keyboards, Jeff Brown on bass and Bodo Schopf—both Schopf and Mann would end up in the Michael Schenker Group.

All told, the record is a form of well-executed hair metal if a bit plodding and laden with dated mid-'80s production tropes. It's ambitious enough to be sure, but trouble is, it's a good six, maybe even seven years too late, with hair metal winding up across the pond at this point and grunge entering its mature phase to boot. The blip in activity for Andy's band results in a video release called *Live at the Capitol*, but soon there are more line-up changes. Meanwhile the band van marshalling Brian Connolly's Sweet around is broken into, March '92, resulting in the theft of four fairly polished demos featuring Brian, songs that would have represented Brian's last recordings, had they been recovered.

Come 1994, Brian manages to get through shows in Dubai and Bahrain, while the following year, Steve's daughter Lisa gets married in England and both Mick and Brian are there for a wobbly bit of a jam with Steve—modest but historic given what was about to happen. Both Andy and Brian manage to get low-key releases out—live stuff, covers, compilations—amidst a regular flow of dodgy Sweet compilations from God knows where. Key among these is *Let's Go*, which finds Brian tentatively vocalising nine

Sweet classics with Brian Connolly's Sweet but also a cover and two new originals. Also, this year, May 26th, Brian's partner Jean gives birth to a son, also called Brian, but soon dad would end his career, playing his last show at the Hippodrome on December 5th of 1996, just after a documentary on his life called *Don't Leave Me This Way* is released, showing how fragile Connolly had become.

February 9th, 1997, the beloved and legendary vocalist for Sweet passes, age 51, due to a combination of liver failure, kidney failure and repeated heart attacks. Cremated, Brian was to be survived by daughters Nicola and Michelle, son Brian, ex-wife Marilyn and girlfriend Jean. This puts the nail, obviously, to the original Sweet getting back together, not that we'd heard anything from Steve for 15 years at this point.

As Andy told Dave Ling, "I still have great memories of Brian, and without warning sometimes they still make me laugh out loud. Things like the hotel receptionist calling our tour manager and asking to retrieve him from a corridor, where he'd been found spread-eagled and stark bollock naked. He'd mistaken a potted plant for his bathroom door, peed on it, and passed out."

"Around that time, Mick and I snuck in to see Brian at some gig down in Windsor," continues Andy, talking to Dave about events from not too long previous. "There was confusion because there were two versions of The Sweet: Brian Connolly and the New Sweet doing their cabaret stuff, and us playing whichever rock venues would take us in England. The strangest thing was that we were already back on the map in Germany. I told him the only solution to everybody's problems was for him to come and play some gigs with my band. We'd play the first half of the set, and he'd come on for the last part. He was really into the idea."

For his part, Andy Scott's Sweet, after losing vocalist Chad Brown in 1998, to be replaced by Jeff Brown, enjoys a period of stability, even coming up with a new studio album in 2002 called *Sweetlife*.

Also, this year however, February 14th, after five years battling leukemia, Mick Tucker passes away, age 54. "He rang me up the night before he died," recalls Gary Moberley. "And he'd had a very high voice from all the medication. And guess what he said to me? 'Get out of my limo' (laughs). While he's lying in bed, and with not long to go, and it was funny; it was good timing. As I say, I liked Mick."

"I think out of the four of us, at least right at that point in those early days, he did have something a bit more special to offer," says Andy, musing on Mick. "I remember talking to him years later when we weren't doing that much in the early '80s, after Steve had gone to America and there was an audition coming up. I have a feeling that it was either Ozzy Osbourne was forming a band or Tony Iommi wanted a drummer to replace Bill, but it was something to do with Black Sabbath. And I said, 'You should definitely go for that, Mick.' And he was kind of, 'What do you mean I should go for that?' And I said, 'Well, you know…' and he said, 'If they want me, they can ask me.' And that was Mick right there, if you know what I mean."

With Andy's band continuing to shuffle members and perform live, Scott also found time to do the aforementioned QSP album with Suzi Quatro and Don Powell from Slade, which was issued in 2006. Then it was Steve's time to start a version of Sweet, this one from his bastion in sunny Los Angeles. The band played their first show on June 12th, at the

Whisky in Hollywood, with the author managing to catch the band twice, first at the Nakusp Music Fest in rural British Columbia and second time in his hometown of Toronto. On August 30th, the band would play a show in Cabazon, California, which would be issued as the *Live! In America*, July of 2009. Also in 2009, Ace Frehley covers "Fox on the Run" on his *Anomaly* record while Sweet sees the release of a proper and fine compilation called *Action: The Sweet Anthology*, issued April 28th of that year.

As Steve explained to me back in the Spring of 2008, "I hadn't been playing for a long time. I'd been mucking around with studios and writing etc., but I went and saw Eric Clapton at the Staples Centre and thought, I've got to get back on stage again. So I got back together with an old friend of mine named Stuart Smith, who I've known since I lived in Los Angeles, and he had a friend who's a drummer, a very good drummer who I've also worked with off and on, and we put a band together with a singer, Joe Retta, and keyboard player and we've been rehearsing for the last few months. Andy is still doing Andy Scott's Sweet, and he's been trying to do it for a while. But I'm afraid our musical and just personalities have gone too far apart for us to tread the same boards; let's put it that way. Nothing in particular where I can actually say, 'Oh, that happened and that happened.' It just happened."

A month later I talked to Steve again, and he informed me that, "We've just done two gigs in Los Angeles, which is The Whisky and the Canyon Club, and they were brilliant (laughs). Great audiences both times, and we just came out swinging. We have rearranged the set list slightly. That was from doing the Soundstage, when we did a little warm-up gig in Ventura, and I said, 'There's something wrong with this. It's not quite mixing.' So, we just juggled a couple of songs around and then all of a sudden it flowed. As for the songs, I was very surprised I didn't have to pull them apart. But there are some very funny timing things; like in 'Teenage Rampage,' there are a couple of bars of 5/4 in there. I mean, I don't remember that (laughs). But it follows the vocals, so it doesn't sort of skip. But it means there is like half a bar here or there that shouldn't be there. 'Action' is not too bad but it's hard work. They all are. I mean, not hard work as in 'I don't like it,' but as in, it's physically hard."

"I hired Joe on Stuart's recommendation because he said he was a good singer," continues Priest. "I said I'm not going to turn this into a Sweet look-alike band. I wanted it to sound alike, but now it's got its own character. And the people who have seen us have said, 'My God, it's even better than the original.' Well, I wouldn't go so far as to say that, but it is good (laughs)."

Remarked Steve to Christopher Tessmer in advance of a gig in Regina, Saskatchewan, "We've got a much harder edge than even the original had. I don't know if that's my influence or what. I've been set on doing the songs as close to the originals as possible, but we tend to add a rawer edge to it. That's what I always wanted. We weren't really allowed to sound too heavy during our original years. It was only on *Give Us a Wink* where we broke away from Mike Chapman, where the harder side of the band started to come out. We weren't really allowed to continue with that because the label felt we needed to go back and make hits and all that crapola. Now whatever is going to come out is going to come out and we'll record it. We're going to do a lot of the hits, plus some slightly obscure album tracks like 'Windy City,' but most importantly we're going to go out and have fun. Basically, we go out on stage and make sure we have fun and hopefully the audience goes along with that. They have so far."

Spring of the following year, Andy is diagnosed with prostate cancer, which he successfully fights off, resuming touring duties, including a trip to Australia and eventually, in 2017, yet another visit down under, this time with QSP. Meanwhile Steve's band continues to play, causing confusion.

"Steve and I aren't really in the kind of communication that we used to be," Andy told me at the time. "It's sad when… well, I always thought that we had a relationship. I'm now learning that maybe there's been a bit of festering of contempt coming from his side for rather a long time, and I've just not been aware of it, you know? I've heard this from a few Sweet fans, who basically said that Sweet is quintessentially a British band. The band that has continued from that original line-up, in the 1970s, is the band that is led by me. Because when Mick and I carried it on in the '80s, nobody left this band. There's been no, 'I am Spartacus,' that kind of thing going on. It's a very straightforward thing. Do you want to play? Yes, I do. Or if you don't, when would you like to play? But you don't find out that there's been some Machiavellian kind of backstabbing thing going on and now we're back as if what had gone on over the last 25 years has meant nothing."

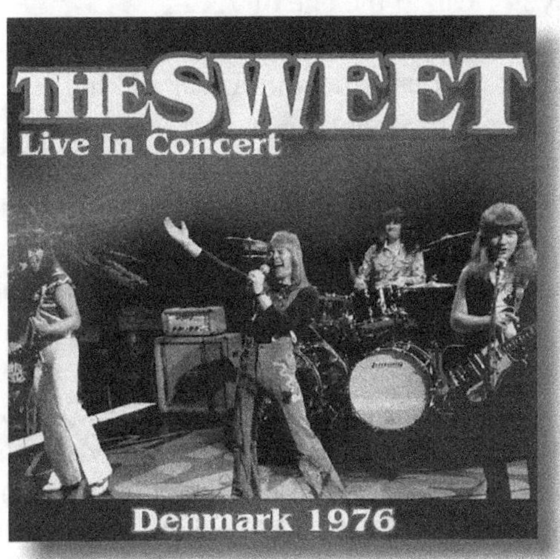

"People are not stupid," continues Andy. "They know that the band's been together in the '70s, and that there was a band from '84, '85, up to date. You don't just come out of the woodwork three or four years ago and say, 'Right, we're back.' You're treating people as if they're stupid. Back then, at that time, it would've been—because we were well up and running—it would've been, 'Steve, get on a plane, bring your bass with you and come and infiltrate into the band and we'll do a few dates and see how it goes.' That would have been the easiest and most graceful way."

"And then out of the blue, we've got a band that doesn't sound like Sweet, coming out and calling themselves Sweet, and trying to conquer the world. Well, I don't know, mate. I don't know how you feel about stuff like that. But it happened before in the past, when people like Rod Evans from Deep Purple went out in America and tried to be Deep Purple. But I'm afraid our history is littered with these kinds of attempts. We just played at Sweden Rock, big festival in Scandinavia and there's a lot of stuff out there. If you go on the Sweet website, it'll take you over to Facebook, and you could see a few of the pictures and a few of the interviews that have gone on. I've also realised that with regards to anything that's happened with Sweet along the way, there's no point now in trying to skirt any issues. You know, here we are, 45 years later, and if you don't know what's gone on by now, then you'll never know. We've been slapped in the face a few times, but we're still here."

Steve's band also went through a bunch of line-up changes, but managed to play live quite a bit, mostly in the US and Canada but also in Germany and South America. But soon it was Steve's turn to leave the stage. On June 4th, 2020, in the early months of the coronavirus pandemic, we would lose Steve Priest, at the age of 72.

"It's become a last man standing situation now with Steve's passing," Andy told me, just after Priest's death. "I was talking to his wife. There's one minor disappointment. Somebody was gonna get me a link, because obviously I can't travel to Los Angeles. But apparently there was some kind of funeral service at the beginning of the week of this week. Now I don't know whether it was private or whether they let the public go. I know nothing, because as I said, I'm not on social media. Somebody did say that they went ahead, but nobody gave me the link. Apparently, there was a kind of Zoom thing going on. So, yeah, that's not important. The only thing that I keep saying to Maureen, his wife, is you just make sure that you get yourself sorted in your head. Because in the end it was a shock."

As for cause of death, Andy says, "I think he ended up getting pneumonia, having done a gig up in Minnesota or something back in the middle of February. Maureen said he should never have gone. He was not really well enough. And he came back, and he got pneumonia but then she thought he could have gotten over that. And then he was rushed into ICU and he was in ICU for a couple of weeks. And I didn't know that. When I contacted her, she said, 'Oh, he's coming out.' So, I'd been aware. Then she said, 'out of the ICU' and I went, 'Oh God.' So anyway, he came out and then he must've had a downturn somewhere. But he was rushed back in and then he never came out again. I think you'd probably be talking about… generally the body decides that, you know, it's had enough."

As for the legacy this last man standing and his fallen Sweet brethren has left for us, "Everyone likes 'Love Is Like Oxygen,'" reflects Gary Moberley, as close to a fifth member of the band classic Sweet ever had. "I remember, I was out at this hotel, the building used in *Towering Inferno* where the lift goes up on the outside. But we come out there, and it was summertime, and someone was standing on the footpath. This guy comes around, sweeping up the road, an African-American, and I said to him, 'Oh, nice day.' 'Yeah, yeah, beautiful day.' And he said, 'Oh, you got a funny accent.' As we talked on from there, he said, 'Oh my son knows all that music. He listens to "Love Is Like Oxygen" and he was copying the guitar and he likes your band.' And I went, 'Oh, okay,' and I said, 'Why don't you and your family come down to the gig tonight?' So, it was nice. And they came backstage and his son met the band and I thought yeah, it's nice when I can do things like that. You know, you're pretty knackered, you spend three, six months on the road… It's like, one night we got up onstage and Steve said, 'Are you ready to rock, Chicago?' I said, 'Steve, it's Cleveland. We were in Chicago last night.'"

I asked Gary if he figured the guys had come out the other end of the circus that was Sweet in the '70s and early '80s with a bit of savings, some security as it were. "That's hard to answer, but I know that at one stage Andy had come around my house with some keyboards, because he needed 400 quid. So, he needed money at that stage. He was the backbone of the band. I don't think much would've been done if he wasn't there. I don't know what Steve was doing, but he did nothing for 30 years. I don't know what the record sales were. I don't see where there can be that amount of royalties. Especially in the digital age now, where people don't pay for anything."

Adds Andy, "One thing I will say, is that along the way, it may not have been everything that we were owed, but we were never completely and utterly—like occurred with some bands—all of a sudden the money dries up. Whatever has happened, it's been on a solid foundation. No, we might not have gotten as much of a cut as we wanted to get, but there's always been a steady through-flow. It was always set up correctly, you know what I mean? We ended up with a little bit of stuff in liquidation. For example, the publishing company, the stupidity of a business manager saying, 'Oh, let it go to liquidation and buy it back cheaply.' And then we realised that it wasn't going be that easy."

In the end, Andy defends his insistence upon continuing to do business as Sweet. "Yes, well, I actually think that of the bands from that era, you've still got Quo doing fantastic business on the road. You've also still got Nazareth and Uriah Heep at the moment doing really good business in Europe. We did some shows with both Nazareth and Uriah Heep last year, which were phenomenal. There are certain bands in this business that kind of get up themselves. They don't want to be considered nostalgia acts. But as far as I'm concerned, it's your music. If you're not in the charts right at the moment, and you're able to go on the road and sell venues, and the people want to hear your hits from the '70s, I'm afraid you're just out of it if you don't serve them. There's no other word for it."

With all the changes that have happened in pop over the decades, I asked Andy what a typical 20-year-old today could possibly get out of the music of Sweet, music that is pretty much delicately preserved in amber now that three of its makers are gone, with Scott fighting his own aging and health issues, and indeed, with live music as a business proposition now shut down by a worldwide pandemic.

"We live in a very, open world," figures Andy. "Musically everything is available to anybody, and that can't be a bad thing. But what it does is it also gives you immense choice that probably wasn't there when I was growing up 50, 60 years ago. The inherent problem with that is that you now have so much, how can you ever listen to it all? But the way that the internet and certain sites are, they push things towards you because of your listening habits. I even find that myself, even though I'm not on any social media. It's the last thing and place I want to be. I don't even like having to answer my phone; I feel like some slave, you know? So why would I ever want to be on any kind of social media where your phone's bloody pinging every 20 seconds and you end up walking into trees in parks?"

"But I loved it when we used to perform gigs and teenagers, 18-year-olds, would come up and say, 'Love it, love it, love your band.' You're just wondering, how did you come by us? And the stories are just wide-ranging. I would say that the legacy that The Sweet are gonna have left behind is that we were one of the few bands that jumped across the genres and would not be put in a box. That's the way I would like to think of us: you'll get from us whatever you want to get from us, not what you're told to get from us, you know? I think that's what it comes down to. It's a matter of taste. And yet somehow the commerciality still comes through. Whether it be Jimi Hendrix or Cream or Sweet or Slade, that commerciality, as long as it comes across on a radio, I think the public will accept it."

"But back to that 20-year-old kid today, and what can he learn from Sweet, I wish I knew. You can't remember what you've learned, and that's why when you look back at bands in their era, you wish that they had stayed there. But you realise why they hadn't, and it's because they're progressing. And some progress in the right way, and some don't. With Sweet, it's been a twisty road—it's not that obvious. I would have hoped that for somebody who likes rock music, but also likes it to be accessible, you couldn't have found a better band than Sweet. You had a band that sounded like the heavier rock bands like Deep Purple and Zeppelin, but you had vocals that sounded like Crosby, Stills and Nash or the Hollies, these four-part harmonies and some of them fairly complex. And the only other band that I can think of like that is Queen, who, again, came slightly after us. I'm not saying that it's completely true that we opened the door for them, but I think it's a natural progression. If you want to be a chart band but you're also into rock, then you're going to start addressing that area, doing harmony vocals on top of a backtrack that sounds like it should have been on Led Zeppelin one or Deep Purple *In Rock*, you know?"

A BLOCKBUSTING
NEW COLLECTION
FULL OF GLITZ, BLITZ
AND ALL THE HITZ!!!

**20 boot stomping, hell raising anthems including
Blockbuster!, Hell Raiser and Ballroom Blitz**

ALSO AVAILABLE:

Their first five studio albums each re-mastered and
re-packaged with bonus tracks, sleevenotes by Andy Scott
and featuring rare photos and artwork.

**FUNNY HOW SWEET
CO-CO CAN BE**

SWEET FANNY ADAMS

DESOLATION BOULEVARD

GIVE US A WINK

OFF THE RECORD

"THE VERY BEST OF SWEET" IS AVAILABLE ON DVD FROM WIENERWORLD WNRD2185

AVAILABLE FROM 17TH JANUARY AT

HMV
top dog for music·dvd·games

I wondered aloud with Andy whether he thought Steve's band would be so bold as to continue without him.

"The thing is, nothing would surprise me," chuckles Scott. "We've already had that happen with Brian's band over here. And that took quite a while to turn to dust in the end. Right at this moment, nobody can make any judgments about anything because there is nothing to be done. It's all very well. Maybe one of them might have said we're going to keep Steve's legacy together. I don't know. But if they're planning to do that, when are they going to be doing it? Because I can't see any gigs coming together until at least next year sometime. Unless there's some kind of vaccine that will kill this off so that people can do what they're used to doing, like 1000, 1200 people cramming into a venue to jump up and down and sing the songs and be close to each other and shout and sweat, there's never going to be a gig like we've experienced in the past. All I'm looking for right now is that the world finds its feet again, and that the people end up with a smile on their bloody face because there's far too many serious faces over here."

And then there it was, a new Sweet record from Andy in 2024 called *Full Circle*, tantalisingly teased with the usual advance single business. Once the album dropped, it was obvious, from the album cover right on down through the top-shelf production and the canny songwriting, that Scott hadn't lost a step. It's an absolutely first-rate classic rock album, punchy and intriguingly, southern rock and even pomp rock at times, something that is a lost art. Indeed, along those lines, the real magic comes with the melodic hooks uplifting songs like "Changes," "Everything" and "Rising Up." In fact, Andy's made something pretty surprising here, not going for the heavy metal jugular as might have been expected.

Five decades on now, there have been plenty of ups and downs, but Andy's main take-away has been to appreciate the good times, because they are bound to drift by and be replaced by new circumstances.

Case in point, "Cheap Trick started out as one of the bands that supported us. And then a couple of years later, we are the sandwich band on their tours; they have an opening act and Sweet play and then Cheap Trick finish. That's what happens, but it's too little too late now, isn't it? But the thing is, we were never on the beat, never on the circuit playing the US regularly enough. If we had been, we would've broken the States wide open. That's the feeling I have, anyway. Similar thing with Kiss. I believe Kiss did a couple of gigs with us before the full masks went on. And then towards the end of the '70s, we're on tour playing before Alice Cooper and Kiss and a few of these others. We also did a couple of gigs with Rush and they were great. I remember chatting to them backstage for quite a while. But yeah, when I think back, it's what I've said to a lot of musicians that I produced and everything: when that moment happens, grasp it with both hands and look around. Whatever you're doing, put it in your memory bank because it ain't going to be there forever."

DISCOGRAPHY

Complicated catalogue to be sure. First section, the official LPs, I suppose is pretty straight-forward. I've included a notes section to show variations between the UK and the US editions, save for *Desolation Boulevard*, which is addressed in Section B.

Second section, kind of messy, but there are two significant US albums that are essentially compilations, namely the first and second albums. I thought *The Sweet's Biggest Hits* from '72 was significant enough to put here as well, plus *Strung Up*. That's it. Four records, two UK and two US—keeping it simple.

Moving to singles, our third section, again, this is a selected discography of only the most important singles on home turf and in the US. It's done this way mainly because the continental singles reflected pretty closely the intent of the UK singles. And then over to the US, I've paid attention to this because America constitutes biggest territory to conquer, and the career trajectory for Sweet there was so different, and so there's more contrast with what the band were doing in the UK and mainland Europe. I tend to not do singles sections in my books, but for Sweet, little records have been a significant part of their business and history.

What else? Quote marks around songs only in Notes section. Spelling and punctuation of song titles (plus timings) as per release, UK issue as priority. Production: just the names, not broken down by tracks. I've skipped providing my usual personnel section as it's a mess of session players in the beginning, but a solid official band line-up throughout, save for the subtraction of Brian at *Cut Above the Rest*, which I pointed out in the notes. I've noted side 1/side 2 designations because all of these albums were released before the CD age. Singles I've kept simple date-wise, along with skipping catalogue numbers, producers etc. As well, we're only working this out up to the end of the official band in 1982.

OFFICIAL STUDIO ALBUMS

Funny How Sweet Co-Co Can Be
November 27, 1971; RCA SF 8238
Produced by Phil Wainman
Side 1: 1. Co-Co (Chinn, Chapman) 3:14; 2. Chop Chop (Chinn, Chapman) 3:00; 3. Reflections (Holland, Dozier, Holland) 2:52; 4. Honeysuckle Love (Connolly, Priest, Scott, Tucker) 2:55; 5. Santa Monica Sunshine (Chinn, Chapman) 3:20; 6. Daydream (Sebastian) 3:13
Side 2: 1. Funny Funny (Chinn, Chapman) 2:46; 2. Tom Tom Turnaround (Chinn, Chapman) 4:07; 3. Jeanie (Connolly, Priest, Scott, Tucker) 2:58; 4. Sunny Sleeps Late (Chinn, Chapman) 2:58; 5. Spotlight (Connolly, Priest, Tucker, Scott) 2:47; 6. Done Me Wrong All Right (Connolly, Priest, Tucker, Scott) 2:57
Notes: German issue is with different cover and entitled *Funny Funny, How Sweet Co-Co Can Be*. As well, this issue includes additional track "Done Me Wrong All Right."

Sweet Fanny Adams
April 1974; RCA LPL1 5038
Produced by Phil Wainman
Side 1: 1. Set Me Free (Connolly, Priest, Scott, Tucker) 3:57; 2. Heartbreak Today (Connolly, Priest, Scott, Tucker) 5:02; 3. No You Don't (Chinn, Chapman) 4:35; 5. Peppermint Twist (Dee, Glover) 3:29
Side 2: 1. Sweet F.A. (Connolly, Priest, Scott, Tucker) 6:15; 2. Restless (Connolly, Priest, Scott, Tucker) 4:29; 3. Into the Night (Scott) 4:26; 4. AC-DC (Chinn, Chapman) 3:29

Desolation Boulevard
November 1974; RCA LPL1 5080
Produced by Mike Chapman and Nicky Chinn
Side 1: 1. The Six Teens (Chinn, Chapman) 4:02; Solid Gold Brass (Connolly, Priest, Scott, Tucker) 5:33; 3. Turn It Down (Chinn, Chapman 3:30; 4. Medusa (Connolly, Priest, Scott, Tucker) 4:45; 5. Lady Starlight (Scott) 3:12
Side 2: 1. The Man with the Golden Arm (Bernstein, Fine) 8:27; 2. Fox on the Run (Connolly, Priest, Scott, Tucker) 4:47; 3. Breakdown (Connolly, Priest, Scott, Tucker) 3:06; 4. My Generation (Townshend) 3:59

Give Us a Wink
February 16, 1976; RCA RS 1036
Produced by Sweet
Side 1: The Lies in Your Eyes (Connolly, Priest, Scott, Tucker) 3:48; 2. Cockroach (Connolly, Priest, Scott, Tucker) 4:51; 3. Keep It In (Connolly, Priest, Scott, Tucker) 5:00; 4. 4th of July (Connolly, Priest, Scott, Tucker) 4:24
Side 2: 1. Action (Connolly, Priest, Scott, Tucker) 3:44; 2. Yesterday's Rain (Connolly, Priest, Scott, Tucker) 5:16; 3. White Mice (Connolly, Priest, Scott, Tucker) 4:58; 4. Healer (Connolly, Priest, Scott, Tucker) 7:17

Notes: North American Capitol issue adds a ninth track, "Lady Starlight," 3:10, over the European issue (and shuffles the order). Japanese Capitol issue adds two extra tracks for a total of ten, namely "Lady Starlight" 3:10, and "Fox on the Run" 3:24, (and follows roughly the order of the North American issue).

Off the Record

April 1977; RCA PL 25072

Produced by Sweet

Side 1: 1. Fever of Love (Connolly, Priest, Scott, Tucker) 4:03; 2. Lost Angels (Connolly, Priest, Scott, Tucker) 4:06; 3. Midnight to Daylight (Connolly, Priest, Scott, Tucker) 3:34; 4. Windy City (Connolly, Priest, Scott, Tucker) 7:30
Side 2: 1. Live for Today (Connolly, Priest, Scott, Tucker) 3:19; 2. She Gimme Lovin' (Connolly, Priest, Scott, Tucker) 4:08; 3. Laura Lee (Connolly, Priest, Scott, Tucker) 4:18; 4. Hard Times (Connolly, Priest, Scott, Tucker) 4:01; 5. Funk It Up (Connolly, Priest, Scott, Tucker) 3:34
Notes: North American issue adds a tenth track, "Stairway to the Stars," 3:05, among other small differences, including a shuffled track order. UK issue front cover does not include record title; title showing on North American copies.

Level Headed

January 1978; Polydor POLD 5001

Produced by Sweet

Side 1: 1. Dream On (Connolly, Priest, Scott, Tucker) 2:53; 2. Love Is Like Oxygen (Scott, Griffin) 6:53; 3. California Nights (Connolly, Priest, Scott, Tucker) 3:45; 4. Strong Love (Connolly, Priest, Scott, Tucker) 3:28; 5. Fountain (Connolly, Priest, Scott, Tucker) 4:44
Side 2: 1. Anthem No. I (Lady of the Lake) (Connolly, Priest, Scott, Tucker) 4:11; 2. Silverbird (Connolly, Priest, Scott, Tucker) 3:26; 3. Lettres D'Amour (Connolly, Priest, Scott, Tucker) 3:30; 4. Anthem No. II 1:02 (Connolly, Priest, Scott, Tucker); 5. Air on 'A' Tape Loop (Priest, Scott, Tucker) 5:59
Notes: The UK version features a Terry Pastor band photograph on the front cover with the cassette illustration used in the gatefold. This is essentially reversed for the North American issue. The band is now on Polydor in the UK but remain on Capitol in North America. Same tracks on North American version but order is shuffled.

Cut Above the Rest

March 1979; Polydor POLD 5022

Produced by Sweet

Side 1: 1. Call Me (Scott) 3:38; 2. Play All Night (Scott, Tucker, Priest) 3:16; 3. Big Apple Waltz (Scott, Priest) 4:03; 4. Dorian Gray (Scott, Tucker, Priest) 4:38; 5. Discophony (Dis-kof-o-ne) (Scott, Moberley, Tucker, Priest) 5:57
Side 2: 1. Eye Games (Scott, Austin) 1:54; 2. Mother Earth (Scott, Priest) 6:27; 3. Hold Me (Scott) 4:46; 4. Stay With Me (Scott, Tucker, Priest) 5:02
Notes: European cover art features a wood-burned image of the band, versus the tape machine illustration used in the UK and North America.

Waters Edge

August 1980; Polydor POLS 1021
Produced by Sweet and Pip Williams
Side 1: 1. Sixties Man (Hutchins, Williams) 4:12; 2. Getting in the Mood for Love (Priest, Scott, Tucker) 3:04; 3. Tell the Truth (Priest, Scott, Moberley) 3:34; 4. Own Up (Priest, Scott, Tucker) 3:19; 5. Too Much Talking (McRiner) 3:57
Side 2: 1. Thank You for Loving Me (Scott, Moberley) 3:43; 2. At Midnight (Scott) 3:20; 3. Waters Edge (Priest, Scott, Tucker) 2:59; 4. Hot Shot Gambler (Priest) 3:34; 5. Give the Lady Some Respect (McRiner) 4:30
Notes: Issued in the US and Canada as *VI*, with completely different cover. The North American version contained the same ten tracks but with a different running order.

Identity Crisis

October 1982; Polydor 2311 179
Produced by Sweet
Side 1: 1. Identity Crisis (Priest, Scott, Tucker) 4:06; 2. New Shoes (Priest, Scott, Tucker) 3:22; 3. Two into One (Priest, Scott, Tucker) 2:37; 4. Love Is the Cure (Scott) 3:40; 5. It Makes Me Wonder (Priest, Scott, Tucker) 3:24
Side 2: 1. Hey Mama (Priest, Scott, Tucker) 3:28; 2. Falling in Love (Priest, Scott, Tucker) 4:42; 3. I Wish You Would (Arnold) 3:12; 4. Strange Girl (Priest, Scott, Tucker) 4:30
Notes: Issued only in Germany and Mexico.

SELECTED COMPILATIONS

The Sweet's Biggest Hits
December 1972; RCA, LSP 10384
Side 1. Wig-Wam Bam (Chinn, Chapman) 2:57; 2. Little Willy (Chinn, Chapman) 3:10;
3. Done Me Wrong All Right (Connolly, Priest, Tucker, Scott) 2:53; 4. Poppa Joe (Chinn,
Chapman) 3:07; 5. Funny Funny (Chinn, Chapman) 2:46; 6. Co-Co (Chinn, Chapman)
3:08
Side 2. Alexander Graham Bell (Chinn, Chapman) 2:50; 2. Chop Chop (Chinn, Chapman)
2:55; 3. You're Not Wrong for Loving Me (Connolly, Priest, Tucker, Scott) 2:44; 4. Jeanie
(Connolly, Priest, Tucker, Scott) 2:53; 5. Spotlight (Connolly, Priest, Tucker, Scott) 2:42
Notes: This first UK compilation is included here because much of it was non-LP,
including the band's latest spate of singles.

The Sweet
July 1973; Bell 1125
Produced by Phil Wainman
Side 1: 1. Little Willy (Chinn, Chapman) 3:13; 2. New York Connection (Connolly, Priest,
Tucker, Scott) 3:35; 3. Wig-Wam Bam (Chinn, Chapman) 3:03; 4. Done Me Wrong Alright
(Connolly, Priest, Tucker, Scott) 2:58; 5. Hell Raiser (Chinn, Chapman)
Side 2: 1. Blockbuster (Chinn, Chapman) 3:12; 2. Need a Lot of Lovin' (Connolly, Priest,
Tucker, Scott) 3:00; 3. Man from Mecca (Connolly, Priest, Tucker, Scott) 2:45; 4. Spotlight
(Connolly, Priest, Tucker, Scott) 2:47; 5. You're Not Wrong for Loving Me (Connolly,
Priest, Tucker, Scott) 2:58
Notes: Effectively the band's debut album in the US and Canada, despite it being a
compilation.

Desolation Boulevard
July 1975; Capitol ST-11395
Produced by Phil Wainman, Mike Chapman, Nicky Chinn, Sweet
Side 1: 1. Ballroom Blitz (Chinn, Chapman) 4:00; 2. The 6-Teens (Chinn, Chapman) 4:04;
3. No You Don't (Chinn, Chapman) 4:32; 4. A.C.D.C. (Chinn, Chapman) 3:24; 5. I Wanna
Be Committed (Chinn, Chapman) 3:12
Side 2: 1. Sweet F.A. (Connolly, Priest, Tucker, Scott) 6:12; 2. Fox on the Run (Connolly,
Priest, Tucker, Scott) 3:24; 3. Set Me Free (Scott) 3:56; 4. Into the Night (Scott) 4:22; 5.
Sold Gold Brass (Connolly, Priest, Tucker, Scott)
Notes: This US album shares the title and (essentially) the cover art with Sweet's third
album, but it is a compilation consisting mostly of tracks from *Sweet Fanny Adams*.

Strung Up

November 1975; RCA SPC 0001

Produced by Phil Wainman, Mike Chapman, Nicky Chinn, Sweet

Record 1: Side 1: 1. Hell Raiser (Chinn, Chapman) 3:50; 2. Burning/Someone Else Will (Connolly, Priest, Tucker, Scott) 5:30; 3. Rock 'n' Roll Disgrace (Connolly, Priest, Tucker, Scott) 4:15; 4. Need a Lot of Lovin' (Connolly, Priest, Tucker, Scott) 3:00

Record 1: Side 2: 1. Done Me Wrong All Right (Connolly, Priest, Tucker, Scott) 8:08; 2. You're Not Wrong for Loving Me (Connolly, Priest, Tucker, Scott) 3:28; 3. The Man with the Golden Arm (Elmer Bernstein, Sylvia Fine) 8:05

Notes: European-issue double album with gatefold sleeve consisting of a live disc recorded December 21, 1973 at the Rainbow Theatre in London, plus a compilation disc.

SELECTED SINGLES

Slow Motion/It's Lonely Out There (1968)

The Lollipop Man/Time (1969)

All You'll Ever Get from Me/The Juicer (1970)

Get on the Line/Mr. McGallagher (1970)

Funny Funny/You're Not Wrong for Loving Me (1971)

Co-Co/Done Me Wrong All Right (1971)

Alexander Graham Bell/Spotlight (1971)

Poppa Joe/Jeanie (1972)

Little Willy/Man from Mecca (1972)

Wig-Wam Bam/New York Connection (1972)

Blockbuster!/Need a Lot of Lovin' (1973)

Hell Raiser/Burning (1973)

Ballroom Blitz/Rock & Roll Disgrace (1973)

Teenage Rampage/Own Up, Take a Look at Yourself (1974)

The Six Teens/Burn on the Flame (1974)

Turn It Down/Someone Else Will (1974)

Peppermint Twist/Rebel Rouser (Australia, 1974

Ballroom Blitz/Restless (US, 1975)

Fox on the Run/Miss Demeanour (1975)

Action/Sweet F.A. (1975)

Action/Medusa (US, 1976)

The Lies in Your Eyes/Cockroach (1976)

4th of July/Restless (Australia, 1976)

Lost Angels/Funk It Up (David's Song) (1976)

Fever of Love/A Distinct Lack of Ancient (1977)
Fever of Love/Heartbreak Today (US, 1977)
Funk It Up (David's Song)/Funk It Up (David's Song) (12-inch Disco Mix)
(US, 1977)
Stairway to the Stars/Why Don't You Do It to Me (1977)
Love Is Like Oxygen/Cover Girl (1978)
California Nights/Show Me the Way (1978)
Call Me/Why Don't You (1979)
Mother Earth/Why Don't You (US, 1979)
Big Apple Waltz/Why Don't You (1979)
Give the Lady Some Respect/Tall Girls (1980)
Sixties Man/Oh Yeah! (1980)

SELECTED POST-1982 PRODUCT

Sweet (Andy Scott's and Mick Tucker's version) – *Live at the Marquee*
(1989)
Andy Scott's Sweet – *"A"* (1992)
Brian Connolly's Sweet – *Let's Go* (1995)
Sweet (Andy Scott's version) – *Sweetlife* (2002)
Sweet (Steve Priest's version) – *Live! In America* (2009)
Sweet (Andy Scott's version) – *Full Circle* (2024)

INTERVIEWS WITH THE AUTHOR

Brown, Phill. July 9, 2020.
Levine, Barry. 2009.
Mack, Reinhold. November 29, 2017.
Moberley, Gary. June 26, 2020.
Platt, Tony. July 3, 2020.
Priest, Steve. May 5, 2008.
Priest, Steve. June 18, 2008.
Priest, Steve. 2009.
Quatro, Suzi. January 24, 2019.
Scabies, Rat. 2009.
Scott, Andy. 2009.
Scott, Andy. June 10, 2013.
Scott, Andy. June 18, 2020.
Smith, Stuart. June 26, 2009.
Verity, John. December 20, 2019.

ADDITIONAL CITATIONS

Berkeley Gazette, The. *Give Us a Wink* record review by Evan Hosie. March 12, 1976.
Billboard. Sweet's Smell of Success Enhanced by Nippon Tour by Nat Freedland. September 25, 1976.
Billboard. *Level Headed* record review. January 21, 1978.
Cash Box. *Desolation Boulevard* record review. May 24, 1975.
Cash Box. Sweet: Label Change Helped the Image. February 7, 1976.
Cash Box. *Give Us a Wink* record review. February 21, 1976.
Cash Box. Sweet live review. April 10, 1976.
Cash Box. Capitol Concentrating on Crop of New Performers by David Budge. May 1, 1976.
Cash Box. Andy Scott interview. March 17, 1978.
Cash Box. *Cut Above the Rest* record review. April 28, 1978.
Circus. Sweet but not Saccharine by Dan Nooger. 1976.
Circus. *Off the Record* record review by Charles Bogle. 1977.
Circus. Sweet's *Level Headed* Marks Classical Shift by Chris Charlesworth. Issue No.179. April 13, 1978.
Creem. *Give Us a Wink* record review by Richard Riegel. Vol. 7, No.12. May 1976.
Dayton Daily News. *Give Us a Wink* record review by David C. Scott. June 13, 1976.
Disc. *Sweet Fanny Adams* record review by FC. May 4, 1974.
Fort Worth Star-Telegram. England's Sweet – Give Them a Wink, and a Listen Too by Gerry Barker. March 12, 1976.
Indianapolis News, The. A Rock 'n' Roll Band, Not an Army: The Sweet by Cameron Crowe. December 1, 1975.
Leader-Post, The. Fans enthusiastic about Priest and latest incarnation of Sweet by Christo-

pher Tessmer. February 26, 2009.

Ling, Dave. Interview with Andy Scott.

Los Angeles Times, The. Good News for Fans of Sweet by Robert Hilburn. March 6, 1976.

Melody Maker. Sweeties! by Chris Welch. January 20, 1973.

Melody Maker. Inside the Hit Factory by Jeff Ward. February 16, 1974.

Melody Maker. Sweet - the hit and run band by Jeff Ward. June 1, 1974.

Melody Maker. "The Six Teens" review by Jeff Ward. July 6, 1974.

Melody Maker. Why Sweet are sour with TV by Allan Jones. March 29, 1975.

Messenger-Press. In the Groove: Original Interview, Sweet, by Steve Wosahla. July 13, 1978.

Miami News, the. *Desolation Boulevard* record review by Jon Marlowe. May 30, 1975.

Muncie Star, The. Critic Discards Scruples to Expose *Off the Record* by Steve Freedman. July 10, 1977.

New Musical Express. "Co-Co" review by Derek Johnson. May 29, 1971.

New Musical Express. "Alexander Graham Bell" review by Derek Johnson. September 25, 1971.

New Musical Express. We're not bitter… SWEET by Julie Webb. March 18, 1972.

New Musical Express. Live review by Julie Webb. June 9, 1973.

Phonograph Record. *The Sweet* record review by Alan Betrock. September 1973.

Phonograph Record. *Sweet Fanny Adams* record review by Ron Ross. August 1974.

Province, The. Rockers return in their own sweet time by Tom Harrison. November 16, 1990.

Record, The. *Give Us a Wink* record review. March 7, 1976.

Record Mirror. Sweet FA? by Genny Hall. April 13, 1974.

Record Mirror. *Desolation Boulevard* record review by L.I. November 2, 1974.

Record Mirror. We're Not Dead Over Here by Jan Iles. December 14, 1974.

Record Mirror. 100 per cent Sweet by Ray Fox-Cumming. July 26, 1975.

Record Mirror. *Give Us a Wink* record review by David Hancock. February 28, 1976.

Record Mirror. *Level Headed* record review by John Shearlaw. February 4, 1978.

Record Mirror. Sweet Hammersmith Odeon by Robin Smith. March 4, 1978.

Record World. Ed Leffler on the Function of Personal Management by Eliot Sekuler. October 11, 1975.

Record Mirror. *Waters Edge* record review by Dante Bonutto. August 9, 1980.

Rolling Stone. *The Sweet* record review by James Isaacs. IssueNo. 146. October 25, 1973.

Rolling Stone. *Desolation Boulevard* record review by Gordon Fletcher. Issue No.192. July 31, 1975.

Rolling Stone. The Sweet's Blitz of Hits: 'They Were All Crap' by Cameron Crowe. No.202. December 18, 1975.

Scrantonian Tribune. Sweet Plans Assault on Concert Audiences by Andy Secher. June 11, 1978.

Scrantonian Tribune. British Rockers Are Sweet by Rob Patterson. October 19, 1980.

Shakin' Street Gazette. *Sweet Fanny Adams* record review by Gary Sperrazza. September 11, 1974.

Sydney Morning Herald, The. Sweet album for giveaway. July 17, 1977.

Times and Democrat, The. Sweet by Stephen Ford. February 23, 1976.

Zoo World. How Sweet It Is! July 5, 1973.

Zoo World. *The Sweet* record review by Jon Tiven. October 11, 1973.

ACKNOWLEDGEMENTS

The author would like to acknowledge his buddy Kevin Julie for his fine research work concerning the Sweet press archive. Also, special thanks to Agustin Garcia de Paredes who applied his eagle eye to a copy edit of this thing.

As for photographers gracious enough to contribute to this project, the esteemed Dick Barnatt has been credited for his pictures in the colour sections. But he is also represented in the body of the book, where pictures are not captioned (hence, this attempt to credit from this remote location at the back of the book!). Ergo those are his live shots in the *Give Us a Wink* chapter, those are his posed christening shots in the *Off the Record* chapter and finally, those are his awesome Clearwell Castle pictures in the *Level Headed* chapter.

The *Cut Above the Rest* contains a bunch of cool candid shots by Phil Matthews (there are two of his from 1974 in the *Sweet Fanny Adams* chapter too) and the Epilogue chapter has a few extras of Brian from 1985.

ABOUT THE AUTHOR

At approximately 7900 (with over 7000 appearing in his books), Martin has unofficially written more record reviews than anybody in the history of music writing across all genres. Additionally, Martin has penned approximately 130 books on hard rock, heavy metal, classic rock and record collecting. He was Editor-In-Chief of the now retired *Brave Words & Bloody Knuckles*, Canada's foremost metal publication for 14 years, and has also contributed to *Revolver, Guitar World, Goldmine, Record Collector, bravewords.com, lollipop.com* and *hardradio.com*, with many record label band bios and liner notes to his credit as well. Additionally, Martin has been a regular contractor to Banger Films, having worked for two years as researcher on the award-winning documentary *Rush: Beyond the Lighted Stage*, on the writing and research team for the 11-episode *Metal Evolution* and on the ten-episode *Rock Icons*, both for VH1 Classic. Additionally, Martin is the writer of the original metal genre chart used in *Metal: A Headbanger's Journey* and throughout the *Metal Evolution* episodes. Martin currently resides in Toronto and can be reached through martinp@inforamp.net or www.martinpopoff.com.

MARTIN POPOFF
A COMPLETE BIBLIOGRAPHY

2024: Judas Priest: Album by Album, Bowie: Rock 'n' Roll Chameleon, Behind the Lines: Genesis on Record: 1978 – 1997, Entangled: Genesis on Record 1969 - 1976, Run with the Wolf: Rainbow on Record, Van Halen at 50, Honesty Is No Excuse: Thin Lizzy on Record, Pictures at Eleven: Robert Plant Album by Album, Perfect Water: The Rebel Imaginos

2023: Kiss at 50, The Electric Church: The Biography, Dominance and Submission: The Blue Öyster Cult Canon, The Who and Quadrophenia, Wild Mood Swings: Disintegrating The Cure Album by Album, AC/DC at 50

2022: Pink Floyd and The Dark Side of the Moon: 50 Years, Killing the Dragon: Dio in the '90s and 2000s, Feed My Frankenstein: Alice Cooper, the Solo Years, Easy Action: The Original Alice Cooper Band, Lively Arts: The Damned Deconstructed, Yes: A Visual Biography II: 1982 – 2022, Bowie @ 75, Dream Evil: Dio in the '80s, Judas Priest: A Visual Biography, UFO: A Visual Biography

2021: Hawkwind: A Visual Biography, Loud 'n' Proud: Fifty Years of Nazareth, Yes: A Visual Biography, Uriah Heep: A Visual Biography, Driven: Rush in the '90s and "In the End," Flaming Telepaths: Imaginos Expanded and Specified, Rebel Rouser: A Sweet User Manual

2020: The Fortune: On the Rocks with Angel, Van Halen: A Visual Biography, Thin Lizzy: A Visual Biography, Limelight: Rush in the '80s, Empire of the Clouds: Iron Maiden in the 2000s, Blue Öyster Cult: A Visual Biography, Anthem: Rush in the '70s, Denim and Leather: Saxon's First Ten Years, Black Funeral: Into the Coven with Mercyful Fate

2019: Satisfaction: 10 Albums That Changed My Life, Holy Smoke: Iron Maiden in the '90s, Sensitive to Light: The Rainbow Story, Where Eagles Dare: Iron Maiden in the '80s, Aces High: The Top 250 Heavy Metal Songs of the '80s, Judas Priest: Turbo 'til Now, Born Again! Black Sabbath in the Eighties and Nineties

2018: Riff Raff: The Top 250 Heavy Metal Songs of the '70s, Lettin' Go: UFO in the '80s and '90s, Queen: Album by Album, Unchained: A Van Halen User Manual, Iron Maiden: Album by Album, Sabotage! Black Sabbath in the Seventies, Welcome to My Nightmare: 50 Years of Alice Cooper, Judas Priest: Decade of Domination, Popoff Archive – 6: American Power Metal, Popoff Archive – 5: European Power Metal, The Clash: All the Albums, All the Songs

2017: Led Zeppelin: All the Albums, All the Songs, AC/DC: Album by Album, Lights Out: Surviving the '70s with UFO, Tornado of Souls: Thrash's Titanic Clash, Caught in a Mosh: The Golden Era of Thrash, Rush: Album by Album, Beer Drinkers and Hell Raisers: The Rise of Motörhead, Metal Collector: Gathered Tales from Headbangers, Hit the Lights: The Birth of Thrash, Popoff Archive – 4: Classic Rock, Popoff Archive – 3: Hair Metal

2016: Popoff Archive – 2: Progressive Rock, Popoff Archive – 1: Doom Metal, Rock the Nation: Montrose, Gamma and Ronnie Redefined, Punk Tees: The Punk Revolution in 125 T-Shirts, Metal Heart: Aiming High with Accept, Ramones at 40, Time and a Word: The Yes Story

2015: Kickstart My Heart: A Mötley Crüe Day-by-Day, This Means War: The Sunset Years of the NWOBHM, Wheels of Steel: The Explosive Early Years of the NWOBHM, Swords and Tequila: Riot's Classic First Decade, Who Invented Heavy Metal?, Sail Away: Whitesnake's Fantastic Voyage

2014: Live Magnetic Air: The Unlikely Saga of the Superlative Max Webster, Steal Away the Night: An Ozzy Osbourne Day-by-Day, The Big Book of Hair Metal, Sweating Bullets: The Deth and Rebirth of Megadeth, Smokin' Valves: A Headbanger's Guide to 900 NWOBHM Records

2013: The Art of Metal (co-edit with Malcolm Dome), 2 Minutes to Midnight: An Iron Maiden Day-by-Day, Metallica: The Complete Illustrated History, Rush: The Illustrated History, Ye Olde Metal: 1979, Scorpions: Top of the Bill - updated and reissued as Wind of Change: The Scorpions Story in 2016

2012: Epic Ted Nugent, Fade To Black: Hard Rock Cover Art of the Vinyl Age, It's Getting Dangerous: Thin Lizzy 81-12, We Will Be Strong: Thin Lizzy 76-81, Fighting My Way Back: Thin Lizzy 69-76, The Deep Purple Royal Family: Chain of Events '80 – '11, The Deep Purple Royal Family: Chain of Events Through '79 - reissued as The Deep Purple Family Year by Year books

2011: Black Sabbath FAQ, The Collector's Guide to Heavy Metal: Volume 4: The '00s (co-authored with David Perri)

2010: Goldmine Standard Catalog of American Records 1948 – 1991, 7th Edition

2009: Goldmine Record Album Price Guide, 6th Edition, Goldmine 45 RPM Price Guide, 7th Edition, A Castle Full of Rascals: Deep Purple '83 – '09, Worlds Away: Voivod and the Art of Michel Langevin, Ye Olde Metal: 1978

2008: Gettin' Tighter: Deep Purple '68 – '76, All Access: The Art of the Backstage Pass, Ye Olde Metal: 1977, Ye Olde Metal: 1976

2007: Judas Priest: Heavy Metal Painkillers, Ye Olde Metal: 1973 to 1975, The Collector's Guide to Heavy Metal: Volume 3: The Nineties, Ye Olde Metal: 1968 to 1972

2006: Run for Cover: The Art of Derek Riggs, Black Sabbath: Doom Let Loose, Dio: Light Beyond the Black

2005: The Collector's Guide to Heavy Metal: Volume 2: The Eighties, Rainbow: English Castle Magic, UFO: Shoot Out the Lights, The New Wave of British Heavy Metal Singles

2004: Blue Öyster Cult: Secrets Revealed! – update and reissued 2009); updated and reissued as Agents of Fortune: The Blue Öyster Cult Story 2016, Contents Under Pressure: 30 Years of Rush at Home & Away, The Top 500 Heavy Metal Albums of All Time

2003: The Collector's Guide to Heavy Metal: Volume 1: The Seventies, The Top 500 Heavy Metal Songs of All Time

2001: Southern Rock Review

2000: Heavy Metal: 20th Century Rock and Roll, The Goldmine Price Guide to Heavy Metal Records

1997: The Collector's Guide to Heavy Metal

1993: Riff Kills Man! 25 Years of Recorded Hard Rock & Heavy Metal

See martinpopoff.com for complete details and ordering information.

SWEET Fanny Adams

Desolation Boulevard
SWEET

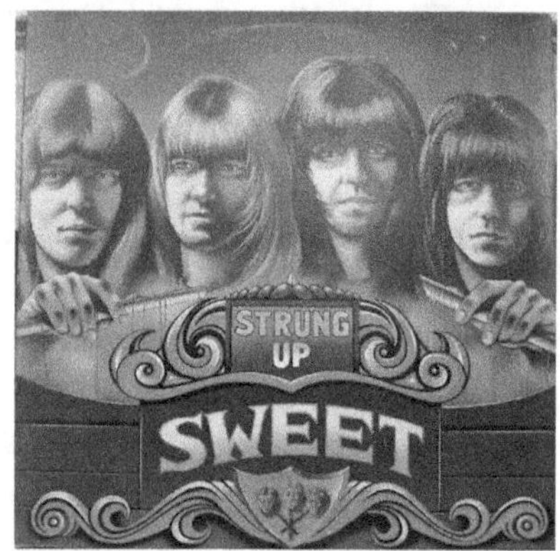
STRUNG UP
SWEET

SWEET
"GIVE US A WINK!"

RCA
SWEET

THE SWEET CHARTS

compiled by
Aleksey A. Kononow

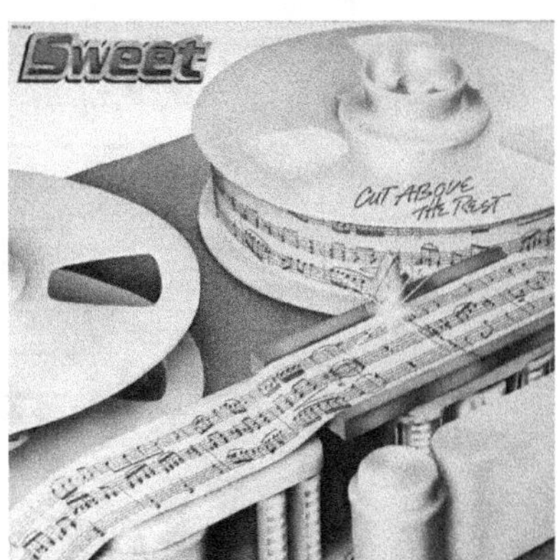

ALBUMS	UK	USA	Canada	Germany	Austria	Switzerland
SWEET FANNY ADAMS	27			2	6	
DESOLATION BOULEVARD		25	5	9		
STRUNG UP				17	10	12
GIVE US A WINK		27	11	9		11
OFF THE RECORD		151	83	11	5	5
LEVEL HEADED		52	52	15	17	4
CUT ABOVE THE REST		151		49		

Singles	UK	USA	Canada	Germany
Funny, Funny	13			5
Co-Co	2	99		1
Alexander Graham Bell	33			24
Poppa Joe	11			3
Little Willy	4	3	1	1
Wig Wam Bam	4			1
Blockbuster!	1	73	30	1
Hell Raiser	2			1
Ballroom Blitz	2	5	1	1
Teenage Rampage	2			1
The Six Teens	9			4
Turn It Down	41			4
Fox On The Run	2	5	2	1
Action	15	20	5	2
The Lies In Your Eyes	35			5
Lost Angels				13
Fever Of Love		118		9
Love Is Like Oxygen	9	8	8	10
California Nights		76	86	23

Singles	Netherlands	Italy	Spain	Ireland	Denmark
Funny, Funny	1		28	7	1
Co-Co	3	2	2	3	1
Alexander Graham Bell	38				
Poppa Joe	1		10	16	1
Little Willy	6			9	1
Wig Wam Bam	6			4	1
Blockbuster!	1	12	12	1	1
Hell Raiser	4		27	2	1
Ballroom Blitz	2		6	1	3
Teenage Rampage	11		19	1	2
The Six Teens	10		28	15	1
Turn It Down			17		2
Fox On The Run	2		7	2	1
Action	5			7	3
The Lies In Your Eyes	9				3
Lost Angels	58				18
Fever Of Love	52				
Love Is Like Oxygen	20	12	13	8	
California Nights					

Netherlands	Italy	Denmark	Norway	Sweden	Finland	Australia	New Zealand
		1	12	4	9	33	
		4	17	2	9	13	17
	25	5	12	4		9	
		4	15	3		17	
			20	14	28	51	
26				26		40	

Austria	Switzerland	France	Belgium (Vlaanderen)	Belgium (Wallonie)
			1	4
	1	15	1	2
	2		1	4
	2		7	19
5	2		3	10
1	3		2	1
4	3		3	26
5	3	13	2	5
16	2	37	10	3
9	6	37	18	6
14				33
3	3	37	4	9
3	4		8	19
17	14		12	33
11	16			34
12	15			
23	6		15	

Norway	Sweden	Finland	Australia	New Zealand	South Africa
2	1	5	93		1
2	2	17	29	2	1
2	2	1	70	14	12
7	3	4	65	7	9
6	18	4	20	10	8
3		4	29	1	7
5		4	49	4	
2	3	12	1	1	3
2	7	5	12	7	
7		8	48		
4	10	11			
2	6	12	1	3	1
2	2	12	4	12	
	6	22	14		
	5		74		
	7				10
			9	4	

charts (source)	debut	peak	weeks	chart-runs & extra notes
Funny Funny single				
UK (Record Mirror)	13/03/1971	13	14	On March 6th 1971 single reached Breakers chart (no.42; like Bubbling Under chart in Billboard on next week enters main singles' chart. (At this time, from February 6th to March 20th the main singles chart was reduced to Top-40, March 27th the chart became Top-50 again). 38-33-30[Mar27]-28-20-15-14-14-13-13-21-37-43- weeks from March 13th to June 12th 1971, when n single Co-Co enters charts!) Single reached no.13 on May 8th and 15th 1971. No.14 in Melody Maker, no.15 in NME.
GERMANY (Der Musikmarkt)	10/05/1971	5	21	10/05/1971: 34 (on May 17th single drop-off fro charts, but then back for 20 weeks!) 24/05/1971: 28-21-18-13-10-9-10-9-7-5-7-11-16- 39-27-33-43-50 (20 weeks from May 24th to Octob 1971) Single reached no.5 on July 26th 1971 (single C no.11 this week).
BELGIUM, Vlaanderen (Ultratop)	10/04/1971	1	14	24-14-7-4-1-1-1-2-2-2-8-16-20-26 (14 weeks fro April 10th to July 10th 1971; on June 26th next Co-Co enters charts) Single reached no.1 for 3 weeks from May 8th to
BELGIUM, Wallonie (Ultratop)	17/04/1971	4	17	29-22-17-14-11-8-6-7-8-7-5-4-7-10-16-29-44 (17 from April 17th to August 7th 1971) Single reached no.4 on July 3rd 1971.
NETHERLANDS (Nationale hitparade)	10/04/1971	1	10	14-4-2-1-1-1-3-6-13-14 (10 weeks from April 10 June 12th 1971) Single reached no.1 for 3 weeks from May 1st to In Nederlandse Top 40 (Radio Veronica) single reached no.1 (for 2 weeks).
SPAIN (Superventas)	19/06/1971	28	2	28-30 "Sólo éxitos. Año a año. 1959-2002" book given that single reached no.12 (but this is the rest combining information from different sources).
IRELAND (Larry Gogan book)	1/05/1971	7	4	
DENMARK (Danmarks Radio Top 10)	26/05/1971	1	14	1-1-1-1-1-1-1-1-2-3-4-7-9-8 (14 weeks from May to August 25th 1971) 8 weeks on Top! On August 18th 1971 next single Co enters charts. (Danmarks Radio Top 10 was based on votes of listeners, not on sales; in October 1972 this c was renamed to Tiparaden)
NORWAY (VG-lista)	23/06/1971	2	13	10-*-6-4-4-5-5-2-3-4-4-7-7 (13 weeks from Jur 23rd to September 22nd 1971; there is no chart June 30th 1971) Single reached no.2 on August 11th 1971 (on this week no.1 was Chirpy Chirpy Cheep Cheep by Midd The Road).
SWEDEN (Kvällstoppen)	25/05/1971	1	12	10-6-2-1-1-2-3-4-4-8-13-20 (12 weeks from May 2 to August 10th 1971) Single reached no.1 on June 15th & 22nd 1971. In Tio i Topp chart single also became no.1.
FINLAND (Suosikki)	Aug/1971	5	11 months	28-11-11-16-11-12-5-7-8-18-19 (11 months from A 1971 to June 1972) Single reached no.5 on February 72 charts (Popp was no.2 this month).
AUSTRALIA (Australian Music Report)	16/08/1971	93	4	
SOUTH AFRICA (Springbok Radio)	28/05/1971	1	16	
Co-Co single				
UK (Record Mirror)	12/06/1971	2	15	On June 5th 1971 single reached Breakers chart (no.52) and on next week enters main singles ch 33-19-9-5-2-2-3-3-5-10-14-22-23-38-44 (15 weeks June 12th to September 18th 1971) Single reached no.2 on July 10th & 17th 1971 (bot week no.1 was Middle Of The Road with "Chirpy C Cheep Cheep") No.2 in Melody Maker, no.2 in NME.
USA (Billboard)	2/10/1971	99	2	On September 11th 1971 single reached Billboard Bubbling Under chart for 3 weeks (106-105-103) then enters Hot 100. 99-99 (2 weeks from October 2nd to 9th 1971) On October 23rd 1971 single again appeared at Billboard Bubbling Under chart for 1 week (no.1 No.85 in Cash Box, no.93 in Record World.

charts (source)	debut	peak	weeks	chart-runs & extra notes
...ANY (Der Musikmarkt)	19/07/1971	1	27	19-11-5-4-2-2-1-1-1-1-1-1-2-1-2-2-6-6-11-10-17-20-26-40-42-48-49 (27 weeks from July 19th 1971 to January 17th 1972) Single reached no.1 for 7 weeks! Stay on Top of charts 6 weeks from August 30th to October 4th and then on October 18th 1971. In October-November 1971 Sweet toured in Germany.
...ERLAND (Swiss National Radio charts «...eller auf dem Plattenteller»)	17/08/1971	1	14	8-4-1-1-1-1-1-1-3-3-4-5-8-9 (14 weeks from August 17th to November 16th 1971) Single reached no.1 for 6 weeks! (from August 31st to October 5th 1971)
...CE (Centre D'Information et de ...entation du Disque)	Sep/1971	15	1 month	
...UM, Vlaanderen (Ultratop)	26/06/1971	1	15	23-14-7-2-2-2-2-2-1-2-7-12-13-20-26 (15 weeks from June 26th to October 10th 1971; on June 26th single Funny Funny was no.16) Single reached no.1 on August 21st 1971. Before this single was no.2 for 5 weeks from July 17th to August 14th (and no.1 was Michel Delpech with Pour un flirt).
...UM, Wallonie (Ultratop)	3/07/1971	2	19	46-30-22-17-11-11-9-6-3-2-3-4-5-10-11-12-17-28-50 (19 weeks from July 3rd to November 6th 1971) Single reached no.2 on September 4th 1971 (no.1 was Gilbert Montagné with The Fool).
...ERLANDS (Nationale hitparade)	19/06/1971	3	11	30-11-5-4-3-4-3-15-15-18-27 (11 weeks from June 19th to August 28th 1971) Single reached no.3 on July 17th & 31st 1971. In Nederlandse Top 40 (Radio Veronica) single also reached no.3.
...(Musica&Dischi)	2/10/1971	2	23	
...(Superventas)	9/10/1971	2	21	30-12-6-4-4-2-2-2-4-6-4-8-6-10-8-9-11-13-13-22-30 (21 weeks from October 9th 1971 to February 26th 1972) Single reached no.2 on November 13th, 20th & 27th 1971 (no.1 on these weeks was Mamy Blue by The Pops Tops). "Sólo éxitos. Año a año. 1959-2002" book given info that single reached no.3 and spent 22 weeks in charts (but this is the result of combining information from different sources).
...ND (Larry Gogan book)	26/06/1971	3	1	
...MARK (Danmarks Radio Top 10)	18/08/1971	1	5	1-2-3-*-3-4 (5 weeks from August 18th to September 22nd 1971; there is no charts on September 8th 1971)
...WAY (VG-lista)	11/08/1971	2	11	9-5-3-3-3-2-3-3-*-*-*-7-*-9-10 (11 weeks from August 11th to November 17th 1971; on August 11th 1971 Funny Funny was no.2; there is no charts on October 6th, 13th, 20th, November 3rd 1971) Single reached no.2 on September 15th 1971 (Funny Funny was no.7 this week, no.1 was still Chirpy Chirpy Cheep Cheep by Middle Of The Road, this single was on Top of Norwegian charts for 11 weeks).
...DEN (Kvällstoppen)	20/07/1971	2	13	20-11-5-2-2-2-2-2-2-2-4-9-15 (13 weeks from July 20th to October 12th 1971) Single reached no.2 on August 10th, 17th, 24th &31st, September 7th & 14th 1971 (no.1 on these weeks was Indian Reservation by The Raiders) and on September 21st 1971 (no.1 on this week was Fireball LP by Deep Purple; Kvällstoppen chart contained both LPs and singles). In Tio i Topp chart single also became no.2.
...AND (Suosikki)	Sep/1971	17	7 months	31-17-20 (3 months from September to November 1971) Feb/72: 19-18-17 (3 months more from February to April 1972) Jun/72: 27 Sisältää hitin book given info that single reached no.15.
...TRALIA (Go-Set)	30/10/1971	29	5	31-30-31-29-31 (5 weeks from October 30th to November 27th 1971) In Australian Music Report chart single reached no.42.
...ZEALAND (The Listener)	27/08/1971	2	11	On August 13th 1971 Co-Co reached Forecast list as no.21, then 1 week was off the charts and on August 27th appeared in main Top-20. 20-18-7-5-4-3-2-3-4-6-11 (11 weeks from August 27th to November 5th 1971) Single reached no.2 on October 8th 1971 (no.1 was Delaney & Bonnie with Never Ending Song Of Love)
...TH AFRICA (Springbok Radio)	30/07/1971	1	18	

charts (source)	debut	peak	weeks	chart-runs & extra notes
All You'll Ever Get From Me single				
SWEDEN (Tio i Topp)	27/11/1971	7	2	
Alexander Graham Bell single				
UK (Record Mirror)	16/10/1971	33	5	43-42-34-33-39 (5 weeks from October 16th to November 13th 1971) Single reached no.33 on November 6th 1971.
GERMANY (Der Musikmarkt)	8/11/1971	24	11	31-33-48-24-29-41-41-25-27-32-40 (11 weeks fr November 8th 1971 to January 17th 1972) Single reached no.24 on November 29th 1971 (Si Co-Co no.10 this week).
NETHERLANDS (Radio Veronica)	13/11/1971	38	2	On October 16th 1971 single reached Tipparade (like Bubbling Under chart in Billboard) for and on November 13th 1971 enters main singles' (Nederlandse Top 40). 38-39
FUNNY, HOW SWEET CO-CO CAN BE album				
DENMARK (Danmarks Radio Top 20)	16/10/1974	15	4	15-18-17-19 (4 weeks from October 16th to Nove 6th 1974)
FINLAND (Suosikki)	Feb/1972	2	9 months	Titled as Funny Funny, How Sweet Co-Co Can Be 6-2-3-3-8-9-16 (7 months from February to Aug 1972) Oct/72: 18-19 (2 charts more) Album reached no.2 in March 1972 (no.1 was Hu compilation from Scandia label). Sisältää hitin book given info that album rea no.1 (because for this book was used informat from several different lists and consolidated one list, but excluded compilations of various artistes).
Poppa Joe single				
UK (Record Mirror)	5/02/1972	11	12	46-30-26-14-11-12-12-17-22-28-38-41 (12 weeks February 5th to April 22nd 1972) Single reached no.11 on March 4th 1972. No.10 in NME, No.11 in Melody Maker.
USA (Cash Box)	18/03/1972	105	5	111-109-105-105-110 (5 weeks from March 18th t April 15th 1972; Looking Ahead chart only, not main Top 100) No.115 in Record World (also 101-150 chart, nc Top 100). Not appeared in Billboard charts.
GERMANY (Der Musikmarkt)	14/02/1972	3	22	48-14-9-6-6-3-4-4-3-3-3-6-3-6-7-6-11-12-21-2 weeks from February 14th to July 3rd 1972) 17/07/1972: 31 Single reached no.3 for 6 times: on March 20th April 10th-17th-24th, May 1st & 15th 1972.
SWITZERLAND (Swiss National Radio charts «Bestseller auf dem Plattenteller»)	15/02/1972	2	14	9-6-3-2-3-3-3-3-3-5-7-7-7-9 (14 weeks from Feb 15th to May 16th 1972) Single reached no.2 on March 7th 1972 (no.1 was Middle Of The Road with Sacramento)
BELGIUM, Vlaanderen (Ultratop)	19/02/1972	1	17	19-11-5-3-2-1-1-1-2-3-4-7-8-9-11-11-21 (17 wee from February 19th to June 10th 1972) Single reached no.1 for 3 weeks! (from March 2 April 8th 1972)
BELGIUM, Wallonie (Ultratop)	26/02/1972	4	19	48-24-15-10-9-8-7-4-5-8-9-9-8-12-15-21-27-33-4 weeks from February 26th to July 1st 1972) Single reached no.4 on April 15th 1972.
NETHERLANDS (Nationale hitparade)	5/02/1972	1	14	22-14-5-2-2-1-1-1-2-7-10-13-24 (14 weeks fro February 5th to May 6th 1972) Single reached no.1 for 4 weeks! (from March 1 April 1st 1972) In Nederlandse Top 40 (Radio Veronica) single reached no.1.
SPAIN (Superventas)	8/04/1972	10	9	28-24-20-13-13-10-15-19-24 (9 weeks from April to June 3rd 1972) Single reached no.10 on May 13th 1972. "Sólo éxitos. Año a año. 1959-2002" book given that single reached no.21 (but this is the res combining information from different sources).
IRELAND (Larry Gogan book)	19/02/1972	16	1	
DENMARK (Danmarks Radio Top 10)	9/02/1972	1	8	1-1-1-1-4-3-5-7 (8 weeks from February 9th to M 29th 1972)

charts (source)	debut	peak	weeks	chart-runs & extra notes
...WAY (VG-lista)	26/01/1972	2	14	10-5-4-2-2-2-2-2-3-3-3-5-8-10 (14 weeks from January 26th to April 26th 1972) Single reached no.2 for 5 weeks on February 16th & 23rd, March 1st, 8th & 15th 1972 (no.1 on these weeks was Sacramento by Middle Of The Road).
...DEN (Kvällstoppen)	1/02/1972	2	13	20-12-5-2-3-4-5-5-6-7-10-11-17 (13 weeks from February 1st to April 25th 1972) Single reached no.2 on February 22nd 1972 (no.1 on this week was Jesus Christ Superstar LP; this chart contains both albums and singles). No.1 in Tio i Topp chart.
...ND (Suosikki)	Jan/1972	1	11 months	20-2-3-1-5-3-4-5-8-11-23 (11 months from January to November 1972) Single reached no.1 at April charts (Funny Funny was no.8 this month).
...RALIA (Australian Music Report)	17/04/1972	70	15	
...ZEALAND (The Listener)	21/04/1972	14	6	On April 7th 1972 Poppa Joe reached Forecast list as no.24, then 1 week was off the charts and on April 21st reached main Top-20. 19-15-15-14-15-14 (6 weeks from April 21st to May 26th 1972) Single reached no.14 on May 12th & 26th 1972.
...H AFRICA (Springbok Radio)	17/03/1972	12	9	

Little Willy single

charts (source)	debut	peak	weeks	chart-runs & extra notes
...(Record Mirror)	10/06/1972	4	14	47-23-8-4-4-6-6-11-17-20-28-37-45-50 (14 weeks from June 10th to September 9th 1972, when next single Wig-Wam Bam debured at charts!) Single reached no.4 on July 1st & 8th 1972. No.3 in NME, No.4 in Melody Maker.
...(Billboard)	20/01/1973	3	23	On January 13th 1973 single reached Billboard Bubbling Under chart (no.119) and on next week enters Hot 100. 99-92-89-86-77-74-60-49-36-32-25-20-12-7-5-3-3-3-7-8-24-23-37 (23 weeks + 1 week Bubbling Under from January 13th to June 23rd 1973) Single reached no.3 for 3 weeks on May 5th & 12th (on these weeks no.1 was Tie A Yellow Ribbon Round The Old Oak Tree single by Dawn feat. Tony Orlando), and on May 19th (no.1 was You Are Sunshine Of My Life by Stevie Wonder). No.3 in Cash Box, no.3 in Record World. In Billboard's 1973-year-end charts (published on December 29th 1973) Little Willy no.18 («Top Pop Singles»), The Sweet no.64 («Top Singles ARTISTS») and no.20 («Top Singles New ARTISTS»). In Cash Box 1973-year-end charts (published on December 29th, 1973) Little Willy no.51 («Singles of 1973» categorie), The Sweet no.6 («Best Artists of 1973 on singles» categorie, «New Groups - Singles» sub-categorie). In Record World's 1973-year-end charts (published on December 29th, 1973) The Sweet became no.3 (End Pop Singles Awards, Top New Male Group).
...ADA (RPM)	10/02/1973	1	22	82-80-77-72-66-59-39-24-18-14-14-9-8-6-6-5-1-4-8-12-27-37 (22 weeks from February 10th to June 30th 1973) Single reached no.1 on May 26th 1973. In RPM's 1973-year-end charts (published on December 29th 1973) Little Willy no.17 («Top 100 Singles of '73»).
...MANY (Der Musikmarkt)	12/06/1972	1	20	33-22-8-5-7-5-2-3-4-1-4-4-4-4-7-10-16-17-27-29 (2 weeks from June 12th to October 23rd 1972; when this single enters charts other Sweet's single Poppa Joe was no.11) Single reached no.1 on August 14th 1972.
...ZERLAND (Swiss National Radio charts «...tseller auf dem Plattenteller»)	27/06/1972	2	12	9-7-6-6-3-2-4-6-8-8-9-9 (12 weeks from June 27th to September 19th 1972) Single reached no.2 on August 8th 1972 (no.1 was Neil Diamond with Song Sung Blue)
...GIUM, Vlaanderen (Ultratop)	17/06/1972	7	12	22-12-10-10-8-7-8-13-20-20-26-28 (12 weeks from June 17th to September 2nd 1972) Single reached no.7 on July 22nd 1972.
...GIUM, Wallonie (Ultratop)	8/07/1972	19	9	43-35-31-26-22-19-25-34-45 (9 weeks from July 8th to September 2nd 1972) Single reached no.19 on August 12th 1972.
...HERLANDS (Nationale hitparade)	3/06/1972	6	7	26-14-11-7-6-13-20 (7 weeks from June 3rd to July 15th 1972) Single reached no.6 on July 1st 1972. No.7 in Nederlandse Top 40 (Radio Veronica).
...AND (Larry Gogan book)	29/06/1972	9	4	

charts (source)	debut	peak	weeks	chart-runs & extra notes
DENMARK (Danmarks Radio Top 10)	12/07/1972	1	11	2-*-1-2-2-1-2-3-3-6-6-3 (11 weeks from July 1 September 27th 1972; there is no charts on Jul 1972) Single reached no.1 on July 26th & August 16th Danmarks Radio Top 10 (Tiparaden) was based o of listeners. In October 1972 Danmarks Radio to compile another charts (titled as Hit-para which was based on sales. Little Willy reache in this chart.
NORWAY (VG-lista)	30/08/1972	7	6	9-8-7-7-9-10 (6 weeks from August 30th to Octo 1972) Single reached no.7 on September 13th & 20th 19
SWEDEN (Tio i Topp)	6/08/1972	3	6	
FINLAND (Suosikki)	Jun/1972	4	10 months	7-5-4-6-4-7-9-11-16-21 (10 months from June 1 March 1973; in June 1972, when single debuted charts, there were Poppa Joe no.3, Funny Funn no.19, Co-Co no.27) Single reached no.4 in August 1972 (Poppa Joe this month) and in October 1972 (Wig-Wam Bam Poppa Joe no.11). Sisältää hitin book given info that single no this is the result of combining information f different sources; in Mitä Suomi soittaa char single reached no.1 in August 1972, in Intro magazine no.2 in September 1972).
AUSTRALIA (Australian Music Report)	23/07/1973	65	4	
NEW ZEALAND (The Listener)	25/08/1972	7	13	On August 11th 1972 Little Willy reached Forec list as no.21, then 1 week was off the charts August 25th appeared in main Top-20. 20-13-8-7-8-7-9-11-11-11-12-12-14 (13 weeks f August 25th to November 17th 1972) Single reached no.7 on September 15th & 29th 19
SOUTH AFRICA (Springbok Radio)	7/07/1972	9	11	

USA: RIAA award single by GOLD disc on April 25th 1973.

Wig-Wam Bam single

charts (source)	debut	peak	weeks	chart-runs & extra notes
UK (Record Mirror)	9/09/1972	4	13	On September 2nd 1972 single reached Breakers (no.54) and on next week enters main singles c 48-25-15-6-4-6-8-10-17-25-36-38-43 (13 weeks f September 9th to December 2nd 1972) Single reached no.4 on October 7th 1972. No.3 in Melody Maker, No.4 in NME.
USA (Cash Box)	13/10/1973	114	3	125-116-114 (3 weeks from October 13th to 27th Looking Ahead chart only, not in main Top 100) Not appeared in Billboard and Record World cha
GERMANY (Der Musikmarkt)	25/09/1972	1	24	19-11-5-5-2-1-1-1-1-1-1-1-1-2-2-2-2-4-11-18- (23 weeks from September 25th 1972 to February 1973; when this single enters charts other Swe single Little Willy was no.10) 12/03/1973: 40 Single reached no.1 and stay on Top for 8 week to October 30th to December 18th 1972!
AUSTRIA (Der Musikmarkt)	15/01/1973	5	3 months	5-5-11 (3 months from January 15th to March 15 1973, when next Sweet's single enters charts)
SWITZERLAND (Swiss National Radio charts «Bestseller auf dem Plattenteller»)	17/10/1972	2	14	10-8-4-3-2-3-2-2-3-4-*-5-6-9-10 (14 weeks from October 17th 1972 to January 23rd 1973; on Decem 26th had no charts) Single reached no.2 on November 14th (no.1 was Hawkwind with Silver Machine), on November 28th December 5th (no.1 on these weeks was The Les Humphries Singers with Mexico).
BELGIUM, Vlaanderen (Ultratop)	23/09/1972	3	17	28-14-7-4-4-4-3-4-4-4-5-9-11-18-22-27-30 (17 w from September 23rd 1972 to January 13th 1973) Single reached no.3 on November 4th 1972.
BELGIUM, Wallonie (Ultratop)	16/09/1972	10	13	38-22-10-11-14-11-13-14-15-20-29-31-41 (13 wee from September 16th to December 9th 1972)
NETHERLANDS (Nationale hitparade)	23/09/1972	6	11	23-8-6-6-6-8-9-10-17-24-27 (11 weeks from Sept 23rd to December 2nd 1972) Single reached no.6 on October 7th, 14th & 21st In Nederlandse Top 40 (Radio Veronica) single reached no.6.
IRELAND (Larry Gogan book)	28/09/1972	4	8	

charts (source)	debut	peak	weeks	chart-runs & extra notes
MARK (Danmarks Radio Hit-paraden)	11/10/1972	1	17	12-5-1-1-1-2-3-3-20-14-12-*-13-12-16-17-17-19 (17 weeks from October 11th 1972 to February 6th 1973; there is no chart on December 27th 1972) Single reached no.1 for 3 weeks! (October 24th, November 1st & 8th 1972)
VAY (VG-lista)	4/10/1972	6	11	9-6-6-7-7-9-9-9-9-10-9 (11 weeks from October 4th to December 13th 1972) Single reached no.6 on October 11th & 18th 1972.
DEN (Kvällstoppen)	5/12/1972	18	2	20-18 No.3 in Tio i Topp chart.
AND (Suosikki)	Sep/1972	4	7 months	4-6-5-4-4-8-14 (7 months from September 1972 to March 1973) Single reached no.4 in September 1972 (Little Willy no.6, Poppa Joe no.8 this month), December 1972 (Little Willy no.9) and January 1973 (Little Willy no.11, Blockbuster no.17). Sisältää hitin book given info that single enters charts in August 1972 and reached no.3 (but this is the result of combining information from different sources; although single reached in Mitä Suomi soittaa charts no.4 and in Intro magazine no.4).
TRALIA (Go-Set)	17/03/1973	20	10	39-35-26-27-26-20-24-*-28-39-33 (10 weeks from March 17th to May 26th 1973; on May 5th 1973 had no charts) Single reached no.20 on April 21st 1973. In Australian Music Report chart single reached no.15.
ZEALAND (The Listener)	24/11/1972	10	6	On October 20th 1972 wig Wam Bam appeared in Forecast list as no.22 (Little Willy was no.11 this week), but then drop-off from the charts. On November 24th reached a main Top-20. 20-10-14-14-15-*-20 (6 weeks from November 24th 1972 to January 5th 1973; on December 29th 1972 had no charts) Single reached no.10 on December 1st 1972.
TH AFRICA (Springbok Radio)	13/10/1972	8	13	

THE SWEET'S BIGGEST HITS compilation

charts (source)	debut	peak	weeks	chart-runs & extra notes
MANY (Der Musikmarkt)	15/01/1973	30	2 months	30-35 (in 70s LP charts in Germany were monthly)
AND (Suosikki)	Nov/1972	3	7 months	6-9-3-9-11-11-20 (7 months from November 1972 to May 1973) Sisältää hitin book given info that album enters charts in October 1973 (because album debuted in Intro magazine chart this month; in Suosikki and Mitä Suomi soittaa charts album debuted at November).
TRALIA (Australian Music Report)	19/03/1973	58	10	

Blockbuster! single

charts (source)	debut	peak	weeks	chart-runs & extra notes
Record Mirror)	13/01/1973	1	15	16-2-1-1-1-1-1-3-5-14-21-31-41-38-49 (15 weeks from January 13th to April 21st 1973) Single became no.1 for 5 weeks! (from January 27th to February 24th 1973!) No.1 in Melody Maker, No.1 in NME!
(Billboard)	16/06/1973	73	7	97-95-87-85-81-79-73 (7 weeks from June 16th to July 28th 1973) When single enters chart (June 16th) other Sweet's single Little Willy was no.23. No.43 in Cash Box, no.52 in Record World.
ADA (RPM)	16/06/1973	30	10	79-69-59-52-44-38-35-32-30-33 (10 weeks from June 16th to August 18th 1973; when single enters charts other Sweet's single Little Willy was no.12)
RMANY (Der Musikmarkt)	22/01/1973	1	20	46-13-5-2-2-1-1-1-2-2-1-4-7-3-7-8-22-23-27-48 (20 weeks from January 22nd to June 4th 1973; when this single enters charts other Sweet's single Wig Wam Bam was no.2) Single reached no.1 for 4 weeks! Stay on Top for 3 weeks from February 26th to March 12th and then on April 2nd 1973.
STRIA (Der Musikmarkt)	15/03/1973	1	5 months	4-1-5-18-18 (5 months from March 15th to July 15th 1973)
TZERLAND (Swiss National Radio charts «Bestseller auf dem Plattenteller»)	30/01/1973	3		9-6-5-4-3-3-4-3-3-4-6-6-8 (13 weeks from January 30th to April 24th 1973) Single appeared on no.3 fourth times: February 27th, March 6th, 20th & 27th.

charts (source)	debut	peak	weeks	chart-runs & extra notes
BELGIUM, Vlaanderen (Ultratop)	20/01/1973	2	13	18-13-5-3-2-2-2-2-2-3-5-14-23 (13 weeks from 20th to April 14th 1973) Single reached no.2 for 5 weeks: on February 24th no.1 was Bonnie St. Claire & Unit Gloria Clap Your Hands And Stamp Your Feet, on March 10th & 17th no.1 was Freddy Breck with his hit Bianca.
BELGIUM, Wallonie (Ultratop)	27/01/1973	1	16	44-37-27-17-14-7-3-1-1-2-3-5-9-15-26-41 (16 weeks from January 27th to May 12th 1973) Single reached no.1 for 2 weeks! (March 17th & 1973)
NETHERLANDS (Nationale hitparade)	20/01/1973	1	11	10-3-1-1-1-2-2-6-11-17-27 (11 weeks from January 20th to March 31st 1973) Single reached no.1 for 3 weeks (from February to 17th 1973)! In Nederlandse Top 40 (Radio Veronica) single reached no.1 for 4 weeks!
ITALY (Ciao)	28/04/1973	12	5	29-17-12-16-16 (5 weeks from April 28th to May 1973)
SPAIN (Superventas)	24/03/1973	12	11	18-13-12-13-13-15-13-17-20-25-29 (11 weeks from March 24th to June 2nd 1973) Single reached no.12 on April 7th 1973. "Sólo éxitos. Año a año. 1959-2002" book given that single reached no.21 (but this is the res combining information from different sources).
IRELAND (Larry Gogan book)	18/01/1973	1	10	
DENMARK (Danmarks Radio Hit-paraden)	24/01/1973	1	12	8-1-1-1-2-2-4-6-10-10-20 (11 weeks from January to April 4th 1973) 18/04/1973: 18 (1 more week) Single reached no.1 for 3 weeks! (January 31st, February 7th & 14th 1973)
NORWAY (VG-lista)	31/01/1973	3	12	10-7-7-6-5-3-5-4-4-4-4-7 (12 weeks from January to April 18th 1973) Single reached no.3 on March 7th 1973.
FINLAND (Suosikki)	Jan/1973	4	6 months	17-4-4-6-10-17 (6 months from January to June in January 1973, when single debuted at charts, there were Wig-wam Bam no.4, Little Willy no.1 Single reached no.4 in February 1973 (Wig-wam no.8 this month, Little Willy no.16) and March (Wig-wam Bam no.14 this month, Little Willy no. Sisältää hitin book given info that single no. this is the result of combining information fr different sources; in Mitä Suomi soittaa charts single reached no.3 in February 1973, in Intro magazine no.2 in March 1973).
AUSTRALIA (Australian Music Report)	12/02/1973	29	26	
NEW ZEALAND (The Listener)	23/02/1973	1	13	On February 9th 1973 Blockbuster reached Foreca list as no.22, then 1 week was off the charts a February 23rd appeared in main Top-20. 10-6-2-2-1-1-1-3-4-6-7-12-16 (13 weeks from Feb 23rd to May 18th 1973) Single reached no.1 for 3 weeks from March 23rd April 6th 1973! In February 1973 Sweet toured i Zealand and Australia. In 1973-year-end-chart Blockbuster became no.1C
GREECE (Billboard)	1973	7		Courtesy of Hellinikos Vorras and Epikera.
SINGAPORE (Billboard)	1973	1		Coutesy by Rediffusion.
HONG KONG (Billboard)	1973	9		Courtesy of Radio Hong Kong.
SOUTH AFRICA (Springbok Radio)	16/02/1973	7	12	

Hell Raiser single

charts (source)	debut	peak	weeks	chart-runs & extra notes
UK (Record Mirror)	5/05/1973	2	11	4-2-2-2-5-8-21-27-35-41-47 (11 weeks from May 5 July 14th 1973) Single became no.2 for 3 weeks on May 12th (no.1 this week was Dawn with Tie A Yellow Ribbon Rou The Old Oak Tree), May 19th & 26th (both weeks n was Wizzard with See My Baby Jive). Interesting coincidence at same time Sweet's si Little Willy became no.3 on Billboard charts an Dawn's single was ahead again! No.2 in NME, No.3 in Melody Maker.
GERMANY (Der Musikmarkt)	14/05/1973	1	19	19-10-5-2-3-2-2-2-2-2-1-1-6-10-10-13-28-19-31 (weeks from May 14th to September 17th 1973; when single enters charts other Sweet's single Blockbuster! was no.22) Single reached no.1 on July 23rd & 30th 1973!

charts (source)	debut	peak	weeks	chart-runs & extra notes
RIA (Der Musikmarkt)	15/07/1973	4	1 month	
ERLAND (Swiss National Radio charts »eller auf dem Plattenteller»)	22/05/1973	3	14	9-8-5-3-3-3-4-4-4-5-6-7-9-9 (14 weeks from May 22nd to August 29th 1973) Single reached no.3 for 3 weeks (from June 12th to 26th 1973).
UM, Vlaanderen (Ultratop)	19/05/1973	3	10	29-11-5-3-4-8-13-16-18-28 (10 weeks from May 19th to July 21st 1973) Single reached no.3 on June 9th 1973.
UM, Wallonie (Ultratop)	26/05/1973	26	6	47-36-28-26-31-45 (6 weeks from May 26th to June 30th 1973) Single reached no.26 on June 16th 1973.
ERLANDS (Nationale hitparade)	12/05/1973	4	7	18-7-4-4-12-15-29 (7 weeks from May 12th to June 23rd 1973) Single reached no.4 on May 26th & June 2nd 1973. Nederlandse Top 40 (Radio Veronica) also no.4.
(Superventas)	20/10/1973	27	4	30-30-27-27 (4 weeks from October 20th to November November 10th 1973) "Sólo éxitos. Año a año. 1959-2002" book given info that single reached no.17 (but this is the result of combining information from different sources).
ND (Morgunblaðið)	3/06/1973	3	5	4-5-3-3-6 (5 weeks from June 3rd to July 1st 1973)
ND (Larry Gogan book)	10/05/1973	2	6	
MARK (Danmarks Radio Top 30)	23/05/1973	1	7	6-1-1-2-1-2-21 (7 weeks from May 23rd to July 4th 1973) No.1 for 3 weeks! (May 30th, June 6th & 20th 1973) From May 1973 Danmarks Radio started compiled new chart called Top 30, this chart based on sales and contained both LPs and singles (before this were two separate charts for singles and for LPs).
VAY (VG-lista)	13/06/1973	5	7	6-5-5-5-6-6-7 (7 weeks from June 13th to July 25th 1973) No.5 on June 20th & 27th, July 4th 1973.
ND (Suosikki)	May/1973	4	5 months	11-4-13-11-23 (5 months from May to September 1973) Single reached no.4 in June 1973 (at same month Mitä Suomi soittaa no.4, Intro magazine no.4). Sisältää hitin book given info that single enters charts in April 1973 (because single debuted in Intro magazine chart this month; in Suosikki and Mitä Suomi soittaa charts single debuted at May).
RALIA (Australian Music Report)	11/06/1973	49	13	
ZEALAND (The Listener)	13/07/1973	4	7	On June 29th 1973 single reached Forecast list as no.21, then 1 week was off the charts and on July 13th appeared in main Top-20. 16-10-4-8-8-10-15 (7 weeks from July 13th to August 24th 1973) Single reached no.4 on July 27th 1973.

THE SWEET compilation (only USA & Canada)

charts (source)	debut	peak	weeks	chart-runs & extra notes
(Billboard)	28/07/1973	191	4	196-191-195-200 (4 weeks from July 28th to August 18th 1973) No.101 in Cash Box.
ADA (RPM)	21/07/1973	46	10	98-93-87-85-54-48-47-46-64-68 (10 weeks from July 21st to September 22nd 1973) LP reached no.46 on September 8th 1973.

Ballroom Blitz single

charts (source)	debut	peak	weeks	chart-runs & extra notes
Record Mirror)	22/09/1973	2	9	2-2-2-3-7-12-25-32-47 (9 weeks from September 22nd to November 17th 1973) Single debuted as no.2 and stay on this position for 3 weeks: on September 22nd no.1 was Angel Fingers by Wizzard, on September 29th & October 6th no.1 was Eye Level by Simon Park Orchestra. No.1 in Melody Maker, No.1 in NME!

charts (source)	debut	peak	weeks	chart-runs & extra notes
USA (Billboard)	14/06/1975	5	25	100-90-80-70-60-49-41-33-29-24-20-16-14-12-1₎ 5-9-33-43-43-59-78 (25 weeks from June 14th t₎ November 29th 1975) Single was issued in America 2 years after Eu₎ release! Single reached no.5 on October 18th ₎ (LP Desolation Boulevard no.27 this week). No.9 in Cash Box, no.11 in Record World. In Billboard's 1975-year-end charts (publishe₎ December 27th 1975) single Ballroom Blitz no.₎ («Top POP singles»), The Sweet no.29 («Top Po₎ Singles Artists»). In Cash Box 1975-year-end charts (December 27₎ 1975) Ballroom Blitz no.46 («Top 100 Singles
CANADA (RPM)	12/07/1975	1	17	98-91-77-73-62-55-42-24-19-16-8-3-1-3-5-7[Oct₎ *-*-*-*-*-71[Dec13] (17 weeks from July 12th t₎ December 13th 1975; there is no charts from No₎ 1st to December 6th 1975) Single reached no.1 on October 4th 1975 (LP Desolation Boulevard no.61 this week). In RPM's 1975-year-end charts (December 27th ₎ Ballroom Blitz no.22 («Top 200 Singles of 197₎
GERMANY (Der Musikmarkt)	1/10/1973	1	20	11-9-6-1-3-5-3-4-3-3-3-4-7-13-15-11-10-27-24-₎ weeks from October 1st 1973 to February 11th 1₎ Single reached no.1 on October 22nd 1973.
AUSTRIA (Der Musikmarkt)	15/11/1973	5	3 months	9-5-17 (3 months from November 15th 1973 to Ja₎ 15th 1974)
SWITZERLAND (Swiss National Radio charts «Bestseller auf dem Plattenteller»)	19/09/1973	3	11	9-8-8-5-3-4-7-8-7-9-10 (11 weeks from Septemb₎ to November 28th 1973) Single reached no.3 on October 17th 1973.
FRANCE (SNEP)	30/09/1973	13	11	46-33-29-20-13-17-19-21-23-33-45 (11 weeks fr₎ September 30th to December 9th 1973) Single reached no.13 on October 28th 1973. No.29 in Centre D'Information et de Documenta₎ Disque charts.
BELGIUM, Vlaanderen (Ultratop)	6/10/1973	2	11	21-11-5-3-2-3-3-3-7-16-22 (11 weeks from Octo₎ to December 15th 1973) Single reached no.2 on November 3rd 1973 (no.1 Demis Roussos with My Friend The Wind).
BELGIUM, Wallonie (Ultratop)	29/09/1973	5	14	29-16-9-7-6-5-6-9-12-14-11-21-29-40 (14 weeks September 29th to December 29th 1973) Single reached no.5 on November 3rd 1973.
NETHERLANDS (Nationale hitparade)	29/09/1973	2	7	8-4-2-3-6-11-18 (7 weeks from September 29th t₎ November 10th 1973) Single reached no.2 on October 13th 1973 (no.1 Demis Roussos with My Friend The Wind). No.4 in Nederlandse Top 40 (Radio Veronica).
SPAIN (Superventas)	9/03/1974	6	25	24-11-14-8-8-7-6-7-6-6-6-6-9-8-12-8-13-12-16-₎ 22-25-28-28 (25 weeks from March 9th to August 1974) Single reached no.6 on April 20th, May 4th, 11th & 25th 1974. "Sólo éxitos. Año a año. 1959-2002" book giver that single reached no.5 and spent 22 weeks in charts (but this is the result of combining information from different sources).
ICELAND (Morgunblaðið)	12/02/1974	1	5	On February 3rd 1974 single reached no.11 (like Bubbling Under chart in Billboard) and then en₎ main Top 10 (same time with Teenage Rampage). 1-1-1-3-6 (5 weeks from Feb.12th to March 10th
IRELAND (Larry Gogan book)	4/10/1973	1	7	
DENMARK (Danmarks Radio Top 30)	26/09/1973	3	18	12-4-3-3-4-12-6-6-5-7-7-10-26-20-*-26 (15 week₎ September 26th 1973 to January 9th 1974) 30/01/1974: 14-18-26 (3 more weeks) Single reached no.3 on October 10th & 17th 1973₎ these weeks no.1 & no.2 was German star Freddy₎ with his two LPs Überall auf der Welt and Rote₎ für dich... Danmarks Radio Top 30 contains bot₎ albums and singles.) Ballroom Blitz reached no.1 in Danmarks Radio'₎ Tiparaden (votes of listeners, not sales).
NORWAY (VG-lista)	3/10/1973	2	14	9-7-5-4-3-2-2-3-3-4-7-8-*-*-10-9 (14 weeks fro₎ October 3rd 1973 to January 16th 1974; there ar₎ charts on December 26th 1973 and January 2nd 197₎ Single reached no.2 on November 7th & 14th 1973₎ (no.1 was Barn av regnbuen by local star Lille Nilsen).
SWEDEN (Kvällstoppen)	6/11/1974	3	17	17-5-4-4-3-7-7-11[Dec25]-xx[Jan1]-10-xx-xx-xx-₎ xx-xx (17 weeks from November 6th 1973 to Febru₎ 26th 1974; from January 1st 1974 records on Top₎ Kvällstoppen charts were numbered, records und₎ Top-10 were just listed, without number of pla₎ Single reached no.3 on December 4th 1973. No.1 in Tio i Topp chart.

charts (source)	debut	peak	weeks	chart-runs & extra notes
...ND (Suosikki)	Sep/1973	12	3 months	13-14-12 (3 months from September to November 1973) Sisältää hitin book given info that single no.10 (but this is the result of combining information from different sources; in Mitä Suomi soittaa charts a single reached no.10 in September 1973, in Intro magazine no.11 in November 1973).
...RALIA (Go-Set)	24/11/1973	1	19	29-16-10-9-13-4-*-*-1-2-9-6-7-7-10-10-10-22-18-34-38 (19 weeks from November 24th 1973 to April 13th 1974; on January 5th & 12th 1974 had no charts) Single reached no.1 on January 19th 1974. No.2 in Australian Music Report.
...ZEALAND (The Listener)	2/11/1973	1	12	On October 19th 1973 Ballroom Blitz reached Forecast list as no.23, then 1 week was off the charts and on November 2nd appeared in main Top-20. 20-8-5-1-1-1-2-4-*-*-7-7-13-19 (12 weeks from November 2nd 1973 to February 1st 1974; no charts on December 28th 1973 and January 4th 1974) Single reached no.1 for 3 weeks from November 23rd to December 7th 1973!
...H AFRICA (Springbok Radio)	26/10/1973	3	15	

...I awarded single by SILVER disc on October 1st 1973.

...: CRIA awarded single by GOLD disc on February 1st 1976 (with Desolation Boulevard album).

Teenage Rampage single

charts (source)	debut	peak	weeks	chart-runs & extra notes
...(Record Mirror)	19/01/1974	2	8	6-2-2-2-4-11-24-34 (8 weeks from January 19th to March 9th 1974) Single reached no.2 for 3 weeks (from January 26th to February 9th 1974), on these weeks no.1 was Tiger Feet by Mud. No.2 in Melody Maker. No.1 in NME (26/01/1974)!
...MANY (Der Musikmarkt)	28/01/1974	1	18	11-4-4-1-1-1-1-1-1-1-2-1-3-9-4-10-17-29-27 (18 weeks from January 28th to May 27th 1974; when this single enters charts other Sweet's single Ballroom Blitz was no.27) Single reached no.1 for 7 weeks! (6 weeks from February 18th to March 25th and then on April 8th 1974.)
...RIA (Der Musikmarkt)	15/03/1974	16	2 months	16-20 (2 months from March 15th to April 15th 1974)
...ZERLAND (Swiss National Radio charts «...seller auf dem Plattenteller»)	23/01/1974	2	12	8-5-4-2-3-2-2-4-5-7-7-10 (12 weeks from January 23rd to April 10th 1974) Single reached no.2 on February 12th (no.1 was Lobo with I'd Love You To Want Me), February 27th & March 6th (no.1 for these weeks was The Les Humphries Singers with Kansas City).
...NCE (SNEP)	10/03/1974	37	5	49-44-41-37-42 (5 weeks from March 10th to April 7th 1974) Single reached no.37 on March 31st 1974. No.29 in Centre D'Information et de Documentation du Disque charts.
...GIUM, Vlaanderen (Ultratop)	2/02/1974	10	8	19-13-12-10-13-18-24-25 (8 weeks from February 2nd to March 23rd 1974) Single reached no.10 on February 23rd 1974.
...GIUM, Wallonie (Ultratop)	2/02/1974	3	14	43-30-15-10-7-5-3-3-3-4-6-11-21-35 (14 weeks from February 2nd to May 4th 1974) Single reached no.3 on March 16th, 23rd & 30th 1974
...HERLANDS (Nationale hitparade)	26/01/1974	11	4	19-13-11-16 (4 weeks from January 26th to February 16th 1974) Single reached no.11 on February 9th 1974. In Nederlandse Top 40 (Radio Veronica) also no.11.
...N ("Sólo éxitos. Año a año. 1959-2002"	1974	19	5	Single didn't chart in Superventas. "Sólo éxitos. Año a año. 1959-2002" book haven't enters date, but given date of peak position (October 7th 1974).
...AND (Morgunblaðið)	12/02/1974	3	4	On February 3rd 1974 single reached no.15 (something like Bubbling Under chart in Billboard) and then enters main Top 10 chart (at same time with Ballroom Blitz). 5-3-4-9 (4 weeks from Feb.12th to March 3rd 1974)
...AND (Larry Gogan book)	31/01/1974	1	5	
...MARK (Danmarks Radio Top 30)	23/01/1974	2	12	Teenage Rampage reached no.1 in other Danmarks Radio's Tiparaden (votes of listeners, not sales).
...WAY (VG-lista)	6/02/1974	2	12	4-3-2-2-2-2-2-3-3-4-4-9 (12 weeks from February 6th to April 24th 1974) Single reached no.2 on February 20th & 27th, March 6th, 13th & 20th 1974 (no.1 on these weeks was En spennende dag for Josefine by local star Inger Lise Rypdal).

charts (source)	debut	peak	weeks	chart-runs & extra notes
SWEDEN (Kvällstoppen)	12/02/1974	7	7	xx-xx-9-7-8-xx-xx (7 weeks from February 12th March 26th 1974; 3 weeks on Top-10 & 4 weeks ... Top-10 without number of place) Single reached no.7 on March 5th 1974. No.2 in Tio i Topp chart.
FINLAND (Suosikki)	Feb/1974	5	6 months	12-9-5-17-22-24 (6 months from February to Ju... 1974) Single reached no.5 in April 1974. No.5 in Mi... Suomi soittaa charts, no.8 in Intro magazine.
AUSTRALIA (Go-Set)	13/04/1974	12	11	32-19-12-13-14-15-16-21-24-29-36 (weeks from 13th to June 22nd 1974; when single enters char... Ballroom Blitz was no.38) Single reached no.12 on April 27th 1974. No.10 in Australian Music Report.
NEW ZEALAND (The Listener)	1/03/1974	7	6	On January 25th 1974 Teenage Rampage in appear... Forecast list as no.21 (Ballroom Blitz was no... but then dop off from the charts. On March 1st single reached main Top-20. 20-19-8-7-7-9 (6 weeks from Mar.1st to Apr.5th Single reached no.7 on March 22nd & 29th 1974.

UK: BPI awarded single by SILVER disc on January 1st 1974.

SWEET FANNY ADAMS album

charts (source)	debut	peak	weeks	chart-runs & extra notes
UK (Record Mirror)	18/05/1974	27	2	37-27 (2 weeks on May 18th & 25th 1974) No.18 in NME.
GERMANY (Der Musikmarkt)	15/06/1974	2	10 months	14-10-2-4-7-7-9-17-50-44 (10 months from June 1974 to March 15th 1975) Album reached no.2 on August 15th 1974 (no.1 w... Otto with his II album)
AUSTRIA (Der Musikmarkt)	15/08/1974	6	3 months	9-9-6 (3 months from August 15th to Ocotber 15... 1974)
DENMARK (Danmarks Radio Top 30)	15/05/1974	1	9	4-1-2-3-5-5-9-22 (8 weeks from May 15th to Jul... 1974) 22/10/1975: 20
NORWAY (VG-lista)	5/06/1974	12	1	
SWEDEN (Kvällstoppen)	14/05/1974	4	23	9-6-6-7-10-xx-xx-xx-xx-xx-xx-xx-xx-10-10-4-8-9-9-xx-xx-xx (23 weeks from May 14th to October 15... 1974; 13 weeks on Top-10 & 10 weeks under Top-... without number of place) Album reached no.4 on August 20th 1974.
FINLAND (Suosikki)	May/1974	9	7 months	16-17-9-11-16-21-21 (7 months from May to Nove... 1974) Album reached no.9 in July 1974. No.4 in Mitä Suomi soittaa charts (in May 1974... No.8 in Intro magazine (September 1974). Sisältää hitin book given info that album no.9...
AUSTRALIA (Australian Music Report)	1/07/1974	33	27	

UK: BPI awarded album by SILVER and GOLD discs on February 1st 1975 (simultaneously).

The Six Teens single

charts (source)	debut	peak	weeks	chart-runs & extra notes
UK (Record Mirror)	13/07/1974	9	7	18-11-9-11-19-36-42 (7 weeks from July 13th to August 24th 1974) Single reached no.9 on July 27th 1974. No.8 in Melody Maker, No.10 in NME.
GERMANY (Der Musikmarkt)	22/07/1974	4	19	16-6-5-4-5-5-4-4-4-5-5-6-4-5-7-13-14-24-26 (19 from July 22nd to November 25th 1974) Single reached no.4 for 5 times: on August 12th September 2nd, 9th & 16th, October 14th 1974.
AUSTRIA (Der Musikmarkt)	15/09/1974	9	1 month	
SWITZERLAND (Swiss National Radio charts «Bestseller auf dem Plattenteller»)	21/08/1974	6	7	10-8-6-7-8-8-8 (7 weeks from August 21st to Oct... 2nd 1974) Single reached no.6 on September 4th 1974.
FRANCE (SNEP)	11/08/1974	37	4	48-37-40-48 (4 weeks from August 11th to Septem... 1st 1974) Single reached no.37 on August 18th 1974. No.30 in Centre D'Information et de Documentat... Disque charts
BELGIUM, Vlaanderen (Ultratop)	24/08/1974	18	6	29-26-25-22-18-28 (6 weeks from August 24th to September 28th 1974) Single reached no.18 on September 21st 1974.

charts (source)	debut	peak	weeks	chart-runs & extra notes
GIUM, Wallonie (Ultratop)	24/08/1974	6	12	30-19-13-9-6-9-9-11-15-17-31-50 (12 weeks August 24th to November 9th 1974) Single reached no.6 on September 21st 1974.
HERLANDS (Nationale hitparade)	27/07/1974	10	10	23-16-15-14-11-10-13-15-16-19 (10 weeks from July 27th to September 28th 1974) Single reached no.10 on August 31st 1974. In Nederlandse Top 40 single reached no.7.
N ("Sólo éxitos. Año a año. 1959-2002"	1975	28	1	Single didn't chart in Superventas. "Sólo éxitos. Año a año. 1959-2002" book haven't enters date, but given date of peak position (February 17th 1975).
AND (Larry Gogan book)	25/07/1974	15	2	
MARK (Danmarks Radio Top 30 / Top 20)	17/07/1974	1	10	3-2-1-2-7-5-8-10(Sep04)-13-14 (10 weeks from July 17th to September 18th 1974; from September 4th 1974 chart was shortened from top 30 to Top 20) Single reached no.1 on July 31st 1974. The Six Teens reached no.2 in other Danmarks Radio's chart - Tiparaden (votes of listeners, not sales).
WAY (VG-lista)	7/08/1974	7	3	10-7-8 (3 weeks from August 7th to 21st 1974)
DEN (Kvällstoppen)	30/07/1974	-	8	xx-xx-xx-xx-xx-xx-xx-xx (8 weeks from July 30th to September 17th 1974) Single can't reach Top-10, appeared under Top-10 without number of place.
AND (Suosikki)	Jul/1974	8	6 months	8-10-12-21-17-23 (6 months from July to December 1974) No.7 in Mitä Suomi soittaa charts (July & September 1974), No.8 in Intro magazine (August 1974). Sisältää hitin book given info that single no.7.
TRALIA (Australian Music Report)	12/08/1974	48	11	

Turn It Down single

charts (source)	debut	peak	weeks	chart-runs & extra notes
Record Mirror)	9/11/1974	41	2	50-41 (2 weeks on November 9th & 16th 1974)
MANY (Der Musikmarkt)	4/11/1974	4	18	32-18-5-5-5-4-5-4-6-18-10-9-11-23-30-25-35-37 (18 weeks from November 4th 1974 to March 3rd 1975; when this single enters charts other Sweet's single The Six Teens was no.13) Single reached no.4 on December 9th & 23rd 1974.
TRIA (Der Musikmarkt)	15/12/1974	14	1 month	
GIUM, Wallonie (Ultratop)	7/12/1974	33	5	48-41-33-42-48 (5 weeks from December 7th 1974 to January 4th 1975) Single reached no.33 on December 21st 1974.
N ("Sólo éxitos. Año a año. 1959-2002")	1975	17	3	Single didn't chart in Superventas. "Sólo éxitos. Año a año. 1959-2002" book haven't enters date, but given date of peak position (November 10th 1975).
MARK (Danmarks Radio Top 20)	30/10/1974	2	6	(6 weeks from October 30th to December 4th 1974) Single reached no.2 on November 6th 1974.
WAY (VG-lista)	27/11/1974	4	8	10-8-*-6-*-*-6-5-4-4-6-8 (8 weeks from November 27th 1974 to February 13th 1975; there are no charts on December 11th & 25th 1974, January 2nd 1975) Single reached no.4 on January 23rd & 30th 1975.
EDEN (Kvällstoppen)	5/11/1974	10	6	xx-xx-10-xx-xx-xx (6 weeks from November 5th to December 10th 1974; 1 week on Top-10 & 5 weeks under Top-10 without number of place) Single reached no.10 on November 19th 1974.
AND (Suosikki)	Nov/1974	11	4 months	11-13-11-22 (4 months from November 1974 to February 1975) No.10 in Mitä Suomi soittaa charts (January 1975), No.11 in Intro magazine (January 1975). Sisältää hitin book given info that single no.10.

Peppermint Twist single (Japan, Australia and New Zealand only)

charts (source)	debut	peak	weeks	chart-runs & extra notes
TRALIA (Australian Music Report)	18/11/1974	4	27	
ZEALAND (The Listener)	15/11/1974	22	1	Single can't reached main Top-20, but appeared in Forecast list.

DESOLATION BOULEVARD album

charts (source)	debut	peak	weeks	chart-runs & extra notes
USA (Billboard)	26/07/1975	25	44	On July 19th 1975 album reached Billboard Bubbl Under chart (no.203) and on next week enters m chart. 132-122-112-100-89-77-67-55-44-38-33-29-27-25- 52-50-43-58-58-58-103-103-97-89-74-64-53-51-51 50-64-80-90-90-115-124-152-162-162-163-180 (44 from July 26th 1975 to May 22nd 1976) Album reached no.25 on October 25th & November 1975 (single Ballroom Blitz no.9 and no.33 on weeks). No.33 in Cash Box, no.34 in Record World. In Billboard's 1976-year-end charts (published December 25th 1976) LP Desolation Boulevard bec no.81 («Top POP Albums»), Sweet became no.54 (Pop Albums Artists»).
CANADA (RPM)	20/09/1975	5	21	100-68-61-39-41-34[Oct25]-*-*-*-*-*-*-29[Dec13 20-32-26-22-14-6-5-13-14-27-31-48-33 (21 weeks September 20th 1975 to March 27th 1976; there is charts from November 1st to December 6th 1975; (March 27th 1976 next Sweet's LP enters charts) Album reached no.5 on February 14th 1976 (singl On The Run no.5 this week). At Top 100 Albums Of '76 (published in RPM on January 8th 1977) LP appeared as no.42.
GERMANY (Der Musikmarkt)	15/01/1975	9	8 months	9-16-20-22-17-31-36-28 (8 months from January to August 15th 1975) When album enters charts LP Sweet Fanny Adams no.17.
DENMARK (Danmarks Radio Top 20)	4/12/1974	4	8	4-6-6-5-*-7-7-12-16 (8 weeks from December 4th to January 29th 1975; there are no charts on Ja 1st 1975)
NORWAY (VG-lista)	16/01/1975	17	1	
SWEDEN (Kvällstoppen)	26/11/1974	2	14	8-3-2-2-3-2-3-2-2-3-5-9-xx-xx (14 weeks from November 26th 1974 to February 25th 1975; 12 wee Top-10 & 2 weeks under Top-10 without number of place) Album reached no.2 on December 10th, 17th & 31st (no.1 on these weeks was Forever And Ever by De Roussos), On January 14th & 21st 1975 (no.1 on t weeks was Flamingokvintetten-5).
FINLAND (Suosikki)	Dec/1974	9	3 months	9-14-24 (3 months from December 1974 to Februar 1975) No.9 in Mita Suomi soittaa charts (in May 1974) No.9 in Intro magazine (September 1974).
AUSTRALIA (Australian Music Report)	10/03/1975	13	41	
NEW ZEALAND (RIANZ)	6/06/1975	17	8	17-23-19-37 (4 weeks from June 6th to 27th 1975 29/08/1975: 26-24-35-39 (4 weeks from August 29 September 19th 1975)

UK: BPI awarded album by SILVER disc on January 1st 1975 (although LP not appeared in UK charts!).
USA: RIAA award album by GOLD disc on May 25th 1976.
Canada: CRIA awarded album by GOLD disc on February 1st 1976 (with Ballroom Blitz single).

Fox On The Run single

	debut	peak	weeks	chart-runs & extra notes
UK (Record Mirror)	15/03/1975	2	10	42-21-10-5-2-2-3-10-21-41 (10 weeks from March to May 17th 1975) Single reached no.2 on 12th & 19th April, on the weeks no.1 was Bye Bye Baby by Bay City Rollers No.2 in Melody Maker, No.2 in NME.
USA (Billboard)	15/11/1975	5	16	47-35-26-11-10-9-8-7-6-5-18-28-48-64-79-92 (16 from November 15th 1975 to February 28th 1976) Single reached no.5 on January 17th 1976 (LP Desolation Boulevard no.89 this week). No.4 in Record World, no.5 in Cash Box. In Billboard's 1976-year-end charts (published December 25th 1976) single Fox On The Run became no.76 («Top POP singles»), Sweet became no.29 (Pop Singles Artists»). In Cash Box 1976-year-end charts (published on December 25th, 1976) single Fox On The Run becam no.63 («Top 100 Singles of 1976»).

charts (source)	debut	peak	weeks	chart-runs & extra notes
DA (RPM)	13/12/1975	2	16	14-8-8-6-3-2-2-2-5-21-28-39-48-58-72-90 (16 weeks from December 13th 1975 to April 3rd 1976; there is not charts from November 1st to December 6th 1975; on December 13th single Ballroom Blitz no.71 & LP Desolation Boulevard no.29) Single reached no.2 on January 24th & 31st and February 7th 1976 (no.1 on these weeks was C.W.McCall with Convoy; Desolation Boulevard LP no.22 & no.14). In RPM's 1976-year-end charts (published on January 8th 1977) Fox On The Run became no.37 («Top 200 Singles of '76»).
ANY (Der Musikmarkt)	17/03/1975	1	25	19-10-7-4-1-2-2-2-1-1-1-1-1-2-2-3-2-2-4-5-12[Aug4]-11-25-26-35 (25 weeks from March 17th to September 1st 1975) Single reached no.1 for 6 weeks! Stay on Top on April 14th and for 5 weeks from May 12th to June 9th.
RIA (Der Musikmarkt)	15/05/1975	3	5 months	13-3-6-7-15 (5 months from May 15th to September 15th 1975, when single Action enters chart!)
ZERLAND (Swiss National Radio charts «seller auf dem Plattenteller»)	30/05/1975	3	11	10-5-3-3-6-7-7-7-10-9-9 (11 weeks from May 30th to August 8th 1975) Single reached no.3 on June 13th & 20th 1975. No.10 in Der Musikmartkt charts (for Swiss).
CE (SNEP)	27/04/1975	37	5	43-37-42-44-50 (5 weeks from April 27th to May 25th 1975) Single reached no.37 on May 4th 1975.
IUM, Vlaanderen (Ultratop)	12/04/1975	4	13	23-12-9-4-4-4-5-6-7-8-14-14-30 (13 weeks from April 12th to July 5th 1975) Single reached no.4 on May 3rd, 10th & 17th 1975.
IUM, Wallonie (Ultratop)	26/04/1975	9	12	37-28-23-21-17-13-11-11-9-12-20-35 (12 weeks from April 26th to July 12th 1975) Single reached no.9 on June 21st 1975.
IERLANDS (Nationale hitparade)	29/03/1975	2	11	25-18-7-4-2-3-4-13-13-17-30 (11 weeks from March 29th to June 7th 1975) Single reached no.2 on April 26th 1975 (no.1 was George Baker Selection with Paloma Blanca). In Nederlandse Top 40 (Radio Veronica) no.2 too.
N (Superventas)	23/08/1975	7	15	25-22-14-11-8-12-10-7-8-12-17-20-21-23-25 (15 weeks from August 23rd to November 29th 1975) Single reached no.7 on October 11th 1975. "Sólo éxitos. Año a año. 1959-2002" book given info that single reached no.8 (but this is the result of combining information from different sources).
AND (Larry Gogan book)	10/04/1975	2	5	
MARK (Danmarks Radio Top 20)	19/03/1975	1	18	18-1-1-1-2-3-3-7-10-9-9-6-8-10-12-12 (16 weeks from March 19th to July 2nd 1975) 23/07/1975: 19-20 3 weeks on Top! (March 26, April 2 & 9 1975)
WAY (VG-lista)	24/04/1975	2	19	10-*-6-6-6-6-5-5-3-7-3-2-2-2-5-3-4-5-4 (19 weeks from April 24th to August 28th 1975; there are no charts on May 1st 1975) Single reached no.2 on July 10th, 17th & 24th 1975 (no.1 on these weeks was Love Hurts by Nazareth).
DEN (Kvällstoppen)	22/04/1975	6	16	xx-9-7-8-6-6-9-9-xx-xx-xx-xx-xx-xx-xx-xx (16 weeks from April 22nd to August 5th 1975; 8 weeks on Top-10 & 8 weeks under Top-10 without number of place) Single reached no.6 on May 20th & 27th 1975. In the end of August 1975 Kvallstoppen charts were closed and from November 14th 1975 the official Swedish music charts were compiled by Sveriges Radio, known as Topplistan and (later) Hitlistan. Fox On The Run reached in Topplistan charts no.10 (10-17-11-11-15-12-19; 7 bi-weeks, from November 14th 1975 to February 2nd 1976).
AND (Suosikki)	Apr/1975	12	3 months	12-15 (2 months from April to May 1975) Jun/75: 21 Sisältää hitin book given info that single no.10 (but this is the result of combining information from different sources; in Mitä Suomi soittaa charts no.12, in Intro magazine no.18).
N (Oricon)	20/12/1975	88		6,000 (sales numbers)
TRALIA (Australian Music Report)	12/05/1975	1	32	
ZEALAND (RIANZ)	16/05/1975	3	21	31-26-9-9-12-8-15-20-20-9-7-5-7-3-6-7-16-6-28-40-37 (21 weeks from May 16th to October 3rd 1975) Single reached no.3 on August 15th 1975. In August 1975 Sweet toured in New Zealand and Australia.
TH AFRICA (Springbok Radio)	6/06/1975	1	14	

USA: RIAA award single by GOLD disc on February 23rd 1976.
UK: BPI awarded single by SILVER disc on April 1st 1976.
CANADA: CRIA awarded single by GOLD disc on May 1st 1976.

Action single

charts (source)	debut	peak	weeks	chart-runs & extra notes
UK (Record Mirror)	12/07/1975	15	6	47-27-17-15-19-21 (6 weeks from July 12th to ̷ 16th 1975) Single reached no.15 on August 2nd 1975. No.14 in NME, No.15 in Melody Maker.
USA (Billboard)	14/02/1976	20	14	80-70-53-40-30-26-23-21-21-20-51-57-59-98 (14 ̷ from February 14th to May 15th 1976) When Action enters charts (14/02/1976) single ̷ The Run was no.64, LP Desolation Boulevard no ̷ Single Action reached no.20 on April 17th 1976 ̷ Give Us A Wink no.27 and LP Desolation Boulev ̷ no.124 this week) On last week of Action (15/05/1976) LP Give U ̷ Wink no.62 and LP Desolation Boulevard no.163 ̷ No.10 in Cash Box, no.18 in Record World. In Cash Box 1976-year-end charts (published o ̷ December 25th, 1976) Action no.93 («Top 100 Si ̷ of 1976»).
CANADA (RPM)	28/02/1976	5	15	81-40-9-6-5-5-15-22-25-31-34-48-52-62-91 (15 ̷ from February 28th to June 5th 1976; on Februar ̷ single Fox on the Run no.28 and LP Desolation ̷ Boulevard no.14) Single reached no.5 on March 27th & April 3rd ̷ (LP Give Us A Wink no.98 & no.41 on these weel ̷ In RPM's 1976-year-end charts (published on J ̷ 8th 1977) Action no.70 («Top 200 Singles of '7 ̷
GERMANY (Der Musikmarkt)	14/07/1975	2	20	33-16-4-2-2-2-2-3-3-4-5-5-10-11-13-22-21-40-3(̷ (20 weeks from July 14th to November 24th 1975 ̷ Action enters charts Fox On The Run was no.2) Single reached no.2 for 4 weeks from August 4 ̷ 25th 1975 (Fox on The Run for this period was ̷ 25-26; no.1 on all these weeks was George Bak ̷ Selection with Paloma Blanca).
AUSTRIA (Der Musikmarkt)	15/09/1975	3	2 months	3-6 (2 months from September 15 to October 15 ̷
SWITZERLAND (Swiss National Radio charts «Bestseller auf dem Plattenteller»)	1/08/1975	4	11	10-7-5-4-5-6-7-7-9-9-10 (11 weeks from August ̷ October 10th 1975) Single reached no.4 on August 22nd 1975. In Der Musikmartkt charts (for Swiss) also no. ̷
BELGIUM, Vlaanderen (Ultratop)	26/07/1975	8	8	25-21-18-10-8-11-18-28 (8 weeks from July 26th ̷ September 13th 1975, reached no.8 on August 23 ̷
BELGIUM, Wallonie (Ultratop)	16/08/1975	19	8	41-26-24-20-19-28-35-50 (8 weeks from August ̷ October 4th 1975)
NETHERLANDS (Nationale hitparade)	19/07/1975	5	7	21-9-6-5-5-11-30 (7 weeks from July 19th to Au ̷ 30th 1975) Single reached no.5 on August 9th & 16th 1975. No.6 in Nederlandse Top 40 (Radio Veronica).
IRELAND (Larry Gogan book)	31/07/1975	7	4	
DENMARK (Danmarks Radio Top 20)	9/07/1975	3	9	9-3-5-4-6-6-7-15-15 (9 weeks from July 9th to ̷ September 3rd 1975) Single reached no.3 on July 16th 1975.
NORWAY (VG-lista)	24/07/1975	2	25	6-4-2-2-2-2-2-3-3-5-6-7-9-8-8-7-10-9-8-7-9-7-5 ̷ 6-10 (25 weeks from July 24th 1975 to January ̷ 1976; there are no charts on January 1st & 8th ̷ on July 24th 1975 Fox On The Run was no.2) Single reached no.2 on August 7th, 14th, 21st & ̷ September 4th 1975 (no.1 on these weeks was sti ̷ Love Hurts by Nazareth, as with Fox On The Run ̷ Nazareth was on Top for 14 weeks).
SWEDEN (Topplistan)	14/11/1975	2	11 bi-weeks	2-3-4-4-5-4-7-8-9-16-19 (11 bi-weeks, from Nov ̷ 14th 1975 to March 29th 1976; no.1 on November ̷ was George Baker Selection with Paloma Blanca, ̷ was first Topplistan issue)
FINLAND (Suosikki)	Aug/1975	12	3 months	12-15-20 (3 months from August to October 1975 ̷ Sisältää hitin book given info that single no. ̷ (but this is the result of combining informati ̷ from different sources; in Mitä Suomi soittaa ̷ a single reached no.19, in Intro magazine no.1 ̷
JAPAN (Oricon)	20/03/1976	98		3,000 (sales numbers)
AUSTRALIA (Australian Music Report)	8/09/1975	4	25	
NEW ZEALAND (RIANZ)	5/09/1975	12	8	12-15-24-20-18-34-34-31 (8 weeks from Septembe ̷ to October 24th 1975; when single enters charts ̷ Sweet's single Fox On The Run was no.16 and LP ̷ Desolation Boulevard no.24)

charts (source)	debut	peak	weeks	chart-runs & extra notes
SWEET SINGLES ALBUM compilation (Australia & New Zealand only)				
RALIA (Australian Music Report)	16/06/1975	2	39	
ZEALAND (RIANZ)	10/10/1975	21	5	21-34-29-30-40 (5 weeks from October 10th to November 7th 1975; when LP enters charts Sweet's single Action was no.34)
STRUNG UP live & compilation album				
MANY (Der Musikmarkt)	15/12/1975	17	4 months	32-17-24-43 (4 months from December 15th 1975 to 15th March 1976, when next Sweet's LP enters charts) LP reached no.17 on January 15th 1976.
RIA (Der Musikmarkt)	15/03/1976	10	1 month	
ZERLAND (Der Musikmarkt)	1/01/1976	12	2 months	On December 1st 1975 album appeared at LP-Warteliste (like Bubbling Under chart in Billboard) order (alphabetical, without places) and next month enters main-LP chart. 16-12 (2 months from January 1 to February 1 1976)
Y (Ciao)	6/12/1975	25	1	In Italy was released 2 separate albums - the compilation set entitled Strung Up (released 1975) and the live set entitled Live In England (1976).
MARK (Danmarks Radio Top 20)	26/11/1975	5	9	19-10-6-5-*-6-6-12-12-19 (9 weeks from November 26th 1975 to January 28th 1976; there are no charts on December 31st 1975)
WAY (VG-lista)	27/11/1975	12	4	27/11/1975: 20-16 18/12/1975: 12-18
DEN (Topplistan)	27/11/1975	4	7 bi-weeks	7-5-4-7-8-15-27 (7 bi-weeks from November 27th 1975 to February 16th 1976; on February 16th Give Us A Wink LP enters charts) LP reached no.4 on December 26th 1975.
RALIA (Australian Music Report)	26/01/1976	9	18	
LIVE IN ENGLAND live album (Italy only)				
Y (Ciao)	5/02/1977	25	1	
The Lies In Your Eyes single				
Record Mirror)	24/01/1976	35	4	On January 17th 1976 single reached Star Breakers chart (no.57) and on next week enters main singles chart. 39-35-35-39 (4 weeks from Janury 24th to February 14th 1976) No.30 in Melody Maker.
MANY (Der Musikmarkt)	9/02/1976	5	18	49-12-6-5-5-6-7-9-16-9-8-20-18-26-35-34-36-46 (18 weeks from February 9th to June 7th 1976) Single reached no.5 on March 1st & 8th 1976.
TRIA (Der Musikmarkt)	15/03/1976	17	1 month	
ZERLAND (Der Musikmarkt)	1/03/1976	14	3 months	15-14-20 (3 months from March 1st to May 1st 1976)
GIUM, Vlaanderen (Ultratop)	7/02/1976	12	9	30-27-27-22-12-12-20-22-27 (9 weeks from February 7th to April 3rd 1976) Single reached no.12 on March 6th & 13th 1976. Billboard (April 17, 1976) given info for single in Belgish charts: no.10 (courtesy by Humo).
GIUM, Wallonie (Ultratop)	6/03/1976	33	5	44-36-34-33-45 (5 weeks from March 6th to April 3rd 1976)
HERLANDS (Nationale hitparade)	7/02/1976	9	7	26-26-15-10-9-13-29 (7 weeks from February 7th to March 20th 1976) Single reached no.9 on March 6th 1976. In Nederlandse Top 40 (Radio Veronica) also no.9.
MARK (Danmarks Radio Top 20)	28/01/1976	3	5	8-3-4-9-15 (5 weeks from January 28th to February 25th 1976) Single reached no.3 on February 4th 1976.
DEN (Topplistan)	1/03/1976	6	7 bi-weeks	8-6-6-9-13 (5 bi-weeks, from March 1st to April 26th 1976; on March 1st single Action was no.9 and LP Give Us A Wink no.5) 8/06/1976: 18 6/07/1976: 20 In total 7 bi-weeks. Single reached no.6 on March 15th & 29th 1976 (single Action was no.16 & no.19, LP Give Us A Wink no.8 & no.10 on these weeks).

charts (source)	debut	peak	weeks	chart-runs & extra notes
FINLAND (Suosikki)	Feb/1976	22	1 month	Sisältää hitin book given info that single no (but this is the result of combining informat from different sources; in Intro magazine cha single reached no.17 and not reached Mitä Suo soittaa charts).
AUSTRALIA (Australian Music Report)	9/02/1976	14	24	

GIVE US A WINK album

charts (source)	debut	peak	weeks	chart-runs & extra notes
USA (Billboard)	6/03/1976	27	13	60-49-40-38-34-30-27-27-31-52-62-80-138 (13 w from March 6th to May 29th 1976) Album reached no.27 on April 17th & 24th 1976 (Action was no.20 and no.51, LP Desolation Boul no.124 and no.152 on these weeks) No.30 in Cash Box, no.30 in Record World.
CANADA (RPM)	27/03/1976	11	14	98-41-37-36-24-19-13-12-11-20-21-26-36-39 (14 from March 27th to June 26th 1976; on March 27t single Action no.5) Album reached no.11 on May 22nd 1976 (single A no.52 this week). In RPM's 1976-year-end charts (published on Ja 8 1977) Give Us A Wink no.78 (Top 100 Albums (
GERMANY (Der Musikmarkt)	15/03/1976	9	4 months	9-12-30-42 (4 months from March 15th to June 1 1976; when album enters charts other Sweet's I Strung Up was no.43)
SWITZERLAND (Der Musikmarkt)	1/03/1976	11	3 months	11-18-17 (3 months from March 1st to May 1st 19
DENMARK (Danmarks Radio Top 20)	4/02/1976	4	4	4-6-4-5 (4 weeks from February 4th to 25th 1976
NORWAY (VG-lista)	26/02/1976	15	2	26/02/1976: 20 11/03/1976: 15
SWEDEN (Topplistan)	16/02/1976	3	8 bi-weeks	3-5-8-10-17-20-32-44 (8 bi-weeks from February to May 25th 1976; on February 16th Action was n
JAPAN (Oricon)	20/03/1976	37	10	19,520 [LP] (sales numbers)
AUSTRALIA (Australian Music Report)	22/03/1976	17	16	

Lost Angels single

charts (source)	debut	peak	weeks	chart-runs & extra notes
GERMANY (Der Musikmarkt)	8/11/1976	13	18	31-23-16-19-15-16-13-19-25-20-30-32-28-31-38-3 50 (18 weeks from November 8th 1976 to March 7t 1977) Single reached no.13 on December 20th 1976.
AUSTRIA (Der Musikmarkt)	15/01/1977	11	1 month	
SWITZERLAND (Der Musikmarkt)	15/12/1976	16	6 half-months	17-16-19-18-24-17 (6 half-months from December 1976 to March 1st 1977)
BELGIUM, Wallonie (Ultratop)	1/01/1977	34	4	46-39-34-42 (4 weeks from January 1st to 22nd 19
NETHERLANDS (Radio Veronica)	13/11/1976	58 (18)	3	On November 13th 1976 single reached Tipparade (30 singles under main chart) for 3 weeks, can reach main singles' chart (Nederlandse Top 40) 63(23)-58(18)-58(18) (3 weeks from November 13 27th 1976) (Positions in Tipparade were numbered from 1 t but no.1 in Tipparade is not the same as no.1 main Top 40! Therefore, it is noted as 58(18).
DENMARK (Danmarks Radio Top 20)	17/11/1976	18	1	
SWEDEN (Topplistan)	16/11/1976	5	8 bi-weeks	9-5-5-5-6-8-8-12 (8 bi-weeks, from November 16 1976 to February 25th 1977) Single reached no.5 on November 30th, December 28th 1976.
AUSTRALIA (Australian Music Report)	13/12/1976	74	14	

Fever Of Love single

charts (source)	debut	peak	weeks	chart-runs & extra notes
USA (Record World)	4/06/1977	118	5	124-119-118-118-149 (5 weeks from June 4th to J 2nd 1977 in Top-101-150-singles chart only, not reached main Record World Top-100) Single reached no.118 on June 18th & 25th 1977. Not charted at Billboard and Cash Box charts.
GERMANY (Der Musikmarkt)	21/03/1977	9	14	40-23-22-9-13-15-11-16-17-19-21-23-30-46 (14 w from March 21st to June 20th 1977) Single reached no.9 on April 11th 1977.
AUSTRIA (Der Musikmarkt)	15/04/1977	12	2 months	12-19 (2 months from April 15th to May 15th 1977

charts (source)	debut	peak	weeks	chart-runs & extra notes
ZERLAND (Der Musikmarkt)	1/05/1977	15	3 half-months	23-15-17 (3 half-months from May 1st to June 1st 1977)
HERLANDS (Radio Veronica)	5/03/1977	52 (12)	5	On March 5th 1977 single reached Tipparade chart (30 singles under main chart) for 5 weeks, can't reach main singles' chart (Nederlandse Top 40). 69(29)-61(21)-58(18)-54(14)-52(12) (5 weeks from March 5th to April 2nd 1977) (Positions in Tipparade were numbered from 1 to 30, but no.1 in Tipparade is not the same as no.1 in main Top 40! Therefore, it is noted as 69(29).)
DEN (Topplistan)	11/03/1977	7	5 bi-weeks	8-7-10-11-16 (5 bi-weeks, from March 11th to May 6th 1977) Single reached no.7 on March 25th 1977.
TH AFRICA (Springbok Radio)	27/05/1977	10	7	

OFF THE RECORD album

charts (source)	debut	peak	weeks	chart-runs & extra notes
(Billboard)	14/05/1977	151	4	180-169-158-151 (4 weeks from May 14th to June 4th 1977) No.109 in Record World, no.150 in Cash Box.
ADA (RPM)	21/05/1977	83	5	98-93-90-83-93 (5 week from May 21st to June 18th 1977) Album reached no.83 on June 11th 1977.
MANY (Der Musikmarkt)	1/05/1977	11	8 half-months	48-13-11-17-21-27-49 (7 half-months from May 1st to August 1st 1977) 15/09/1977: 45 (1 more half-months) Album reached no.11 on June 1st 1977.
TRIA (Der Musikmarkt)	15/05/1977	5	1 month	
TZERLAND (Der Musikmarkt)	1/05/1977	5	5 half-months	5-8-9-6 (4 half-months from May 1 to June 15 1977) 15/07/1977: 15
WAY (VG-lista)	5/05/1977	20	1	
DEN (Topplistan)	22/04/1977	14	5 bi-weeks	16-14-20-33-34 (5 bi-weeks from April 22nd to June 17th 1977; on April 22nd single Fever Of Love was no.11) Album reached no.14 on May 6th 1977 (single Fever Of Love was no.16 this week).
AND (Suosikki)	Jul/1977	28	1 month	Sisältää hitin book given info that album no.29. (Album not reached Mitä Suomi soittaa charts and Intro magazine charts).
TRALIA (Australian Music Report)	18/07/1977	51	7	

Stairway To The Stars single

charts (source)	debut	peak	weeks	chart-runs & extra notes
MANY (Der Musikmarkt)	8/08/1977	15	10	44-23-15-21-21-22-20-34-42-43 (10 weeks from August 8th to Ocotber 10th 1977) Single reached no.15 on August 22nd 1977.
TZERLAND (Der Musikmarkt)	1/09/1977	18	1 half-month	

Funk It Up (David's Song) single

charts (source)	debut	peak	weeks	chart-runs & extra notes
(Billboard)	13/08/1977	88	5	95-94-93-93-88 (5 weeks from August 13th to September 10th 1977) No.90 in Cash Box, no.102 in Record World.
ADA (RPM)	17/09/1977	87	3	100-94-87 (3 weeks from September 17th to October 1st 1977)

Love Is Like Oxygen single

charts (source)	debut	peak	weeks	chart-runs & extra notes
Record Mirror)	28/01/1978	9	9	48-21-18-9-10-9-16-23-32 (9 weeks from January 28th to March 25th 1978) Single reached no.2 twice on February 18th & March 4th 1978. No.7 in Melody Maker, No.8 in NME.

charts (source)	debut	peak	weeks	chart-runs & extra notes
USA (Billboard)	18/02/1978	8	25	81-71-60-58-56-51-49-42-38-35-28-21-18-16-15-1 10-8-8-15-34-51-57-93 (25 weeks from February to August 5th 1978, and next single California Nights enters Hot 100 next week) Single reached no.8 for 2 weeks on June 26th & 1st 1978 (LP Level Headed no.63 and no.53) No.8 in Cash Box, no.12 in Record World. In Billboard's 1978-year-end charts (published December 23rd 1978) single Love Is Like Oxygen became no.23 («POP singles»), Sweet became no.! («Pop Singles Artists»). In Cash Box 1978-year-end charts (published on December 30th 1978) single Love Is Like Oxygen became no.71 («Top 100 Singles»).
CANADA (RPM)	11/03/1978	8	26	97-69-63-58-45-39-34-28-28-28-27-24-21-17-17-9 8-13-29-42-60-62-65-85 (26 weeks from March 11' September 2nd 1978) Single reached no.8 on July 15th 1978 (album Le Headed no.56 this week). In RPM's 1978-year-end charts (published on De 30th 1978) Love Is Like Oxygen became no.63 (To Singles Of '78).
GERMANY (Media Control)	6/02/1978	10	18	24-21-11-10-13-15-13-15-11-12-13-15-17-20-25-3: 44 (18 weeks from February 6th to June 5th 1978) Single reached no.10 on February 27th 1978.
AUSTRIA (Der Musikmarkt)	15/04/1978	23	1 month	
SWITZERLAND (Swiss National Radio charts «Bestseller auf dem Plattenteller»)	25/02/1978	6	10	15-11-7-6-*-6-10-13-14-13-14 (10 weeks from Fel 25th to May 6th 1978; on March 25th had no charts Single reached no.6 on March 18th & April 1st 19 In Der Musikmartkt charts (for Swiss) single re no.4.
BELGIUM, Vlaanderen (Ultratop)	25/02/1978	15	6	23-17-15-17-22-27 (6 weeks from February 25th t April 1st 1978) Single reached no.15 on March 11th 1978.
NETHERLANDS (Nationale hitparade)	25/02/1978	20	4	20-20-22-28 (4 weeks from February 25th to Marc 1978) No.16 in Nederlandse Top 40 (Radio Veronica).
ITALY (Musica&Dischi)	15/04/1978	12	15	No.22 in Ciao charts.
SPAIN (Superventas)	8/04/1978	13	13	28-26-19-14-?-13-15-16-16-16-20-25-30 (13 weeks April 8th to July 1st 1978; don't have info for 6th 1978) Single reached no.13 on May 13th 1978.
IRELAND (Larry Gogan book)	23/02/1978	8	7	
AUSTRALIA (Australian Music Report)	27/03/1978	9	24	
NEW ZEALAND (RIANZ)	14/05/1978	4	18	40-21-25-31-9-5-4-8-12-6-11-14-17-20-23-28-27-3 weeks from May 14th to September 10th 1978) Single reached no.4 on June 25th 1978.

UK: BPI awarded single by SILVER disc on March 1st 1978.

LEVEL HEADED album

charts (source)	debut	peak	weeks	chart-runs & extra notes
USA (Billboard)	18/02/1978	52	28	162-149-139-129-121-111-106-104-169-160-157-147 127-117-93-83-73-63-53-52-58-61-72-97-119-119-1 (28 weeks from February 18th to August 26th 1978 Album reached no.52 on July 8th 1978 (single Lov Like Oxygen no.15 this week). On last week in charts of Level Headed (26/08/1 single California Nights reached no.76. No.58 in Cash Box, no.107 in Record World.
CANADA (RPM)	24/06/1978	52	9	98-81-76-56-52-65-60-76-85 (9 weeks from June 2 to August 19th 1978; on June 24th single Love Is Oxygen no.9) Album reached no.52 on July 22nd 1978 (single Lo Is Like Oxygen no.13 this week).
GERMANY (Media Control)	15/03/1978	15	6 half-months	36-15-16-24-30-31 (6 half-months from March 15th June 1st 1978) Album reached no.15 on April 1st 1978.
AUSTRIA (Der Musikmarkt)	15/03/1978	17	1 month	
SWITZERLAND (Der Musikmarkt)	1/03/1978	4	5 half-months	4-6 (2 half-months from March 1st & 15th 1978, ar drop off from charts for 1 half-months on April 15/04/1978: 7-21-21 (3 half-months from April 1 to May 15th 1978)
NETHERLANDS (Nationale hitparade)	25/02/1978	26	4	30-26-26-28 (4 weeks from February 25th to March 1978) In Veronica's LP Top 50 album reached no.38.

charts (source)	debut	peak	weeks	chart-runs & extra notes
EN (Topplistan)	24/02/1978	26	1 bi-week	
RALIA (Australian Music Report)	27/03/1978	40	20	

California Nights single

charts (source)	debut	peak	weeks	chart-runs & extra notes
Billboard)	12/08/1978	76	4	83-78-76-76 (4 weeks from August 12th to September 2nd 1978) No.77 in Record World, no. 88 in Cash Box.
DA (RPM)	26/08/1978	86	5	97-90-88-86-88 (5 weeks from August 26th to September 23rd 1978; on August 26th single Love Is Like Oxygen no.65) Single reached no.86 on September 16th 1978.
MANY (Media Control)	31/07/1978	23	5	23-39-35-40-46 (5 weeks from July 31st to August 28th 1978)

Call Me single

charts (source)	debut	peak	weeks	chart-runs & extra notes
MANY (Media Control)	9/04/1979	29	6	31-37-29-32-34 (5 weeks from April 9th to May 7th 1979) 21/05/1979: 44 Single reached no.29 on April 23rd 1979.

CUT ABOVE THE REST album

charts (source)	debut	peak	weeks	chart-runs & extra notes
Billboard)	12/05/1979	151	5	175-164-154-151-171 (5 weeks from May 12th to June 9th 1979) No.112 in Cash Box, no.155 in Record World.
MANY (Media Control)	11/06/1979	49	2	11/06/1979: 50 25/06/1979: 49
RALIA (Australian Music Report)	6/08/1979	53	16	

TEENAGE RAMPAGE compilation (Australia & New Zealand only)

charts (source)	debut	peak	weeks	chart-runs & extra notes
RALIA (Australian Music Report)	26/10/1981	53	16	

SWEET 16 - IT'S IT'S ... SWEET'S HITS compilation

charts (source)	debut	peak	weeks	chart-runs & extra notes
Record Mirror)	22/09/1984	49	6	74-49-68-63-74-93 (6 weeks from September 22nd to October 27th 1984)
RALIA (Australian Music Report)	8/07/1985	17	9	

It's It's The Sweet Mix single

charts (source)	debut	peak	weeks	chart-runs & extra notes
Record Mirror)	19/01/1985	45	6	96-69-49-49-45-65 (6 weeks from January 19th to February 23rd 1985) No.35 in NME.
RALIA (Australian Music Report)	1/07/1985	36	12	

Sweet 2th single

charts (source)	debut	peak	weeks	chart-runs & extra notes
Record Mirror)	25/05/1985	85	2	85-85 (2 weeks on May 25th & June 1st 1985)

STARKE ZEITEN compilation

charts (source)	debut	peak	weeks	chart-runs & extra notes
MANY (Media Control)	28/03/1988	26	9	26-34-39-39-42-46-60-51-57 (9 weeks from March 28th to May 23rd 1988)

THE BALLROOM BLITZ & MORE SWEET HITS compilation

charts (source)	debut	peak	weeks	chart-runs & extra notes
TRALIA (ARIA)	17/01/1993	19	6	31-19-24-28-39-47 (6 weeks from January 17th to February 21st 1993)

GOLD - 20 SUPER HIT compilation

charts (source)	debut	peak	weeks	chart-runs & extra notes
GERMANY (Media Control)	1/11/1993	44	9	1/11/1993: 81 (1 week and then for 1 week dro from charts) 15/11/1993: 44-60-49-60-65-78-80-83 (8 weeks November 15th 1993 to January 10th 1994)

BALLROOM HITZ - THE VERY BEST OF SWEET compilation

charts (source)	debut	peak	weeks	chart-runs & extra notes
UK (Official Charts)	20/01/1996	15	15	20-15-28-41-54-66-186 (7 weeks from January 2 March 2nd 1996) 13/04/1996: 173-133-177-186 (4 weeks from Apr to May 4th 1996) 21/09/1996: 165-116-112-156 (4 weeks from Sep 21st to October 12th 1996) In total 15 weeks.
DENMARK (IFPI)	8/06/2001	13	5	38-19-13-16-32 (5 weeks from June 8th to July 2001)

UK: BPI awarded compilation by SILVER disc on July 22nd 2013 (together with other compilation The Greatest Hits, released in 1999).

THE VERY BEST OF compilation

charts (source)	debut	peak	weeks	chart-runs & extra notes
UK (Official Charts)	29/01/2005	72	2	72-130 (2 weeks on January 29th & February 5th In 2018 compilation appeared in Budget Album and reached no.18.

THE GREATEST HITS compilation

charts (source)	debut	peak	weeks	chart-runs & extra notes
UK (Official Charts, Budget Album Chart)	3/09/2005	13	8	Not charted in main albums chart. 5/09/2005: 28-43 (2 weeks on September 3rd & 2005) 25/03/2006: 41 23/06/20012: 13-25-31-27-32 (5 weeks from June to July 21st 2012)

UK: BPI awarded compilation by GOLD disc on July 22nd 2013.

ACTION - THE ULTIMATE STORY compilation & DVD

charts (source)	debut	peak	weeks	chart-runs & extra notes
GERMANY (GfK Entertainment)	25/09/2015	17	6	17-37-76-82-82-97 (6 weeks from September 25th October 30th 2015)
SWITZERLAND (Media Control DVD chart)	27/09/2015	2	3	2-4-8 (3 weeks from September 27th to October 2015)
NETHERLANDS (Nationale hitparade DVD)	26/09/2015	5	5	5-12-19-18-18 (5 weeks from September 26th to Ocotber 24th 2015)

ARE YOU READY? – THE RCA ERA box

charts (source)	debut	peak	weeks	chart-runs & extra notes
GERMANY (GfK Entertainment)	21/04/2017	61	1	

SENSATIONAL SWEET. CHAPTER ONE: THE WILD BUNCH box

charts (source)	debut	peak	weeks	chart-runs & extra notes
GERMANY (GfK Entertainment)	24/11/2017	28	2	28-97 (2 weeks from November 24 to December 1st 2017)

9 781915 246691